Digital Transformation
and Knowledge Management

Lucia Marchegiani

Digital Transformation and Knowledge Management

LONDON AND NEW YORK

G. Giappichelli Editore

First published 2021
by Routledge
2 Park Square, Milton Park, Abingdon, Oxon OX14 4RN

and by Routledge
711 Third Avenue, New York, NY 10017

Routledge is an imprint of the Taylor & Francis Group, an informa business

and by G. Giappichelli Editore
Via Po 21, Torino – Italia

© 2020 Lucia Marchegiani

The right of Lucia Marchegiani to be identified as author of this work has been asserted by her in accordance with sections 77 and 78 of the Copyright, Designs and Patents Act 1988.

All rights reserved. No part of this book may be reprinted or reproduced or utilised in any form or by any electronic, mechanical, or other means, now known or hereafter invented, including photocopying and recording, or in any information storage or retrieval system, without permission in writing from the publishers.

Trademark notice: Product or corporate names may be trademarks or registered trademarks, and are used only for identification and explanation without intent to infringe.

British Library Cataloguing-in-Publication Data
A catalogue record for this book is available from the British Library

ISBN: 978-88-921-3478-2 (hbk-G. Giappichelli Editore)
ISBN: 978-88-921-8903-4 (ebk-G. Giappichelli Editore)
ISBN: 978-0-367-62832-1 (hbk-Routledge)
ISBN: 978-0-367-62828-4 (ebk-Routledge)

Typeset in Simoncini Garamond
by G. Giappichelli Editore, Turin, Italy

The manuscript has been subjected to the double blind peer review process prior to publication.

*To my beloved parents,
who say they have overly intelligent children*

CONTENTS

	page
List of Figures	xi
List of Tables	xiii
List of Boxes	xv
Foreword	xvii
Introduction	1

1. Origins and evolutions of KM
- 1.1. Where do we stand? — 5
  - 1.1.1. The internet Revolution, when It All Started — 6
  - 1.1.2. The 4th Industrial Revolution — 9
  - 1.1.3. The Rise of the Knowledge Economy — 11
- 1.2. Where Do We Go from Here? The Digital Age — 12
  - 1.2.1. Innovative Organizing: Tacit and Explicit Knowledge — 16
  - 1.2.2. Innovative Organizing: Intermediate and Multi-Sided Markets — 18
  - 1.2.3. Innovative Organizing: Networks and Platform Organizations (by Lucia Marchegiani and Andrea Grieco) — 21
  - 1.2.4. Innovative Organizing: Mass Collaboration — 25
- 1.3. Evolution of Knowledge in Management — 26
  - 1.3.1. Data, Information, Knowledge — 27
  - 1.3.2. Approaches to Knowledge Management — 31
  - 1.3.3. Network Perspective in Knowledge Management — 36
- 1.4. Why Do We Still Need to Manage Knowledge? — 40
  - 1.4.1. Knowledge Management and Innovation — 42
  - 1.4.2. Knowledge Management and People Management — 43
  - 1.4.3. The Pyramid of Knowledge, Revisited — 44
  - 1.4.4. Much Ado about Knowledge, here Comes the Pandemic! — 48

2. Why is knowledge the strategic asset?
- 2.1. Leveraging the Technological Trigger — 51
- 2.2. Digital-enabled Business Opportunities — 53
  - 2.2.1. Data-Based Innovation — 53
  - 2.2.2. Servitization — 55

		page
2.2.3.	Faster Innovation Cycles	55
2.2.4.	Open Collaboration and Digital Business Ecosystems	56
2.3.	Which Technology? What Are the Exponential Technologies?	63
2.3.1.	Big Data	64
2.3.2.	Business Intelligence	66
2.3.3.	Cloud computing (by Lucia Marchegiani and Andrea Grieco)	67
2.3.4.	Internet of Things (or of Everything)	72
2.3.5.	Artificial Intelligence (AI)	75
2.4.	Diffusion of (Digital) Innovations	77
2.5.	All that Glitters Is not (Technological) Gold!	92
2.5.1.	Information Systems in Organizations	93
2.5.2.	Technology Acceptance Models	98
2.5.3.	IS and Change Management	102

3. Knowledge and (digital) learning organizations

3.1.	Digital Transformation	105
3.1.1.	The Hype of Digital Transformation	106
3.1.2.	Digitization, Digitalization, and Digital Transformation	108
3.1.3.	Chief Digital Officer, who?	111
3.2.	Organizational Learning and Learning Organizations	112
3.2.1.	Organizational Learning	112
3.2.2.	Learning Organizations	117
3.2.3.	Learning through Experience	119
3.2.4.	Knowledge Intensive Firms	121
3.2.5.	Agile Organizations	125
3.3.	Digital technologies for Human Resources Management	130
3.3.1.	Managing the Knowledge Workers, Revisited. Cognitive Computing and Machine Learning	137
3.3.2.	Digital Workplaces	139
3.3.3.	Flexible Working, Smart Working?	144

4. Km and digital transformation in contexts

4.1.	Introduction	149
4.2.	Operations & industry 4.0: Navantia and Shell	150
4.3.	HR-TECH: IBM, Generali, Company X	152
4.3.1.	Artificial intelligence	152
4.3.2.	People analytics	153
4.3.3.	Impact on Employees' motivation	153
4.4.	Marketing and Sales	154
4.5.	Supply chain and Logistics	157
4.6.	Internet of Things (IoT)	160
4.7.	When Innovations are disruptive: The Evolution of the mobile TLC Sector	161

		page
4.7.1.	The Actors of the new Mobile TLC Industry	171
4.8.	KM practices as a tool to overcome organizational silos	173

Conclusions 183

References 185

Index 197

LIST OF FIGURES

page

Figure 1.1.	The rise of the Internet Revolution	7
Figure 1.2.	The four Industrial Revolutions, over time	9
Figure 1.3.	The determinant of the knowledge-based economy	12
Figure 1.4.	Innovative organizing in the Digital Age	15
Figure 1.5.	Main changes of IS/IT in the Digital Age	17
Figure 1.6.	The Pyramid of Knowledge	28
Figure 1.7.	The SECI model	35
Figure 1.8.	A framework for knowledge network research	38
Figure 1.9.	Knowledge, innovation, and people management	41
Figure 1.10.	Human and non-human interactions in cyber physical systems	45
Figure 1.11.	From data to wisdom	47
Figure 1.12.	The DIKW Pyramid, human vs. non-human impact	47
Figure 1.13.	Workers who regularly work from home, per Country, 2018	49
Figure 2.1.	Three rings of nodes in online social networks	60
Figure 2.2.	The central core of an online social network	61
Figure 2.3.	The 3Vs of Big Data	65
Figure 2.4.	Models and characteristics of cloud computing	69
Figure 2.5.	General network effects	78
Figure 2.6.	The Bass model	84
Figure 2.7.	The Chasm Model	88
Figure 2.8.	The Technology Acceptance Model (TAM)	99
Figure 2.9.	The UTAT model	100
Figure 2.10.	The depth and rapidity of change	103
Figure 3.1.	Trend in academic publications on digital transformation (2000-2019)	106
Figure 3.2.	Publications on digital transformation by subject area (2000-2019)	107
Figure 3.3.	Publications on digital transformation by country (top 15 countries, 2000-2019)	107
Figure 3.4.	The Digital Transformation Framework	110
Figure 3.5.	Nonaka's hypertext organization	114
Figure 3.6.	Characteristics of Learning Organizations	119
Figure 3.7.	Evolution of workplaces over time per focal activity	141
Figure 3.8.	Categories of coworking users	143
Figure 4.1.	Evolution of mobile phone Generations	166
Figure 4.2.	From KM to actual network	175
Figure 4.3.	From KM to actual networks including TAM	176
Figure 4.4.	Evolution of the network over time	180

LIST OF TABLES

		page
Table 1.1.	How are information and knowledge different?	27
Table 1.2.	Taxonomy of Knowledge Management Schools	32
Table 1.3.	Comparison between Zeleny and Ackoff pyramids of knowledge	46
Table 2.1.	Comparison between closed and open innovation paradigms	57
Table 3.1.	Digitization vs. digitalization	109
Table 4.1.	Homophily indexes over time	181

LIST OF BOXES

		page
Box 1.1.	Examples of two/multi-sided markets	19
Box 1.2.	From a traditional business model to a platform model	25
Box 1.3.	Characteristics of knowledge	28
Box 2.1.	The design thinking approach in new product development	62
Box 2.2.	Forbes case study	71
Box 2.3.	Diffusion of Innovation, the case of Apple	90
Box 3.1.	Learning opportunities in divestment processes	120
Box 3.2.	Focus on the HR-tech market in Italy	131
Box 3.3.	The Docebo case study	139
Box 3.4.	The TAG case study	143
Box 4.1.	The Navantia case study	150
Box 4.2.	The Shell case study	151
Box 4.3.	The IBM case study	152
Box 4.4.	The Generali case study	153
Box 4.5	A case study on Digital Transformation and Motivation	153
Box 4.6.	The NBA case study	154
Box 4.7.	The Biogen case study	156
Box 4.8.	Impact of DT on supply side and logistics	157
Box 4.9.	The Unilever case study	158
Box 4.10.	AccuWeather Case Study	159
Box 4.11.	iRobot Case Study	160

FOREWORD

> «Considerate la vostra semenza: fatti non foste a viver come bruti ma per seguir virtute e canoscenza»
>
> Dante, *Divina Commedia*, Canto V Inferno

While I was finally writing the last paragraphs of this book, one of my kids asked me what I was doing. "I am writing a book," was my reply. As curious as any 5-year-old kid, this reply was not enough for him. "What is this book about?" he asked. I did not know how detailed my answers could be for him to understand anything about knowledge management and digital technologies. "It is about knowledge and technology," I tried. He pressed: "What has technology got to do with knowledge?" It was clear that the debate had just begun. "Uhm, let's see" – I tried to buy some time – "sometimes the technology can help in finding new knowledge." He thought a bit and then said "Ah, it is like a robot who knows someone and recognizes who knows someone. Or, a telephone that knows someone's password." It made me smile. At first, I did not understand what he meant. I tried to deepen the conversation and I got it. For him, technology and people go hand in hand, and there must be something useful in this relation.

Actually, I believe that he is not far from the essence of knowledge management. We are living in a world of Information and Knowledge. These years will be remembered as the Knowledge Age. And yet Wisdom is a foremost prize that we human beings tend to seize. In an era when sources of data are diffused, quantity of data available is massive, information seems to be widespread and innovation is spreading at an unprecedented speed, it has become crucial to distinguish between valuable and ignorable data, between trustworthy and unreliable sources of information. Now that information overload is a tangible threat to our productivity, attention has become a significant success factor for individuals, as well as for organizations. In this complex world of big data and Information and Communication Technologies, we humans have become acquainted to interacting with non-human artefacts. We refer to the youngest generations as the native digital. Indeed, my youngest child, who at this time is not even one, fights with his siblings to hold my smartphone and stares at its screen turning on and off. The interactions between humans and ICT have become a familiar habit, almost natural, and probably continuous. While we unconsciously use such non-humans artefacts, we leave behind a digital footprint, which is far more interesting than the digital fingerprint. While retrieving data, we produce new data. It may be worthy to understand the path that leads from those data to knowledge, and which kind of knowledge. At an organizational level, businesses have started to embrace the digital revolution in a variety of ways. Not always following a planned strategy, contemporary organizations have been forced to deal with the digital disruption. Also, exponential technologies are paired with exponential organizations, but the average company is probably unaware of how to exploit the full potential of the digital technologies and to convey proper knowledge-creation processes.

Recently, the whole world has been in lockdown to overcome the Covid-19 pandemic. Digital Technologies have been necessary to continue normal daily activities such as working, attending schools and universities, and meeting family and friends. Knowledge sharing and creation have increasingly been intermediated by digital technologies, such as video conferencing platforms, shared documents, and distant learning solutions. Whether this experience has left us wiser is difficult to assess. Nonetheless, the pandemic emergency has opened Pandora's box showing the shortfalls of massive usage of digital technologies. This unique social experiment has, among other things, revealed the flaws of a digitally interconnected – and always connected – world. We, as humans, experience the limit of human brains in terms of computational capacity, memory, and speed. Digital technology, on the contrary, is fast, ubiquitous, and capable of massive quantities of data. But when it comes to knowledge and wisdom, technology alone is not the solution. I believe that Ulysses' words are still valid. In the Divine Comedy, Dante makes Ulysses warn his companions: "You were not made to live like beasts, but to follow virtue and knowledge." Undoubtedly, it is in our human nature to aspire to know more and do better. To achieve this goal, digital technology can be a great help. But brutally using technology would leave us in the dark living like modern, digital, connected… beasts.

My interest for a Knowledge-based Economy traces back to my very first professional experience, working first for a telecommunication company, and completing my PhD in Organizations and Information Systems. At that time, we were at the dawn of this completely new way of organizing the global economy. Fifteen years later, disruptive and massive digital technologies have brought radical changes in the world economy. The Information Economy has become reality, and the Knowledge-based perspective of firms is nowadays mature. The fourth Industrial Revolution has imposed new challenges on firms and on the ways in which people interact, produce, and organize their lives and the whole economy. Yet the dynamics of knowledge creation, both at individual and organizational levels, deserve scrutiny and research.

This work is the result of the interaction between myself and the brilliant colleagues and students whom I have encountered so far in my professional life. My friend and colleague Michela Marchiori has taught me the value of rigorous research paired with a critical approach, while at the same time practicing the immense art of working together respectfully.

I am thankful to all the students who accepted to engage in the nontraditional, interactive, and highly demanding courses that I teach. I deeply believe that learning only comes through continuous interaction and knowledge sharing, and I try to put this in practice in my courses, asking students to be curious and provocative and always ask questions. The naughtier, the better. From these students I have learnt a lot. Some of their inputs have also fed this book and they are fully credited in the coming chapters. Among the others, I am thankful to Laura Pileggi, Flavia Mozziconi, Valentina Podestà, Sara Pennacchini, and Pietro Pratense, for their feedback and stimulus to be constantly up-to-date. I started teaching very young and I have soon realized that being a teacher is more about learning than passing knowledge, more about receiving than giving. Of this I am extremely grateful to God. Working at Roma Tre University and being hosted as a visiting scholar in prestigious Business Schools gave me the chance to engage in very interesting academic debates that have left me a bit wiser but also much more curious to know more. More than 2400 years ago, Socrates, conscious of human limitations, said: "One thing only I know, and that is that I know nothing." Hopefully, the nothing that I know is clearly illustrated in this book and will provide occasions for further academic debates. The rest that I do not know has probably led me to make some mistakes as well, for which I deeply apologize.

A special thanks is devoted to my family: Matteo, Chiara, Leonardo, Ginevra Anna, Romeo, Margherita, and Adriano, and to my parents, who have been so patient to stand by my side, and who gave me the most valuable stimulus for my job. Being a researcher gives me opportunities to increase my knowledge. Being the wife to a researcher gives me chances to debate my understanding. Being a mom gives me opportunities to be challenged and contested. Hopefully, this will lead to wisdom, eventually.

Lucia Marchegiani

Roma – Italy
May 2020

INTRODUCTION

> «On ne reçoit pas la sagesse, il faut la découvrir soi-même après un trajet que personne ne peut faire pour nous, ne peut nous épargner.»
>
> Marcel Proust

For human beings, knowledge has always been a distinctive trait. The quest for more advanced knowledge has motivated human actions over the course of history. As Proust wrote in his masterpiece "*À la recherche du temps perdu*," we [human beings] are not provided with wisdom, we must discover it for ourselves, after a journey through the wilderness which no one else can take for us, an effort which no one can spare us. Nowadays, knowledge is at the core of the socio-economic global system, and unexplored areas of socio-economic development have appeared. For profit and not-for-profit firms, institutions, and organizations in general face unique opportunities and threats related to knowledge. Digital technologies and digital transformation offer a wide array of opportunities for value creation. At the same time, organizations need to foster newer, faster, and more dynamic ways of mobilizing and managing knowledge. In this scenario, knowledge management can be considered as a powerful tool to face the journey through the wilderness that can lead to (organizational) wisdom. The interplay between human and non-human actors in sharing knowledge requires extraordinary organizational change and renewal. Emerging trends, such as artificial intelligence, collective intelligence, agile methodologies, open innovation, and co-creation enable new business models and managerial paradigms that need to be understood and conceptualized.

This book offers an extensive overview of the most recent trends in knowledge management that take into account the interplay between human and non-human actors. It aims at offering an up-to-date conceptualization and guidance for the implementation of knowledge management in an era of unprecedented human/non-human interaction.

This book conveys the results of more than a decade of research and applied experience in the field of knowledge management carried out by the author. It is intended not only for students and academics but also for managers and practitioners who are interested in deepening their understanding of knowledge and learning in the contemporary economy.

It covers a comprehensive view of the most advanced theoretical approaches while, at the same time, offering a wide array of case studies and evidence-based knowledge management practices.

This book thereby takes up the theoretical debate about knowledge management in light of the most recent technological and managerial advances that support the digital transformation of organizations.

This book offers a broad understanding of the theoretical underpinnings of knowledge management in the digital era while also providing an overview of the interrelation between ICT and knowledge management challenges, in terms of human/non-human interactions.

This integrated perspective combines a theoretical framework with practical solutions and benchmarking. Moreover, in an innovative way, this book adopts a new multi-layered perspective on the organizational implications of the adoption of digital technologies and of the digital transformation.

The work is divided into four chapters. It starts with an overview of the origins and evolutions of the discipline of KM and an understanding of the current challenges. The first sections cover the history of knowledge management, explaining why it has emerged as a stream of research and as a business practice. Moreover, these chapters highlight the current and foreseeable trends related to new needs that emerge from the evolution of business-related technology. Starting from the seminal contributions of Nonaka and Takeuchi, Davenport, Senge and other founding fathers of organizational knowledge and learning, these chapters will cover the more recent contributions that have deepened the understanding of how organizational learning works and what challenges knowledge management poses to contemporary organizations. The concept of non-human knowledge is also introduced here, as well as the interrelation between human and non-human actors in sharing business-related knowledge. These chapters are written adopting a critical perspective in order to provide the readers not only with an academic overview but also to introduce and discuss relevant practice-oriented challenges.

The second chapter aims to answer the question "Why is knowledge the strategic asset?" The sections in this part cover topics that are relevant from a managerial perspective. Well known concepts such as digital transformation and organizational learning are discussed with a new flavor. The latter is related to the increasing centrality of digital technologies in defining strategic orientation and in guiding organizational decisions. The technologies that are emerging as standards are introduced. The aim of these chapters is not only to provide the students with an overview of these important technologies, but also, and mostly, to discuss how these technologies disrupt the ways in which businesses are managed and organized.

The third chapter focuses on the concept of knowledge and learning organizations. This part deepens the managerial challenges and discusses the toolkits that are available to face the technology related managerial challenges. In particular, these sections adopt an organizational viewpoint and deepen the understanding of the emerging trends in managing organizational learning and knowledge. Again, these sections focus on the new trends of managing human and non-human actors, and their interrelation. Old concepts such as knowledge workers are revisited with a perspective of the new technologies that interact with the human workers.

The fourth chapter focuses on contexts. Although case studies are scattered throughout the whole book, this part is specifically reserved to the discussion of cases that constitute good practices at the operational level. Each case study is related to a specific operation. This provides the readers with a ready-to-use example of how digital technologies have disrupted the operational level of organizations (for profit but also not-for-profit) and what managerial decisions have been adopted in good practices. Moreover, the chapter offers an overview of the evolution of the telecommunication sector through the innovation waves that have disrupted the sector over time. Finally, a specific study is reported, that focuses on how knowledge management practices can overcome the problem of organizational silos, and foster intra-organizational knowledge sharing.

Chapter 1
ORIGINS AND EVOLUTIONS OF KM

SUMMARY: 1.1. Where Do We stand? – 1.1.1. The Internet Revolution, when It All Started. – 1.1.2. The 4th Industrial Revolution. – 1.1.3. The Rise of the Knowledge Economy. – 1.2. Where Do We Go from Here? The Digital Age. – 1.2.1. Innovative Organizing: Tacit and Explicit Knowledge. – 1.2.2. Innovative Organizing: Intermediate and Multi-Sided Markets. – 1.2.3. Innovative Organizing: Networks and Platforms Organizations. – 1.2.4. Innovative Organizing: Mass Collaboration. – 1.3. Evolution of Knowledge in Management. – 1.3.1. Data, Information, Knowledge. – 1.3.2. Approaches to Knowledge Management. – 1.3.3. Network Perspective in Knowledge Management. – 1.4. Why Do We Still Need to Manage Knowledge? – 1.4.1. Knowledge Management and Innovation. – 1.4.2. Knowledge Management and People Management. – 1.4.3. The Pyramid of Knowledge, Revisited. – 1.4.4. Much Ado About Knowledge, Here Comes the Pandemic!

1.1. Where Do We Stand?

We currently live in a world where digital technologies and the Internet play a fundamental role in our daily lives. Technological advancements offer benefits and advantages to us all-be it as individuals, communities, businesses, or organizations-by expanding the boundaries of information availability, enhancing efficiency and agility, and reducing costs.

As a society, we perceive that we are surrounded by constant and rapid technological innovations, especially thanks to our continuous exposure to media. In spite of our perception, and despite living in the so-called Digital Age, the transition to a fully-fledged digital society is not yet complete. The term Digital Transformation has become familiar as one of the most compelling managerial trends. Yet, the organizations that embrace this transformation most of the time underestimate the organizational consequences and the impact on human resources. Generally speaking, the digital transformation requires a profound organizational change that includes, but does not end with, digital information technology. In order to understand this complexity, it is necessary to step back and look at the past decades, when the seeds of the digital age were laid.

Information Technology refers to the technological applications that are developed to drive information and to favor the exchange of information among remotely connected points. The advent of the Internet and electronic settings (e-business, e-commerce, e-marketplaces, etc.) boosted the relevance of information technology, and Information Systems started to be at the center of academic and managerial attention. Those are systems where the different Information-based components are intertwined and integrated. The overall aim of such complex systems is to optimize the exchange of information, selecting the relevant contents, in a connected input-output series of nodes.

1.1.1. The Internet Revolution, when It All Started

In the late '90s, the convergence between Information Technology and Telecommunication gave birth to Information and Communication Technology. The pace of innovation activities dramatically boosted and Moore's law became famous, stating that the power of ICT doubled every second year.

The first notion of Information Age can be traced back to the early '80s, when the advent of more and more refined technological applications for Information processing, alongside with social transformation, gave rise to the idea that a completely new world was about to be born (Naisbitt & Bisesi, 1983). It is interesting to recall the Megatrends of the Information Society that were detected at the end of the 1980s:

1. A clear pattern emerged from the Industrial Society to Information Society;
2. From mechanical relations with Forced Technology to High Tech/High Touch (FAXs that can be touched, cut, pasted, colored, etc.);
3. From a limited National Economy to the broader World Economy;
4. From perspectives based on the Short Term to Long Term views;
5. From a general approach towards Centralization to Decentralization;
6. From the belief on Institutional Help to the emergence of Self-Help;
7. From passive forms of Representative Democracy to more active Participatory Democracy;
8. From Hierarchies to Networking;
9. From a North-centric perspective to South;
10. From the dyad "Either/Or" to Multiple Option.

Over twenty years later, these megatrends are still valid. The Interconnected world (Malhotra, 2000; Muegge, 2013) has become indeed a commonly used expression. This impels a deep investigation of what happens in a large complex system of interconnected agents. This kind of society has plenty of consequences, from social life to the economic sphere. From a sociological perspective, it has been said that the whole world has become smaller, and that distances may have been nullified by the existence of digital highways. A widely appraised author is Manuel Castells, who traced back the origins of the Information Economy to three interrelated processes, namely:

- the IT revolution,
- the fall of capitalism and statism, and
- the rise of new social movements.

According to the Author, together these three processes have caused a new social structure (a network society), a new economy (a global informational economy), and a new culture (a culture of 'real virtuality') (Castells, 1996, 1997, 1998).

Figure 1.1. The rise of the Internet Revolution.

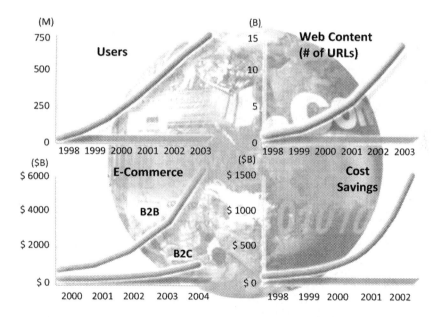

Source: author's elaboration.

The **Internet Revolution** started at the beginning of the 21st century with a boom in informatics, in terms of a rapidly increasing number of Internet users and of web content (Figure 1.1). These changes brought heavy impacts on the economy, but also on society and individual lives. The rise of e-commerce was favored both by an increasing offer through websites and by the users who welcomed this new way of shopping online.

Such a Copernican revolution implied that information flows are at the center of the economic cosmos, instead of the firms' assets and competencies. Information flows are not only internal to firms. Instead, they are ubiquitous, and firms should be able to capture relevant information, where it appears and grows. At a closer look, the revolution laid on technological as well as socio-economic drivers, such as:

- Technology:
  - The diffusion of the Internet, and of high-speed Internet connections;
  - The increasing amount of data available on the World Wide Web;
  - The diffusion of devices such as PC and mobile devices: these are the gateways to access the Internet and WWW and serve multiple purposes, such as typewriters, archives, libraries, post offices, banks, supermarkets, newspapers, weather forecasting, TV, cinemas, games, financial markets, videoconferences.
- Economic drivers:
  - The increasing globalization of markets;
  - The decreasing regulation;
  - The privatization of former public monopolist TLC companies.
- Sociological drivers:
  - New lifestyles;
  - Standardization;
  - The increasing appeal of instant communication.

If the revolution started with technologies that drive information and knowledge, it then became pervasive and caused a radical change, such as:

- The shift from industrial capitalism to cultural capitalism;
- The emergence of a new renaissance, which considers man and technology at the core of the universal values;
- The rise of innovation and creativity: the revolution allowed the re-invention ofgoods and services, new businesses emerged, and e-commerce boomed.

These are the basics of the dawn of the **Digital Age**. With Information becoming one of the strategic assets of firms, a large part of the economics principles has changed. When it comes to understanding the kind of revolution that firms have had to embrace to capture their competitive advantage, it is straightforward that information plays a pivotal role. Nowadays it is meaningless to ponder access to natural resources or scale and scope economies as sources of competitive advantage. Most of the time what makes the difference is the ability to orchestrate intangible assets, such as knowledge and competencies, and to deploy them over time in what are called dynamic capabilities (Teece, 2007; Teece et al., 1997).

1.1.2. The 4th Industrial Revolution

The Internet Revolution was just a preamble to a wider industrial revolution. In the history of modern economies, this is labeled as the 4th Industrial Revolution (Figure 1.2).

Figure 1.2. The four Industrial Revolutions, over time.

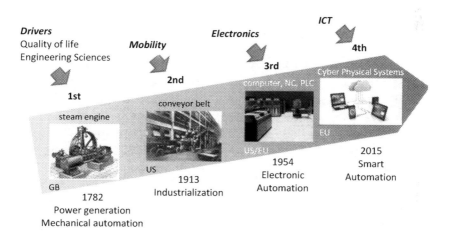

Source: author's elaboration.

The 1st Industrial Revolution, that marked the proto-industrialization period, started at the end of the 18th century to the beginning of the 19th century in Great Britain. Due to mechanical automation, the handicraft model of production converged into a machine model of production, with prevalence in the textile-metallurgical sector and the use of inanimate energy sources such as coal, steam, and waterpower. The invention of the steam engine created a new type of energy that later on also helped to speed up the manufacturing of railroads. The changes that affected the structure of the production system also influenced the economic structure, completely changing the set-up of the social system with the birth of the working class and the expansion of cities.

The 2nd Industrial Revolution occurred between the end of the 19th century and the beginning of the 20th century, mainly in the United States. It brought major innovations in transportation, communication, and manufacturing, thanks to advancements in the field of industries that helped the emergence of new sources of energy: electricity, gas, and oil. The production system changed in 1908 when Henry Ford planned the production of cars in bulk due to mass production. In 1913 the process of industrialization took off, with the increasing usage of the conveyor belt and mass manufacturing. The Bessmer process to produce steel and new plastic materials was responsible for the expansion of the rail and telegraph networks, which later culminated in inventions such as the telephone, aircraft, and cars. The increasing interactions of trades, ideas, and people led to a new socio-economic scenario, where mobility started to affirm itself as a societal value. Nonetheless, despite the improved standards of living, unemployment and the social divide increased.

The 3rd Industrial Revolution started in the middle of the 20th century with the rise of electronics, telecommunications, and computers. Through these new technologies, the third industrial revolution opened the doors to space expeditions, research, and biotechnology. Two major inventions, Programmable Logic Controllers (PLCs) and Robots, helped give rise to an era of high-level automation. Also, the first experimentation of digital technologies appeared, leading the way to the Information Age.

What we are currently living in is referred to as the 4th Revolution, although some authors state that we are still living in the long effects of the third revolution. Indeed, we are living a revolution that is completely different from the previous ones, as digital technologies have completely disrupted the old ways of doing business, and the living standards as well. Mechanical or electronic-analogical systems have become obsolete, and digital is now the key. This is the time of the Smart Automation due to fully digital Cyber-physical systems that are central to the development of a Digital Age. For the first time, the world has become fully interconnected, and efficient mobile communication systems have made the world smaller.

Innovative digital technologies (which will be extensively discussed in Chapter Two) are the new enablers of this new phase called the **Digital Age**.
One of the key factors driving the development of the economy in the digital age, also referred to as knowledge-based economy or digital economy, is **data**: a resource which can be fully exploited by means of appropriate analytical tools, and at the same time through a radical change in the organizational culture of businesses and public institutions.

1.1.3. The Rise of the Knowledge Economy

The term Knowledge Economy or Knowledge-based Economy (KBE) emerged with reference to the industrial organization and management dynamics of the knowledge-intensive industries that face the competitive challenges of the 4th Industrial Revolution. Those are economic settings characterized by a high density of knowledge and information. In particular, with the digitalization waves, knowledge became a valuable assct per sè, whereas in the older industrial settings it was included in the products that were commercialized. In other words, the digital waves provoked a dematerialization of the industrial world, raising the relative importance of the service-based industries.

The importance of knowledge and networks of relations for firms' growth processes has received much attention by economists and management researchers. In particular, value-adding processes of firms (such as the internationalization one) are increasingly based on the creation and exploitation of knowledge and of the connections with other economic actors. Thus, the Knowledge-based view of the firms is intrinsically correlated with the Relational view of the firm (Dyer & Singh, 1998; Inkpen & Tsang, 2005; Yli-Renko et al., 2001).

Knowledge-intensive products and services (Bettis & Hitt, 1995; Rylander & Peppard, 2003) and relations (especially external ones), see for example (Zheng, 2010), represent a good vehicle to acquire and combine new knowledge.

In other words, the emphasis of knowledge leads to focus on the ways by which it can be generated or accumulated, taking into consideration the environment where the firms act. In this perspective, relations are one of the principal means through which external knowledge is acquired, which in turn sustains the creation of new, internal know-how (see later par. 1.3.3). How firms are organized, and knowledge is funneled and new knowledge is created is at the basis of the firms' competitive advantage (A.H. Gold et al., 2001; Nahapiet & Ghoshal, 1998).

While there has always been a recognition that managing knowledge is important in organizations, some emergent forces have caused a resurgence in this idea (Figure 1.3). Not only managing knowledge is now recognized as an important strategic issue, but knowledge itself is central in wider debates about the sources of wealth creation in contemporary society and the management of knowledge workers.

Figure 1.3. The determinant of the knowledge-based economy.

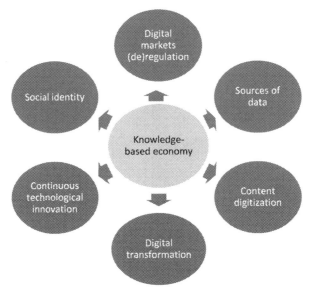

Source: author's elaboration.

The knowledge-based Economy has several characteristics, such as:
i) Deregulation of markets;
ii) Increased number of sources of data and information;
iii) Content digitization;
iv) The awareness that a digital transformation is needed for firms to stay competitive;
v) Technological innovations that lowered the costs of information;
vi) The affirmation of a social identity.

For firms, and organizations in general, coping with these characteristics requires embracing a flexible organizational culture and adopting coherent managerial practices. Flexibility, continuous innovation, and agility have become keywords of this new economic landscape.

1.2. Where Do We Go from Here? The Digital Age

The huge development and diffusion of digital technologies has created new business opportunities for companies, making internal processes and organizations more efficient. It has facilitated the emergence of new competitive spaces, on the one hand, and redefined the mode of development of pre-existing businesses, on the other. Technological progress has, therefore, allowed the identification of new and more powerful internet-based instruments for professional applications related to how to conduct successful business. In fact, patterns of Business to Business (B2B) and Business to Consumer (B2C) relationship management emerged over time. In particular, the acceleration of Web 2.0 has brought out aspects of management and marketing of the possibility of thinking outside the box.

In general, the introduction and implementation of the new digital technologies, and their widespread circulation, have brought deep changes in how we humans behave and relate with each other. The human experience on one side is now characterized by a high degree of efficiency due to the use of data and of integrated cloud systems, which are capable of connecting people and objects, physical and virtual places. On the other side, these technologies have also brought about sociological changes, which can be debatable. This is, however, well beyond the scope of this book [1].

Technology has impacted economic development in many ways and for a long time, as reported in many economic history studies. Structural change that has occurred modified the importance of knowledge and its management. Since the 1960's liberalization has opened up markets for goods and services: this means that tariff and non-tariff barriers have been lowered, and the costs of transportation have diminished. More importantly, the information about market opportunities can spread faster and more easily. Through these developments, competition has been sharpened. This was also due to the increasing development of intermediate products that were made possible by new market opportunities. This process has been boosted by developments in computer and information technology, which have enabled the design of new financial products and the execution of complex transactions. Moreover, the globalization of markets has increased the number of potential suppliers at home and abroad.

In general, the economic structure has shifted from being essentially based on manufacturing, to the processing of intangibles, such as information, in order to develop and transfer new knowledge. So, diminishing returns activities have been replaced by activities characterized by increasing returns and this is paramount in knowledge-based industries. The increasing returns phenomena is driven by the following factors:

---

[1] There is plenty of academic production and books on this theme. It is impossible to give even an essential list of readings here. Just to name one book that I found extremely insightful, I suggest reading (Turkle, 2017).

- Standard and network externalities – The higher the acceptance of the standard, the greater the consumer benefits (network externalities), and the higher the likelihood that the standard becomes dominant.
- Customer lock-in – Providers will compete hard for the original sale.
- Large up-front costs – This is the case of high tech industry and software products.
- Producer learning – Producers become more efficient as experience is gained.

New technologies have triggered a real paradigm shift in the relationship between the company and internal and external stakeholders (Harrison & St. John, 1996).

From the point of view of intra-organizational relations, to have the most effective tools of communication and knowledge management has direct consequences on human resource development and improvement of internal processes.

From an external perspective, the most interactivity is evidenced in the relationship between business partners and increased business opportunities for the firm.

With the introduction of digital technologies, increase in productivity has occurred alongside with the extension of the use of the Internet from simple trade to covering all operations of the business (e-business). This implies that the adoption of new technologies goes beyond the mere possibility of selling/buying on the Internet (e-commerce) and changes the internal work processes and culture of each company. This shift results in increased productivity and quality in all business activities: from marketing to sales, management of customer relationships, logistics and operations management, from education and training to knowledge management. The Internet-based applications and infrastructure, in addition to e-commerce systems, include systems such as: electronic delivery (e-procurement), Supply Chain Management (management of orders, production and distribution), Customer Relationship Management (order management systems, networks and distribution channels), Enterprise resource Planning (management of resources such as finance, human resources, operations), logistics, planning and management of knowledge (knowledge management, business intelligence), and training.

Most importantly, competitive assets have dematerialized. The most successful companies of the Digital Age do not own physical infrastructures. As noted by Tom Goodwin in 2015, *"Uber, the largest taxi company in the world, does not own cars. Facebook, the owner of the most popular social network, does not create content. Alibaba, the most popular online retailer, has no inventory. And Airbnb, the most popular vacation rental broker, has no real estate*" (McAfee & Brynjolfsson, 2017, p. 13). These companies defined a disruptive business model that lays on an incredibly thin layer. In fact, their strength is basically due to their evanescence: they do not possess physical assets, but they rather control lines of code and applications. In other words, their valuable asset is their knowledge.

Figure 1.4. Innovative organizing in the Digital Age.

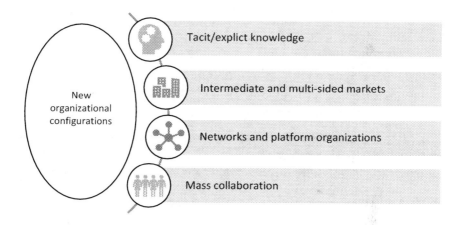

Source: author's elaboration.

It is extremely important to understand the extent to which information and knowledge modifies the drivers that determine firms' competitiveness in the digital age. Successful companies, like those mentioned above, demonstrate that strategic agility and organizational flexibility are powerful drivers for a sustainable competitive advantage. From an organizational point of view, it is extremely fascinating, and useful, to understand the drivers that demand new, and innovative, organizational configurations. Throughout this book, new organizational arrangements, design, and general solutions will be discussed. We refer to the broad term "organization" also including human resources policies.

Figure 1.4 shows the main factors that determine a need for innovative organizing and new organizational configurations.

1.2.1. Innovative Organizing: Tacit and Explicit Knowledge

Tacit and explicit knowledge refers to the need to access a knowledge base that is continuously evolving according to the rapid evolution of competitive environments. To fully leverage the opportunities in the Digital Age, firms need to invest in new organizational capabilities and practices. New skills and adjustment to existing organizational structures are needed to become more agile and foster knowledge creation that boosts creativity and innovation.

Not only new sectors are emerging, with the birth of new firms like start-ups (see later in this chapter), but also firms in traditional sectors are undergoing organizational changes to:

a) attract a workforce with digital capabilities in order to master new innovation domains, and
b) renew their competencies to operate new business models.

In order to attain these objectives, companies undergo a strategic knowledge renewal that can take the form of:

i) internal knowledge development, through a massive retraining of the existing workforce. While this approach has more stable effects in the long term, it is also more time consuming and it may be not adequate when innovation is sought in a very short term.
ii) external knowledge acquisition on the job market, by recruiting digital talents (e.g. software engineers, data analysts). This is the most effective approach in terms of time, but it may be difficult to pursue by traditional firms. In fact, the most talented resources may be more attracted to tech firms and start-ups. Also, digital talents must be then integrated into the existing workforce and this may happen with some friction and organizational inertia.
iii) external knowledge access, by partnering with external actors, such as collaborators or even competitors, in the creation of digital business ecosystems.

The Digital Age has also caused an important redefinition of the role of the Information Systems (IS) Department in organizations. Also from a broader socio-economic perspective, technology experts, "IS/IT people" and "geek" people have been empowered. From an organizational viewpoint, the role of the IS Department has been redefined as well as the power relations with the whole organization. As shown in Figure 1.5, a whole new set of values have been created and internalized in IS Departments within organizations. In fact, back in the 1960's, the so-called IT craftsmanship age saw a sharp definition of roles that relegated the IT people to focus on pure technology, with a clear expertise on programming and system management. They used to work in isolation and their work was more or less routine with some sporadic innovations from time to time. Later, around the 1990's, the IT industrialization started to emerge with a redefinition of roles and capabilities. The focus shifted towards a view on the whole process, thus requiring a collaboration between departments and an increasing cross-functional alignment. Concepts such as IT management and service management referred to the ability to complement the IT skills with a managerial approach. The relations between the departments, though, remained very formal with an internal client approach. Indeed, relations with external stakeholders were not considered important. The IT outcomes were sought in terms of services and solutions to the internal clients' needs and efficiency and effectiveness were considered as parameters of IT success.

Only with the Digital Age, the IT Department has become fully integrated with the whole organization and a focus on business models has come to be common and serve as the basis for internal collaboration. The focus on business models is also related to the new concept of **digital leadership**. In fact, the ability to strategically leverage the digital assets of a company to achieve the business goals is the core capability that is sought in digital leaders.

Figure 1.5. Main changes of IS/IT in the Digital Age.

IT craftmanship

Focus on technology

Core capabilities:
  Programming, systems management

Relations:
  no relational approach, work in isolation

Only sporadic automation and innovation

IT industrialization

Focus on process

Core capabilities:
  IT and service management

Relations:
  very formal client-base internal relations, no external relations

Outcomes as services and solutions; attention to efficiency and effectiveness

Digital Age

Focus on business models

Core capabilities:
  digital leadership

Relations:
  partnership with colleagues; engaged external relations

Outcomes as digital business innovation and new concepts of value like sustainability

Source: author's adaptation based on Gartner, 2014.

1.2.2. Innovative Organizing: Intermediate and Multi-Sided Markets

There have always been markets involving two groups of participants who need to interact via intermediaries. They have been growing in number and relevance in recent years, due to either the increasing technological innovation pace or the growing importance of service industries in western countries. Hence, the managerial literature has been fed over the last years by noticeable contributions on the competitiveness in the two-sided markets (Armstrong, 2006; Rochet & Tirole, 2006). More specifically, the interest of research has been focused both on the number and nature of those markets, and on the different managerial problems that affect the firms competing in those markets.

Two-sided markets (or multi-sided markets) always compel the presence of a core actor, which generally owns the platform. In broad terms, the latter may be viewed as a ground on top of which modular components should be added by both the buyers and the sellers. The two-sidedness characteristic thus raises questions about the positions held by the customers on one side and the other sellers on the other. In fact, when it comes to the supply-side, it is fundamental that complementary components are developed by the sellers and attached to the platform. From this perspective, the concept of complementors comes handy.

Hence, a taxonomy could be provided, with respect to the two variables referring to the suppliers and the customers. As a first step, the variables could be defined as

i) customers' stickiness with the bundle of products and services. It is correlated with the strength of the (positive) network externalities related to the products and services consumption. Moreover, this impacts the diffusion of the products. Potentially, also the level of switching costs may eventually rise. Hence, the greater the positive network externalities of the products and services, the greater the customers' stickiness with them.

ii) the potential strength of complementors. It is related to the ability of the platform owner, or the focal firm, to attract a wide system of related sellers to develop complementary services and products to enrich the platform.

In other words, the platform owners need to reconcile its competitive strategy both to the end user and to the other suppliers, because it cannot possess a wide array of capabilities to offer a whole services and products bundle on its own. It is rather more convenient for the platform owner to combine the diverse sets of competencies, to deliver the products or services to the end market in connection with other suppliers.

The literature on two-sided markets has mostly analyzed problems such as pricing and platform competition. Regarding pricing, razor-and-blade strategies have particularly emerged as the attitude to sell underpriced platforms and overpriced additional components. Prices in two-sided markets are often uneven, and price distortion may be unavoidable between one side and the other. Moreover, the way two-sided businesses set their prices may also vary depending upon their competitive attitude towards complementors. In fact, complementary markets have traditionally been at the core of consolidated streams of economic research. Nevertheless, they have recently gained new momentum, due to recent ICTs innovation, that have contributed to boosting diverse multi-sided markets.

Box 1.1. Examples of two/multi-sided markets

Example 1 – CONFERENCES: Surplus is usually created when speakers address an audience at a conference. Normally both sides enjoy a direct benefit from the interaction: the audience learns what the speakers have to say, while the speakers enjoy disseminating their work and being the focus of attention. Typically, conferences compete for speakers and audiences. A common way to organize the interaction is for the audience to pay to attend and for the speakers to be paid. Is there a good explanation for this feature? (Note that conferences in which most of the audience also present a paper, and where most of the speakers also listen, do not fit the theme of this paper well since there are not then two distinct groups that need to be attracted, but only the single group of 'participants') Institutions such as music (or other arts) festivals would also fit into this framework.

Example 2 – ACADEMIC JOURNALS: Journals compete both for authors and for readers. In the economics field, a common (but not universal) way to organize the interaction is for readers to pay and for (successful) authors to publish for free. But in other scientific disciplines, it is commonplace for (successful) authors to pay a substantial per-page charge for publication.

Example 3 – UNIVERSITY TEACHING: Universities have to compete for both students and for professors. As with the previous examples, quality as much as quantity is perhaps the relevant dimension here: students care about the "quality" of professors and professors care about the "quality" of their students. (A separate issue is the fact that professors also care about the quality of their fellow professors.) If a university is successful in attracting top students, it may have to offer a lower salary to a professor of given quality than otherwise. It is sometimes suggested, for example, that PhD programs at business schools often run at a loss, and this is acceptable as it gives a more "academic" atmosphere to the institution. All three of these academic examples share the feature that intermediaries might not be maximizing profits.

Example 4 – SOFTWARE: Software such as text editing is used for writers to disseminate content and for readers to be able to read the content. It is feasible to sell different software to these two groups. Writers are more likely to buy the "writing" software if there are many people with access to the "reading" software, and readers are more likely to invest in the reading software if they expect to receive many documents in the relevant format.

Example 5 – ADVERTISING IN MEDIA MARKETS: Advertisers/retailers wish to gain access to potential consumers to tempt them to buy products. Often advertising is 'bundled' with other services, such as newspapers, magazines, radio or TV, who act as intermediaries between advertisers and consumers. Revenues from advertising are often used to subsidize the media product for readers/viewers. (Historically, for the case of broadcasting, technology meant that viewers/listeners could not pay directly for the service, and so broadcasters without public funding more-or-less had to find funding from advertisers. But this is less true now for television.) In some special cases, viewers/readers might not benefit directly from advertising, or might actually dislike intrusive advertising. But, for instance in the case of informative advertising, viewers/readers might well benefit from the presence of advertising, as is the case in the next example.

Example 6 – SHOPPING MALLS: Matching consumers to retailers, shopping malls are a good example of two-sided markets. Often, there are several malls in the relevant area which therefore compete for consumers and/or retailers. Typically, retailers pay rent to malls while consumers have free entry (and might also have additional features, such as free convenient parking, offered to attract them). Consumers care about the number and quality of retailers when they decide which mall to visit, and obviously retailers care about the number of consumers coming through the mall.

Example 7 – PAYMENT SYSTEMS: The various methods of paying for products fall under the category of two-sided markets on the theme of facilitating interactions between consumers and retailers. Both consumers and retailers may derive direct benefits (in terms of convenience or security) from using one method over another. To the extent that a consumer only chooses a limited number of payment instruments, he/she will have regard for the number of retailers who choose to accept a given payment method. Similarly, if there are set-up costs in being able to accept a given payment method, a retailer will have regard for the number of consumers who use that method. A common contractual arrangement is for consumers to be able to use a payment card with little or no charge, and for retailers to be asked to cover the costs of the transaction. Aside from traditional credit cards, more recent examples of payment systems include eBay's PayPal. The more sellers (merchants) accept PayPal (Visa credit cards) payments, the more valuable opening a PayPal account (having a Visa card) is for eBay users (consumers); and conversely, the value of having a PayPal account (installing a Visa card reader) for a seller (merchant) is directly proportional to the fraction of eBay buyers (consumers) who have PayPal accounts (carry Visa cards).

Example 8 – VIDEOGAME CONSOLES: Videogame consoles slash shared costs for third-party game developers on one side, and users of games. It would be terribly inefficient if developers had to build a console for each game. Indeed, up until the end of the 1970s, each videogame was hardwired into a game machine. This only changed when Fairchild and Atari introduced the first multi-game machines in 1976 and 1979 respectively. Since then, the role of consoles has always been to take care of the base level functionalities which are needed by all (or most) games – 3D graphics and sound rendering capabilities, translation of high-level programming code into console-readable instructions, etc.

Source: author's elaboration based on (Armstrong, 2006; Hagiu, 2009).

1.2.3. Innovative Organizing: Networks and Platform Organizations (by Lucia Marchegiani and Andrea Grieco)

Platforms have become more and more popular in the Digital Age (Parker & Van Alstyne, 2018), as digital technologies have boosted the opportunities to fully leverage the positive externalities of the sides of the markets.

More recently, recognizing that innovation impels multi-faceted products and services, the perspective on multiple sides of the markets has emerged and gained momentum. The practice, and the managerial literature, shows the relevance of the so-called **multi-sided platforms (MSP)**.

An MSP is defined as a company that provide "*a support that facilitates interactions (or transactions) among the two or more constituents (sides) that it serves, such that members of one side are more likely to get on board the MSP when more members of another side do so*" (Hagiu, 2009, p. 3).

MSPs perform one or both among two fundamental functions: reducing search costs and reducing shared transaction costs among its multiple sides (Hagiu & Wright, 2015).

More in general, **platform organizations** enable or facilitate the interaction between two groups of its customer base: the "buyers" and the "sellers". Each of them can be subdivided in different relevant groups of customers that can be served with fundamental services that the platform needs to perform for those customers. The platform can leverage positive network effects among the various customer groups. As an example, the Xbox videogame serves the following relevant customer groups (or sides):

- the end users, that can be further distinguished in the teenager segment and the young adult segment;
- the independent game developers.

Any user would benefit of greater value the higher the number of games developed for the console. This holds true also vice versa, as Xbox is a more attractive platform for independent game developers if it has a larger installed base of users) (Hagiu, 2009).

The application of big data, new algorithms, and cloud computing will change the nature of work and the structure of the economy. But the exact nature of that change will be determined by the social, political, and business choices we make (Parker & Van Alstyne, 2018). Companies such as Amazon, Etsy, Facebook, Google, Salesforce, and Uber are creating online structures that enable a wide range of human activities. This opens the way for radical changes in how we work, socialize, create value in the economy, and compete for the resulting profits.

These **digital platforms** are multi-sided digital frameworks that shape the terms on which participants interact with one another.

The transformation of services started with the Internet and the intense competition among producers of similar services. These organizations found themselves in a new market with few to none rules, but with strict competition about the creation of the best computable algorithms to emerge as the best supplier of services such as consumption, leisure, and manufacturing.

The shift towards the cloud enabled an easier access to the algorithms and created the infrastructure on which, and out of which, the platform ecosystems and markets operate. Cloud is indeed reconfiguring the globalization of services being a part of the so-called "third globalization".

Not every platform has the same scope; they are indeed diverse both in function and in structure. Starting from search platforms like Google or social media platforms like Facebook, one could argue that they are providing a specific service but both Google and Facebook offer tools to build other platforms on them, like Google Cloud Platform and Facebook Shops. Amazon and eBay are big marketplaces, specifically Amazon is the biggest Internet Company in the world, but it also provides Amazon Web Services, that is the biggest public cloud provider in the world.

Companies like Airbnb and Uber leveraged these platforms to change traditional business models; they are indeed reorganizing the markets, the contractual arrangements, and the value creation. Thinking of Uber and a traditional taxi company one could easily find that Uber has a stronger market positioning because it does not have traditional drivers under a regular contract but is acting like an intermediary, enabling Uber to have better control on working compensations, that are different from salaries, and on the market itself, for example by providing different fees based on the availability of drivers in a particular zone and/or timeslot.

Platform Economy is reshaping business, political, and social interactions much like the Industrial Revolution. The difference is that instead of a factory, that is a tangible asset, Platform Economy companies are built around digital platforms that are mutable, in structure and function, in a fast and an efficient manner. This continuous reshaping creates powerful consequences on the market in which the platform operates like the already cited Amazon, eBay, Uber, and Airbnb.

Another strong point of difference for companies that use cloud computing is that every single piece of data could be analyzed to create better algorithms and finally to create more value; an example are the algorithms of marketplaces that recommend products or apply discounts automatically.

The extension of these algorithms to manufacturing created the Internet of Things, the Internet of Everything, or the Industrial Internet. This concept is applied by leveraging networks of sensors that analyze data all over the productive cycle.

Another aspect of the digital platform is the extensive use of open-source software and technologies and public cloud providers. By using them, individuals could work with industrial-grade technologies and pay just for the consumption, effectively destroying barriers of entry.

Digital platforms usually provide shared technologies, techniques, and standards to build new services over them. Application marketplaces like Apple App Store and Google Play store are indeed open to app builders that could publish their works on them.

Platforms can indeed grow on platforms. The effect of this is the creation of "**Complementors**" that contribute actively in the ecosystem of the main platform creating, if successful, profit for the main platform and, at the same time, usually locking the Complementor in the platform.

As already said, Platform Economy companies should be considered just firms a platform; for example, Uber and Lyft are not taxi operating companies but firms that provide algorithms for a fleet of drivers and their customers; they could create delivery fleets with the same platform leveraging the same algorithms used to provide real-time road conditions and traffic and price estimate. At the same time, the drivers could be paid by the same methods.

Kenney and Zisman categorize digital platforms in 5 types (Kenney & Zysman, 2016):

1. **Platforms for platforms**: examples are the Internet itself that is the foundation with Google acting like a cataloger platform. Mobile Operating Systems like Apple iOS and Google Android enable app developers to sell their work in massive markets. Big players in IT like Google, Microsoft, and Amazon offer cloud technologies with the tools to build architectures and ecosystems on them.
2. **Platforms that make digital tools available online and support the creation of other platforms and marketplaces**: many tools that in the past were provided on the infrastructures of the customers are now

available online free of charge or with consumption models. A famous example is GitHub, that provides a free repository for everyone but also the sharing of open source software effectively becomes the reference platform for all open-source communities.
3. **Platforms mediating work:** platforms could also intermediate human-only jobs like headhunting. For example, LinkedIn is nowadays used by recruiters to find and screen candidates. Another example is Amazon Mechanical Turk that crowdsources tasks that could only be completed by using human judgement.
4. **Retail platforms**: digital platforms like Amazon and eBay but also Yoox and Zalando.
5. **Service-providing platforms**: the highly cited Airbnb, Uber, and Lyft, but also services for Finance and Crowdfunding like Kickstarter.

How is value created?

The set of economic relations is radically changing thanks to the Internet, cloud computing, and data. The ecosystem is indeed the source of value for the platform and the usership is the term by which a platform is judged.

For the platforms there are several ways to capture profit, for example levy a fee on all the transactions or monetize advertisement; usually platform founders try to raise the value of the platform to sell them to big companies or enter the stock market.

"Employees" of a platform, excluding the staff, are usually contractors that are paid according to how much they work with zero to none benefits.

Platforms also create the so-called "consignment workers" that publish their works on platforms like YouTube or application stores.

Who controls the platforms?

This question could have several answers; some companies like Wikipedia are non-profit and are based on shared community rules, others like Uber are owned by a few entrepreneurs and venture capitalists with the aim of maximizing corporate value.

How is work packaged?

Employees in companies like Microsoft, Amazon or Google retain traditional contracts, salaries, and benefits; albeit they are Platform Economy companies. Instead the contractors that work with companies like Uber and JustEat are out of government-regulated contracts and work like self-employed workers with no corporate benefits; in the same fashion developers and publishers on YouTube or application stores could become very successful. But it is very hard to emerge in this competitive environment.

> **Box 1.2.** From a traditional business model to a platform model
>
> Japan Railways East is a company creatively transforming its single-sided business into an MSP. It is the largest train operator in the Tokyo area, which carries more than 10 million passengers daily. In November of 2001, JR East started embedding a contactless technology created by Sony, and called FeliCa, into its transit fare cards: it allowed commuters to zip through train station turnstiles with a simple wave of their card. The new commuter card, dubbed Suica (Super Urban Intelligent Card), was a hit: 6.5 million commuters were carrying it as of June 2003. Then, starting in the spring of 2004, JR East leveraged its success with train passengers to convince physical merchants (convenience stores, cafes, restaurants) located within or in close proximity to JR stations to install contact- less readers enabling Suica holders to use it as a prepaid payment system when shopping there. Today there are over 15 million Suica users and 2,500 merchants accepting it.

Source: author's elaboration based on (Hagiu, 2009).

1.2.4. Innovative Organizing: Mass Collaboration

The boundaries of the firm are becoming more and more blurred as new digital technologies and horizontal relations are replaced by mutual interdependence and circular relations. Firms engage in circular and open collaboration, as technological development becomes faster and more disruptive. In terms of knowledge management, opening up to mass collaboration allows firms to:

a) Gain access and exposure to a richer pool of expertise. In fact, innovation in the digital era often requires skills that go beyond traditional sectoral competence strengths, notably but not only in the field of data analytics. By engaging with external actors (e.g. start-ups, universities), firms search for opportunities to access complementary skills, spur creativity, and channel R&D efforts towards areas that would not have been explored.

b) Share the risks and costs of uncertain investments in digital innovation: Firms are often confronted with a variety of potential research and technology development paths, the mastery of which requires large-scale investments with very uncertain outcomes. Collaboration with others allows firms to expand into different areas while sharing costs.

There are several configurations and operational solutions to engage in mass collaboration.

First of all, **incubation** and **acceleration** programs allow established firms to engage with newcomer, smaller, and more innovative start-ups. The latter are at an early stage of development and do not have the financial resources to grow by themselves. At odds, they possess new R&D capabilities, and fresher ideas to develop digital innovations and new solutions. This kind of collaboration is particularly effective in those regions where social capital has spurred over time and proper innovation ecosystems have been established, such as Silicon Valley, Tel Aviv, Berlin, and London. Normally, this kind of collaboration brings together a variety of actors, such as big high-tech companies, start-ups, but also venture capital, universities, research centers. Thus, this is also referred to as the triple-helix or multiple-helix of innovation model.

Another solution is the creation of industry platforms and standards for digital innovation. They can be defined as *products, services or technologies that provide the foundation upon which different actors can innovate by developing complementary products, services or technologies using digital tools* (Gawer & Cusumano, 2014). The platform can become the standard de facto, which enables faster innovation rates and lower time-to-market for new products.

Moreover, through crowdsourcing platforms and hackathons, firms can source new ideas from external actors. Generally, these solutions are sought when firms need to tackle a specific problem or challenge or find new design ideas. In these cases, firms launch a challenge through online channels and collect the proposals coming from a pool of innovators. These proposals are then selected and eventually adopted by the firm, granting an award to the winning proposal. The innovators can be designers, scientists, experts, or even simply customers. The prizes can be monetary rewards, but also other kinds of reward. Adopting this approach, firms can access a wide pool of skills and a vast knowledge base, and foster knowledge flows across scientific or sectoral communities. Moreover, these solutions lower the cost and time devoted to developing a solution or innovation. Finally, they allow firms to be aware of the latest technological developments and trends.

1.3. Evolution of Knowledge in Management [2]

The concept of knowledge is as old as mankind. It would be interesting to

---

[2] The author acknowledges the valuable insights to this paragraph provided by Laura Pileggi, during the supervision of her Master thesis at the Faculty of Economics at Roma Tre University.

go back to the ancient Greek philosophers, such as Plato and Aristotle, to engage in an articulated debate around knowledge. The relation, then, between *epistêmê* and *technê* in ancient philosophy offers an interesting contrast with our own notions about theory (pure knowledge) and (experience-based) practice. Unfortunately, this debate is well beyond the scope of this book. Yet, the managerial literature has engaged in long, and sometimes philosophical, debates around the definition of knowledge. It is impossible to come up with one single definition.

1.3.1. Data, Information, Knowledge

Knowledge appears both as a difficult concept to define and as a bearer of many nuances and paradoxes. Knowledge does not deteriorate but, on the contrary, it is increased and enhanced with use and can be used without limit without running out (Davenport & Prusak, 2000b; Rullani, 2004). Consequently, knowledge can generate potentially infinite value, and it is created by individuals, from whom an organization cannot disregard.

The distinction between information and knowledge can be summarized in Table 1.1.

Table 1.1. How are information and knowledge different?

	Information	Knowledge
Source	DATA: Information is data that is processed	INFORMATION: Knowledge is information that is modeled to be useful
Purpose	Connection: Information deals with the way that data is related	Meaning: Knowledge examines the patterns within a set of information

Source: author's elaboration.

Despite the variety of definitions, the different authors agree in the distinction among data, information, and knowledge that are sometimes used interchangeably but are rather three different concepts. The mainstream literature identifies the hierarchical order that links data, information, knowledge, and wisdom (or intelligence) (Figure 1.6). Although several graphical renderings have been proposed, generally speaking data represent raw numbers and facts which can be transformed into information, information stems from processing data, and knowledge is information made actionable (Hicks et al., 2006).

> **Box 1.3.** Characteristics of knowledge
>
> - Knowledge does not deteriorate with use, it actually increases its value when shared;
> - The marginal cost of reproducing an additional piece of knowledge is very low;
> - Knowledge cannot easily be stored;
> - Knowledge involves the processing, creation, or use of information in the individual mind;
> - Knowledge is information combined with experience, context, interpretation, reflection, and perspective;
> - Knowledge is ineffective if it's not used.

Source: author's elaboration.

Figure 1.6. The Pyramid of Knowledge.

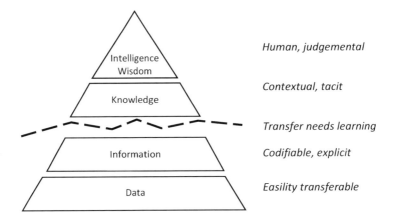

Source: author's elaboration.

One of the original formulations of the pyramid of knowledge has been elaborated by Ackoff back in 1989. The author defines data, information, knowledge, understanding, intelligence and wisdom and explores the transformation between these elements. Wisdom is located at the top of a hierarchy (Figure 1.6). "*Descending from wisdom there are understanding, knowledge, information, and, at the bottom, data. Each of these includes the categories that fall below it – for example, there can be no wisdom without understanding and no understanding without knowledge.*" (Ackoff, 1989, p. 3).

Ackoff offers the following definitions of data, information, knowledge, and wisdom, and their associated transformation processes (Rowley, 2007):

- Data are defined as symbols that represent properties of objects, events, and their environment. They are the products of *observation*. But are of no use until they are in a usable (i.e. relevant) form. The difference between data and information is functional, not structural.
- Information is contained in descriptions, answers to questions that begin with such words as who, what, when, and how many. Information systems generate, store, retrieve, and process data. Information is inferred from data.
- Knowledge is know-how and it is what makes possible the transformation of information into instructions. Knowledge can be obtained either by transmission from another who has it, by instruction, or by extracting it from experience.
- Intelligence is the ability to increase efficiency.
- Wisdom is the ability to increase effectiveness. Wisdom adds value, which requires the mental function that we call judgement. The ethical and aesthetic values that this implies are inherent to the actor and are unique and personal.

Elaborating more in detail, we offer the following descriptions.

Data represent the objective output of any operation and they are the symbolic representation of numbers, letters, facts, and images referring to an event. Data on their own possess limited relevance and purposes. Data do not have an independent meaning as they can describe events only partially, not providing any judgment or interpretation on them and therefore not providing any basis for actions. Nevertheless, data are extremely important for organizations as they are considered to be the raw material for information. In fact, by interpretation, contextualization, and structuring, data are transformed into information (Kane et al., 2014).

Information indeed, is data owning a meaning as it is able to reduce ambiguity and uncertainty typical of data. According to Davenport and Prusak (2000), information is data able to "make the difference," as it has gained the added value of a meaning through different possible processes such as contextualization, the recognition of the aim of data gathering, categorization, the recognition of data key unit of analysis, calculation, mathematical or statistical analysis conducted on data, revision, the mistakes elimination from data and concentration, or the data summary in a concise form (Davenport & Prusak, 2000b; Profili, 2004a). Information provides a new point of view for interpreting events or objects (data) which makes visible previously invisible meanings or sheds lights on unexpected connections; therefore it can be seen as a flow of messages (Nonaka & Takeuchi, 1995b).

Knowledge can be considered the product of the process of learning, deriving from interpretation of information on cause-effect relationships and from application of that information. It is information that has been authenticated and is thought to be true. Knowledge is made of interpretations, beliefs, perspectives, and expectations. It is intangible and personal: knowledge production especially, implies an information rehash process upon which actors' cognitive traits have a strong impact. According to Nonaka and Takeuchi, indeed, knowledge is strictly related to human action and to the context in which it developed. Knowledge is a function of the beliefs, commitment, and intention of actors, it always involves action as it always has a specific meaning and aim. Hence the dynamic and relational nature of knowledge emerges as much as it can be defined as a dynamic human process of justifying personal beliefs toward the truth.

Intelligence is the ability to increase efficiency.

Finally, **Wisdom** is the ability to increase effectiveness. Wisdom adds value, which requires the mental function that we call judgement. The ethical and aesthetic values that this implies are inherent to the actor and are unique and personal (Rowley, 2007).

The dynamic nature of knowledge strongly marks its difference between information and knowledge itself. Information is either static, as it is made of a set of data related to the world state and the deriving consequences, and atomistic, as it considers individuals as independent from their context and from their history. On the other hand, knowledge is dynamic because, in order to keep being valued, it needs to be continuously regenerated, rehashed and expanded through learning processes and it is relational because it emerges from an interpretation process which collocates a single phenomenon into a conceptual web made of schemes, expectations and memories embedded in the individuals and in social systems. Davenport and Prusak define knowledge as "a combination of a fluid mix of framed experience, contextual information, values and expert insight that provides a framework for evaluating and incorporating new experiences and information". Again, from this definition, the complex nature of knowledge emerges: it is an intuitive entity and therefore it is tough to be explained in logic terms (Davenport & Prusak, 2000b).

1.3.2. Approaches to Knowledge Management [3]

According to Davenport and Prusak (1998), Knowledge Management means identifying, managing and enhancing what the organization knows or could know. In other citations, Knowledge Management concerns the critical issues of organizational adaptation, survival, and competence in the face of growing and discontinuous environmental change. Essentially it represents organizational processes that seek a synergistic combination between the ability to process information and the creative and innovative ability of people. Knowledge Management considers the synergies between the technological and behavioral aspects, necessary for the development of the company (Romer, 1990). Based on these assumptions, Knowledge Management can be defined as an element of coordination of the resources necessary for the creation of added value. Knowledge Management has highlighted the importance of learning as a fundamental resource for the survival of organizations. Therefore, the creation and sharing of knowledge is the keystone for effective Knowledge Management.

Although many taxonomies and classifications of Knowledge Management have been proposed, one of the most cited has identified seven different schools of Knowledge Management or strategies (Earl, 2001a). Each approach shows an orientation and a particular focus, but the schools are not mutually exclusive, as it is possible to observe different approaches applied in one organization at the same time. Indeed, each school is outlined through several parameters, such as the focus, the aim, the unit of analysis, the success factors and the philosophy followed. Earl clusters the 7 Knowledge Management schools in 3 main categories, as it is shown in Table 1.2:

- technocratic schools, consisting of systems school, cartographic school and engineering school;
- economic school, consisting of the commercial school;
- behavioral schools, including the organizational school, the spatial school, and the strategic school.

The technocratic category includes schools of thought based primarily on information and Communication Technologies (ICT), supporting and conditioning employees in their everyday tasks. In the technocratic approaches, ICT represents an interface between knowledge owners and knowledge seekers. This is best exemplified by the creation of relevant re-

---

[3] The author acknowledges the contribution of Laura Pileggi and Matteo Pagnani to this paragraph.

cording systems in different formats to suit each school as they strive to achieve their goals of managing tacit knowledge. Achievement of such goals is made possible through the codified systems in the form of knowledge bases, knowledge directories, and knowledge processes. It is through these codified systems that aspects of tangibility, shareability, transferability, and storability are achieved due to the tacit knowledge being converted into explicit knowledge (Njiraine & Le Roux, 2011).

Table 1.2. Taxonomy of Knowledge Management Schools.

	Technocratic			Economic	Behavioral		
	Systems	Cartographic	Process	Commercial	Organizational	Spatial	Strategic
FOCUS	Technology	Maps	Processes	Income	Networks	Space	Mindset
AIM	Knowledge Bases	Knowledge Directories	Knowledge Flows	Knowledge Assets	Knowledge Pooling	Knowledge Exchange	Knowledge Capabilities
UNIT	Domain	Enterprise	Activity	Know-how	Communities	Place	Business
PHILOSOPHY	Codification	Connectivity	Capability	Commercialization	Collaboration	Contactivity	Consciousness

Source: author's elaboration based on (Earl, 2001).

The three schools belonging to the technocratic category in Earl's taxonomy are grouped together, as they are considered to be based on the belief that one of the constraints on business performance improving is the lack of information and knowledge which is recognized as available in the organization or reachable within its boundaries; moreover, it is assumed that such information and knowledge can be transferred accurately and effectively through technical systems although it is possible to realize in different ways, by repositories, directories and maps, or by processes descriptions (Blackman & Henderson, 2005). The common goal of the technocratic approach's branches is the transformation of knowledge in such a form which can be available and accessible for individuals who are in need of it. Although Earl uses the term codification only for the systems school, preferring to separate this concept from the connectivity of the cartographic school and from the capability philosophy of the process school, it can likewise be used to describe all the three schools, if taken in a broader sense. Davenport and Prusak (Davenport & Prusak, 2000a),in fact, define codification as the activities of transformation of knowledge in an accessible and applicable format in order to foster its spreading process: it can be considered as coinciding with Earl's technocratic school's aims. In this sense in fact, the term codification is suitable for all three schools because all of them aim for this objective with different modalities: creating knowledge databases, mapping knowledge owners, or providing processes descriptions. As already highlighted by Earl, IT plays an essential role in such activities because it allows their easier implementation.

As emerged from the description of the first three schools, the real challenge is about the possibility of implementing codification of knowledge without making its properties weaker and without letting it become a poor container for information and data. An essential issue is the identification of the knowledge source in order to make it possible to use, and the validation which leads to defining its usefulness. (Davenport & Prusak, 2000a)

As already highlighted by Earl, IT plays an essential role in such activities because it allows their easier implementation. Technologies precisely are able to overcome spatial and temporal barriers making communication easier and allowing the creation of an organizational memory to which all organization members can access and contribute in order to share and update their experiences and problems' solutions. The creation of such memory and the possibility to access it is strongly related to categorization methods which have to be functional to the information seeking in order to make it easier and faster without cost and time loss. As it has been described in Earl's taxonomy's review, Knowledge Management System can assume different forms such as shared-based databases, acting as repositories, typical of the system school approach; skills directories which enable organizational skills localization, as shown in the cartographic school description; computer-based technologies to support processes (Profili, 2004b).

The **commercial school** is the only entry proposed by Earl in the economic category. The commercial school knowledge Management Model aims to mainly to exploit knowledge and intellectual property directly and not exploit their mediating effect on organizational processes. Essentially, a newly created knowledge, a discovery, carried out in an empirical context is constructed in a protective patent or any similar defendable form of intellectual property. In models belonging to this economical approach, knowledge is not a process but it is rather a product for sale which needs to be exploited by itself and not through its effect on people or processes. Therefore, the exploitation of knowledge in such an approach is made by restriction and not by sharing processes:(Blackman & Henderson, 2007) The main idea is not sharing knowledge in order to make its property wider, but it is rather about protecting and commercializing knowledge: following commercial logic, it mostly concerns with protecting and exploiting a firm's knowledge or intellectual assets in order to produce revenue streams. Knowledge is considered only as an asset to be managed as any other firm's asset and it can be identified as intellectual property comprising patents, trademarks, copyrights and know-how. Therefore, critical success factors in this school are concerned with the successful commitment in deploying the knowledge asset. An essential element is the development or acquisition of capabilities, techniques, and procedures necessary to successfully manage intellectual assets as a routine process: in this manner, firms can avoid losing time on measuring intellectual capital and focus time and resources on effectively developing and exploiting it (Earl, 2001b). The philosophy underlying an economical approach is obviously concerned with commercialization, and as well as with all the other resource management approaches, knowledge management economic approach is also based on protecting and exploiting from a commercial point of view the asset called knowledge, exactly as it happens for any other asset that a firm can own.

The third category proposed by Earl is the **behavioral category** where he includes the three Knowledge Management schools most focusing on stimulating managers and management to be active in the creation, sharing, and usage of knowledge as a resource. In Earl's taxonomy it includes three schools: organizational, focusing on themes largely investigated by literature, spatial school, and strategic school.

One of the main contributions to the behavioral approach stream is probably the knowledge creation model proposed by Nonaka and Takeuchi (Nonaka & Takeuchi, 1995a), the SECI model (Figure 1.7). This model explains how knowledge is continuously created on the basis of the epistemological distinction between explicit and tacit knowledge and on their interaction (Handzic, 2011).

Figure 1.7. The SECI model.

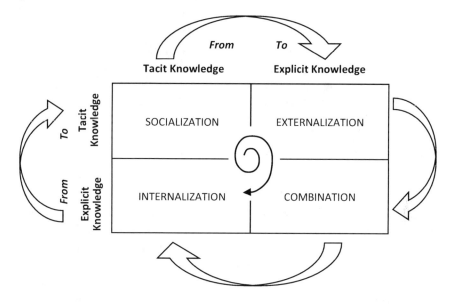

Source: author's elaboration based on Nonaka and Takeuchi (1995).

Arising from the epistemology distinction between explicit and tacit knowledge, Nonaka and Takeuchi recognize the need for a knowledge creation theory able to explicate the organizational level knowledge creation as a dynamic interaction between tacit and explicit knowledge. The key premise of the model is that explicit and tacit knowledge are not totally separate but they rather interact with each other in the creative human activities: the assumption is that human knowledge can be expanded in quality and quantity through a process of dynamic and social interaction between explicit and tacit knowledge, called "knowledge conversion". It needs to be highlighted that this dynamic and social conversion happens between individuals and not within individuals as single entities. Although human cognition is considered to be a deductive process of individuals and therefore ideas are considered to be formed in minds of individuals, an individual is never isolated, and the social interaction is able to influence all the happening minds perceptions and elaborations. Interaction between individuals typically plays a crucial role in developing ideas and in enhancing concepts: communities of interaction contribute to amplify and develop new knowledge. Thus, the recognition of the importance of social interaction in knowledge transfer, sharing, and creation is the reason why Nonaka and Takeuchi's model is considered as an essential contribution to the behavioral approach to Knowledge Management.

As mentioned earlier, the model explains knowledge creation as a process of interaction between tacit and explicit knowledge. The knowledge conversion is constituted of 4 modes: socialization process, conversion from tacit knowledge to tacit knowledge, externalization, from tacit knowledge to explicit knowledge, combination, from explicit knowledge to explicit knowledge, internalization from explicit knowledge to tacit knowledge. The process is carried out as a spiral and continuous process, as shown in Figure 1.7.

1.3.3. Network Perspective in Knowledge Management

In some cases, the knowledge is possessed by a few individuals and could therefore, be more difficult to distribute internally in the company. This is not necessarily a problem for companies, because some researchers state that new knowledge can be created from existing knowledge.

The new tools web-based such as the online Business Social Networks may be classified as a set of reporting tools that do not serve only to a mere communicative function. And the relationship between the people who participate in these networks to make a difference as a social network tip, rather than on the set of individuals who are part of, the complex relations that are to be triggered. They are characterized by the convergence of three networks:

i) ICT Network;
ii) Social Network;
iii) Knowledge Network.

These types of networks are made possible by the Internet and World Wide Web technologies, which use pre-existing links and basic social, professional, business collaboration, and networking among governments, researchers, and businesses. In practice, the single firm establishes an interactive relationship with the client that will enable it to meet the multiple needs of the latter by providing tools, mainly in the form of content and information, useful to ensure the success of their business. This is made possible by the characterization of the Web 2.0 and its development towards the web 3.0 that, encouraging interaction site-user allows it to an active involvement that often takes the form of a real creation of personalized content. In this review, the potential of the individual user is enhanced as a system of promotion and dissemination.

Because of the relationship between the company and customers, the strategy of learning must be seen as a two-way, as the company not only transmits its knowledge but learns itself from the customer. So this is not an idea of learning as a mere individual process that consists of a transfer of knowledge and skills default through mechanisms controlled stimuli and responses (Midoro, 2002). The creation of knowledge through collaboration is realized rather as a realignment of experience and expertise between all participants in a successful network. When experience and expertise are too far apart or too close, it triggers an imbalance that makes it difficult to create and the consequent sharing of knowledge. In the system outlined by the use of the Digital Business Ecosystem (DBE), knowledge is created and diffused collectively, thanks to the dynamic processes of cooperation that are established between the different actors of the system. The significance of each actor is found in its ability to provide impulses for innovation and the generation of innovative ideas. The sharing of creative ideas can be used to create both competitive advantages for existing businesses and opportunities for new business.

The lever capable of ensuring the success of the company in the medium to long term results in the creation of a new organizational model. It must be based on interactivity and be more appropriate to the context than the hierarchical organizations and informal processes, that they represent a model for a shift to the Enterprise 2.0 model.

In summary, Web 2.0 has highlighted the attitude of human resources within the company to use mechanisms and platforms to be connected, manage, and expand their social system. In the process of creation of the value of firms assume considerable importance relational networks of knowledge that have the function to receive, store, process, and/or transmit information. In this context, the digital technologies offer powerful instruments for the management of knowledge from external sources, helping to increase the body of knowledge that the firm develops through the relationship with the market and, in general, with all the stakeholders with which it operates, as holders of elements of relevant knowledge. New knowledge, then, stems from the interaction and sharing of bits of information through the network.

Knowledge is the most valuable asset companies keep in the contemporary world where every piece of information is very valuable. But knowledge wouldn't necessarily exist without networks. Through networks, it is easier to distribute the relevant knowledge to people that can make good use of the information. This is particularly true if we consider the huge value of social networks in expanding knowledge networks.

The research within the field of knowledge network is based on three important dimensions: knowledge outcome, knowledge network properties, and level of analysis (Figure 1.8).

Figure 1.8. A framework for knowledge network research.

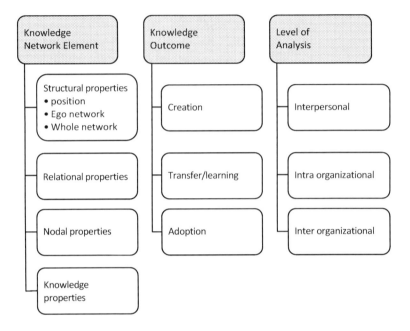

Source: author's elaboration based on (Phelps et al., 2012).

1) The first dimension refers to knowledge network elements. These include properties of network structure, relations, nodes, and knowledge flows. In knowledge networks, nodes are considered as connection points between different sources of knowledge. The knowledge network element has to do with different properties that will eventually form a knowledge network. There are different properties according to what previous research has shown.

These are a) Structural, b) Relational, c) Nodal, and d) Knowledge properties.

A) **Structural properties** are subdivided in three different categories:
- Network Position,
- Ego,
- Whole network.

Network position refers to a persons' social proximity to other persons in an individuals' network. This proximity has been measured in previous studies as length or strength of the paths that connect individuals in a network. The position can also capture the similarity of individuals based on similarities of these individuals. According to this theory, individuals with direct ties have a better knowledge flow than individuals with indirect ties. Direct ties enable a better frequency of communication and sharing, and with more relevant and detailed information at the end.

While in the literature position gets some consistent support, **Ego** properties have very conflicting results.

The **whole network** element refers to the density in a network. Previous research papers show that networks that are well connected, have a better rate of good quality information. This, in turn, will often foster innovation. Also, the shorter the pat4h length of a network is, the better is the information that is distributed through the whole network. Therefore, close ties between individuals will foster better innovation and better information flow.

B) **Relational properties** and the research done in this area is aimed to understand the similarity and the st4rength of ties between individuals in a network. These proxies can then be used for estimating the knowledge outcomes.

C) **Nodal properties** refer to the connection between networks and individuals. One of the main resources to create and maintain knowledge networks are Nodes. Nodes are connection points between different knowledge resources. These nodes are crucial for knowledge networks. Nodes are considered ambassadors who search, adopt, transmit, and eventually create knowledge. Therefore, one could consider the nodes as sources and recipients that gather information and knowledge. Nodes are usually individuals or a group of people for example teams, in some cases, nodes can be considered as patents and other knowledge elements. Nodes can also consist of unde4r units in organizations, the whole organization can also be a node. To conclude, nodes can be found usually in bigger units of people, which usually makes the knowledge creation process more efficient and the knowledge network stronger.

These can also be non-human resources such as patents and catalogs. Nodes are important for organizations and other individuals who want to create innovation and knowledge.

D) **Knowledge properties**. A large part of the research has shown that experience is a valuable source of knowledge. Thus, in organizations, it is important to store and retrieve knowledge in order to learn by doing. The experience gained will eventually become knowledge.

Experience and knowledge can be stored in organizations even if they are geographically dispersed, leveraging the cloud storage that is now available. Knowledge can, therefore, be harnessed, for example in a manual for new employees.

2) The second dimension is represented by **knowledge outcomes**, which include knowledge creation, knowledge transfer, learning, and adoption of knowledge.

More in detail, the first knowledge outcome is knowledge creation, which refers to a wave of new knowledge. In practical terms, it means ideas that will eventually create new products and services, organizational practices, technical inventions and innovations, and also products that will create knowledge by using them.

The transfer of knowledge refers to information sharing by a source, for example a person or a written manual. This source shares the information and knowledge with the receiver, and the transfer is complete when the receiver has acquired and learned the information that has been shared.

The third type of knowledge outcome is the adoption of knowledge. The adoption of knowledge is the decision and the ability to use or implement a specific element of knowledge. The adoption is often made in the form of a product practice or a paper. As for the adoption of knowledge, innovations are more likely to be adopted by new users when an innovator has a central position. The reason for this is that the more central position an innovator has, the more information is available about the innovator. A really good example is Apple. Apple is a front-runner in technologies. What Apple does, usually with high quality, a lot of companies try to replicate those products and adopt those innovations of Apple, into their products.

3) Finally, the third dimension is the **level of analysis**, which includes interpersonal, intra-organizational, and inter-organizational levels of analysis.

All of these three are fundamental for the creation of knowledge networks. When the knowledge is created, different resources are needed to prepare the transformation and translation of the existing knowledge to be transferred. These steps are often necessary to create knowledge that can be easily adopted and used in the long-run.

1.4. Why Do We Still Need to Manage Knowledge?

A common trait of the rich body of knowledge on these subjects lays in the recognition that the traditional manual trades and blue-collar work have declined to the benefit of knowledge work across occupations. For knowledge workers, knowledge is simultaneously an input, medium, and output of their work. The knowledge economy is one where economic value is found more in the intangibles, such as new ideas, software, services, and relationships, and less in tangibles, like physical products, steel or land (Newell et al., 2009).

Knowledge management is at the core of innovation management since no innovation could occur without proper management of the firm's knowledge base, and its fruitful combination with other external actors.

Figure 1.9. Knowledge, innovation, and people management.

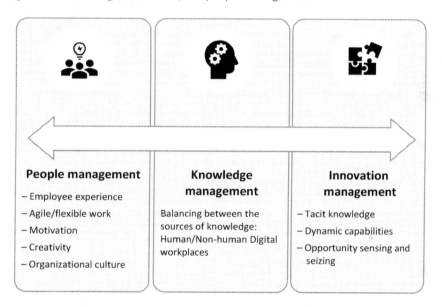

Source: author's elaboration.

On the other side, threats of information overflows are to be considered. It is useful to recall what Simon wrote back in 1971:

"... in an information-rich world, the wealth of information means a dearth of something else: a scarcity of whatever it is that information consumes. What information consumes is rather obvious: it consumes the attention of its recipients. Hence a wealth of information creates a poverty of attention and a need to allocate that attention efficiently among the overabundance of information sources that might consume it". (Simon, 1971, pp. 40-41).

Thus, knowledge management is needed, now more than ever, to assist people within the organizations to make the most of the digital technologies for their work activities. It could be stated that knowledge management has a direct connection in terms of innovation (activities and outcomes) and people (human resources within the organization) (Figure 1.9).

1.4.1. Knowledge Management and Innovation

New information technology and the adoption of standards is greatly assisted by global connectivity: once every person and every business is connected electronically through networks, information can flow more readily. Sufficient information can be collected by mail or on the Internet to enable customers to engage in comparative shopping. In the old analog age, the transfer of information required proximity and specialized channels to customers, suppliers, and distribution, but now network computing, supported by an advanced communication infrastructure, can facilitate collaborative entrepreneurialism by stripping out barriers to communication. Recurrent reorganization becomes the norm, not the exception.

In the Digital Age, knowledge management is critical in its ability to capture value from innovative activities. Firms can put in place proper structures, incentives, and management to generate innovation and build knowledge assets. Thus, the critical activity lays in the deployment and use of knowledge assets. Knowledge is undoubtedly embedded in individuals' experience and expertise. The task of the firms is to provide the right mix of physical spaces, social resources, and allocation structure so that competences can stem from knowledge.

The competitive advantage of firms in the digital age does not stem from market positions, but from firms' ability to deploy knowledge assets that are difficult to replicate. In this vein, tacit knowledge is the most difficult to be imitated.

Complementary assets become relevant in this context. They matter because knowledge assets are typically an intermediate good and need to be packaged into products or services to yield value. When the services of complementary assets are required, they can play an important role in the competitive advantage equation. Because the market for complementary assets is itself riddled with imperfections, competitive advantage can be gained or lost on how expertly the strategy for gaining access is executed. The difficulty to replicate complementary assets can represent a second line of defense against imitators and an important source of competitive advantage.

In many sectors in today's global market, the competitive advantage also requires dynamic capabilities. This is the ability to sense and then to seize new opportunities, and to reconfigure and protect knowledge assets, competencies, and technologies to achieve sustainable competitive advantage. For an organization to exhibit dynamic capabilities, it must sense the opportunity and the need for change, properly calibrate responsive actions and investments. During sensemaking the organization receives information about the market and technologies and evaluates them: it is a critical function but, well-performed, it can enable the organization to connect with its environment thereby generating superior returns. Sensemaking can be assisted with some tools like scenario planning as well as the insights of brilliant outsiders; scenario planning can help managers to develop mental maps of possible complex future realities, to understand the drivers of change. Then, an organization can choose action plans. The openness of markets, stronger intellectual property, increasing returns, the unbundling of artifacts and information, and the possibilities for integration using new information technology are necessarily a part of sensemaking. There is also the need to identify relevant external technology and bring it into the firm. In short, internal and external R&D are complements rather than substitutes.

Once an opportunity is sensed, it must be then sized. This is where the organization's ability to quickly contract up the requisite external resources and direct the relevant internal resources come into play. Enhancing the ability to sense and seize is at the core of an innovative organization. Finding innovative ways of organizing implies searching for leaner processes and more effective ways to boost information flows within the boundaries of the firm, as well as with external stakeholders. The firm is a repository of knowledge (the knowledge being embedded in business routines and processes). Distinctive processes undergird firm-specific assets and competences.

The firm's capacity to sense and seize opportunities, to reconfigure its knowledge assets, competencies, and complementary assets, to select appropriate organization forms and to allocate resources astutely and price strategically all constitute its dynamic capabilities. Configuring the dynamic capabilities allow firms to renew the knowledge base and combine it with complementary assets, which ultimately can lead to gain a competitive advantage. The emphasis on the development and exploitation of knowledge assets shifts the focus of attention from cost minimization to value maximization.

1.4.2. Knowledge Management and People Management

Under the premises of the knowledge economy, the essence of the firm is not only its ability to create, transfer, assemble, integrate and exploit knowledge assets, but also to select relevant information and to avoid negative effects that are related to (Roda, 2010; Roda & Nabeth, 2008):

- people negative perception and cognitive limitations (Roscoe et al., 2019);
- social interaction overload (Misra & Stokols, 2012);
- interruption (Hall et al., 2015);
- excessive multitasking (Rosen, 2008).

The Digital Age has brought non-human sources of knowledge in business organizations and workplaces. Globally interconnected networks of humans (natural intelligence) and artificial intelligence provide unprecedented opportunities for knowledge creation. Thus, this interconnection does not come easy. It rather requires new management styles, new leaderships, and new organizational cultures. Here lies the great challenge for Human Resources Management, or People Management.

Firms can successfully cope with the digital transformation only if they are able to leverage their intangible assets, which are the most important. Above all, knowledge and networking are the most important intangible assets. There is only one element that expresses simultaneously knowledge and networking, and it is the human capital. Thus, also in the digital age, when robots and artificial intelligence are becoming a substitute for human jobs, yet humans appear to be impossible to be fully substituted.

In such new contexts, firms need to nurture a fully collaborative organizational culture, that fosters continuous innovation and the emergence of new ideas from the whole organization. Innovation is not confined in the R&D Department, rather it is a global organizational attitude.

On the other side, people need to be motivated towards the development of dynamic capabilities that allow the organization to stay competitive and updated. In other words, firms need to take into account the Employee Experience (EX) (Plaskoff, 2017). The EX is also data-driven, as it leverages the data and information emerging through informal conversation with employees to fully understand the drivers of the individual motivations to work and individual expectations. This would lead to more satisfied employees, in a virtuous circle of growth and prosperity, in the co-construction of the EX (Rosario Sica, 2019).

1.4.3. The Pyramid of Knowledge, Revisited

The latest technological advancements that are at the core of the Digital Age define an unprecedented interaction between human and non-human actors (Figure 1.10). Cyber-physical systems are defined as computational collaboration systems connected with the surrounding physical world and its on-going processes (Rüßmann et al., 2015), providing and using, at the same time, data accessing and data-processing services available on the internet (Barbosa et al., 2017).

Figure 1.10. Human and non-human interactions in cyber physical systems.

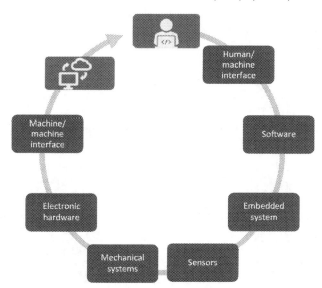

Source: author's elaboration.

Paragraph 1.3.1 discussed the pyramid of knowledge and showed that the old paradigm was based on the assumption that the human mind's capacity for decision-making allows humans to generate knowledge out of information and data. In light of the innovations introduced in the Digital Age, this human exclusivity is actually threatened. In fact, an increasing evidence base shows that machines are able to formulate more accurate decisions than experts, thanks to access to increasing volumes of data and the development of algorithms (McAfee & Brynjolfsson, 2017). Therefore, companies should gradually replace their opinion-based decisions with data-based decisions. Of course, machine learning is a rapidly developing field that still has many limitations, but these are gradually being overcome. Hence, although there are examples of business processes that have changed profoundly with the application of these techniques, there is still enormous room for evolution.

Although machines have been able to improve their contributions in the field of creativity, they are still incapable, and presumably will continue to be, for a long time to understand the world through the human prism. Therefore, the application of dimensions such as empathy or leadership is protected terrain for human beings. We could state that referring to the Pyramid of knowledge, only the upper levels are restricted to human actors. Considering the model proposed by Zeleny, the upper level is called enlightenment. It is interesting to compare Ackoff's and Zeleny's models (Table 1.3), to see how they define the different levels and how these levels have clearly become easily delegated to machines and non-human actors (Ackoff, 1989; Zeleny, 1987).

Table 1.3. Comparison between Zeleny and Ackoff pyramids of knowledge.

	Zeleny	Ackoff
Data	Know nothing	Symbols
Information	Know what	Data that are processed to be useful; provides answers to who, what, where, and when questions
Knowledge	Know how	Application of data and information; answers how questions
Understanding		Appreciation of why
Wisdom	Know why	Evaluated understanding
Enlightenment	Attaining the same sense of truth, the sense of right and wrong, and having it socially accepted, respected, and sanctioned	

Source: author's elaboration based on (Rowley, 2007).

The nature of wisdom or enlightenment attains the moral values and principles that are embedded in human nature. Thus, although non-human actors such as artificial intelligence, robots, and computers are now able to reach the stage of knowledge, the upper level of the pyramid still requires the attainment of human components that machines do not (yet) possess (Figure 1.11 and Figure 1.12).

Figure 1.11. From data to wisdom.

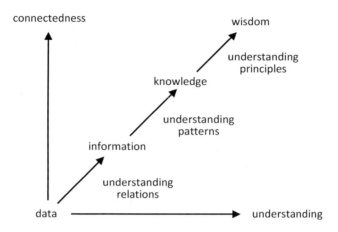

Source: https://www.systems-thinking.org/dikw/dikw.htm.

Figure 1.12. The DIKW Pyramid, human vs. non-human impact.

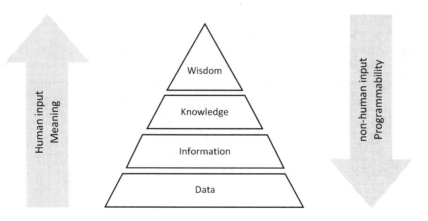

Source: author's elaboration based on (Rowley, 2007, p. 164).

The inherent ethical aspect of wisdom prevents computers from having the ability to possess wisdom. It is surely true that "[…] *wisdom is a uniquely human state, or as I see it, wisdom requires one to have a soul, for it resides as much in the heart as in the mind*" (Bellinger et al., 2004); although more recent study begins to show that Artificial Intelligence enables turning vast amounts of data into information for superior knowledge creation and knowledge management (Paschen et al., 2020).

1.4.4. Much Ado about Knowledge, here Comes the Pandemic!

The power of the drivers of the Digital Age is almost the same that caused the 2020 Covid-19 pandemic emergency. Having just welcomed the new year, in January 2020 the citizens of the western countries began to read worrying news about a new virus that was spreading a remote city in China (Wuhan). This new coronavirus seemed to be, back at that time, remotely confined in China, or better in a single Chinese area. Soon enough, it was evident that indeed the virus was spreading well beyond Wuhan, and it soon reached Europe, starting from Italy. Consequently, to avoid the dangerous uncontrolled spread of the unknown virus, the European national governments decided to lockdown their countries. In some cases, the lockdown was extremely severe, as in Italy, in other cases the lockdown was milder. In any case, the emergency exceptionally forced citizens of all ages to stay at home. Daily activities like working and attending classes became impossible without a device connected to the Internet. Work became smart work, flexible work, or remote work. Schools became smart schooling or distant schooling. Work and education were therefore exceptionally performed through a technological medium. We all discovered the beauty, and the beast, of working/studying, being physically separated and digitally connected from other human beings, such as co-workers, schoolmates, or simply friends and distant relatives.

From the perspective of Knowledge Management, this is an extraordinary example of the importance of being prepared to sharing knowledge through digital technologies. Those who were already accustomed to using such technologies, more easily adapted to the emergency. Those who did not have either the competencies or the infrastructure to deal with the emergency have been left behind.

It is interesting to compare the number of workers who regularly worked from home, per country (Figure 1.13).

Figure 1.13. Workers who regularly work from home, per Country, 2018.

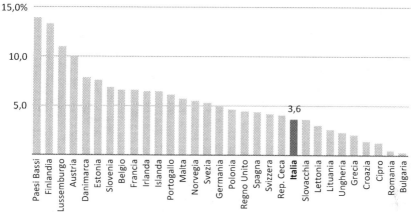

Source: elaboration on data Eurostat.

It is evident that the situation is very diverse across Europe. Indeed, a diverse situation is also persistent within each country. The digital divide persists, especially in some Countries, and hinders the possibility that equal opportunities are given to all workers. Places where the fast internet connection is still not available, or where infrastructural problems persist, do not permit to fully leverage the opportunities brought by the digital technologies.

Chapter 2
WHY IS KNOWLEDGE THE STRATEGIC ASSET?

SUMMARY: 2.1. Leveraging the Technological Trigger. – 2.2. Digital-enabled Business Opportunities. – 2.2.1. Data-based innovation. – 2.2.2. Servitization. – 2.2.3. Faster Innovation Cycles. – 2.2.4. Open Collaboration and Digital Business Ecosystems. – 2.3. Which technology? What Are the Exponential Technologies? – 2.3.1. Big Data. – 2.3.2. Business Intelligence. – 2.3.3. Cloud Computing. – 2.3.4. Internet of Things (or of Everything). – 2.3.5. Artificial Intelligence (AI). – 2.4. Diffusion of (Digital) Innovations. – 2.5. All that Glitters Is not (Technological) Gold! – 2.5.1. Information Systems in Organizations. – 2.5.2. Technology Acceptance Models. – 2.5.3. IS and Change Management.

2.1. Leveraging the Technological Trigger [1]

As shown in the previous chapter, digital technologies have brought to businesses a whole new world of possibilities. Technological advances such as Big Data, Internet of Things (IoT), or Internet of Everything (IoE), Artificial Intelligence (AI) are redefining some basic principles on decision-making in organizations, allowing organizational change towards simpler and leaner organizations.

As far as knowledge in organizations and knowledge management are concerned, obviously, these digital technologies boost the possibility to effectively implement proper Knowledge Management Systems (KMS).

Two main dimensions are essential in knowledge management:

- enablers, and
- processes.

Enablers are mechanisms that facilitate knowledge management activities, such as codifying and sharing among individuals and teams. Moreover, they stimulate knowledge creation, sharing, and protection, and provide the infrastructure necessary to improve the knowledge processes (Yeh et al., 2006).

---

[1] We are grateful to Alessio Balducci and Pietro Pratense for the inputs provided for this chapter.

Knowledge management processes refer to the structured coordination of managing knowledge effectively, such as knowledge creation, sharing, storage, and application (Lee & Choi, 2003).

The management of knowledge can be strongly supported by advanced ICTs. KMS is essentially based on ICTs (Alavi & Leidner, 2001), because innovative ICTs (for example the internet, data mining techniques, and software agents) can be used to systematize knowledge. KMS refers to information systems applied to manage organizational knowledge and to improve the creation, storage, transfer, and application of knowledge (Meihami & Meihami, 2014; Santoro et al., 2018).

Considering knowledge exploration, retention, and exploitation inside and outside the organizational boundaries and relying on previous relevant studies, six different knowledge management capacities are identified:

1. inventive capacity, which regards the firm's ability to internally explore or generate new knowledge (Chebbi et al., 2013);
2. absorptive capacity, which refers to a firm's ability to explore and utilize external knowledge (Cohen & Levinthal, 1990);
3. transformative capacity, which is the firm's ability to internally store knowledge;
4. connective capacity, which represents the firm's ability to store knowledge in inter-organizational relationships (Kale & Singh, 2007);
5. innovative capacity, which is the final process stage of developing new products and services (Santoro et al., 2018); and
6. desorptive capacity, which regards the outward knowledge transfer (Lichtenthaler & Lichtenthaler, 2010).

Several studies on knowledge management suggest that the advantages of establishing a successful KMS include the ability of organizations to be flexible, to respond more quickly to changing market conditions, and the ability to be more innovative, as well as improving decision making and productivity leveraging internal knowledge. Also, KMS is proved to foster ambidexterity in knowledge-intensive firms (Vrontis et al., 2017).

KMS leverage on effective ICTs. In particular, the flexibility of modern digital technologies can foster knowledge inventiveness, knowledge absorption, knowledge transformation, and knowledge connection (Alavi & Leidner, 2001; Lichtenthaler & Lichtenthaler, 2009). This is because digital technologies applied to KMS can encourage the employees to become proactive. Moreover, access to an increasing amount of information allows them to improve capacities and ideas creation (Del Giudice & Della Peruta, 2016).

Although KMS by itself rarely creates a competitive advantage, it has been proved that KMS is positively associated with the creation of an open and collaborative ecosystem, and it helps exploit internal and external flows of knowledge (Vrontis et al., 2017).

2.2. Digital-enabled Business Opportunities

Digital technologies represent a disruption in the economic landscape, as the digitalization has direct impacts on the emergence of new business models, new organizational configurations, and new market segments. It must be highlighted that the opportunities offered by digital technologies may be very different across sectors, with different impacts on products, processes, and business models. Moreover, the adoption and diffusion of digital technologies may happen under different conditions across industries (see later par. 2.4 and 2.5.2). Also, regulatory conditions have a great impact on how digital technologies redefine the competitive landscape, and in many cases, the lack of legislation may create uncertainty or barriers for innovation in some sectors.

It is possible to identify five trends for innovation in the digital age across all sectors of the economy (Paunov & Planes-Satorra, 2019):

1) Data-based innovation;
2) Servitization;
3) Faster innovation cycles;
4) Open collaboration and Digital Business Ecosystems;
5) New organizational capabilities.

2.2.1. Data-Based Innovation

Data is the new oil![2] The massive use of digital technologies has the direct and immediate consequence of producing a wealth of data, which is diverse (personal, business, research, fun, family, etc.) and in time. The digital technologies not only allow for the generation of these huge amounts of data, but they also enable storing, analyzing, retrieving, and combining those data to produce continuous information and knowledge (as seen in Chapter One). Thus, data are a core input for innovation, and the possibilities to exploit such database enables data-driven innovation and new business models.

---

[2] See par. 2.3.1.

As an example, analytics based on Artificial Intelligence and other computational based simulation techniques open up new possibilities of prototyping and innovating. Examples such as Airbnb, Booking.com, Uber, and other platform organizations rely on data continuously updated both at the demand and the offer side of the market. The possibility to compare customer data offers updated knowledge about changing consumer preferences and needs. This also offers the opportunity to continuously customize products and services. Customization may refer to versioning, i.e. offering different versions of the same product/service; or to pricing, i.e. offering different products and services according to time, exploiting the information on price elasticity.

The unprecedented wealth of data is redefining manufacturing. Real-time shop-floor data are used to identify patterns and connections within the production processes. This allows for production optimization, reducing waste, saving energy, and increasing flexibility.

Distributed technologies are also enabling the transformation of existing businesses. For example, blockchain technology feeds global immutable, encrypted, and timestamped databases (Pólvora et al., 2020). Data are validated and replicated all over a decentralized network of nodes. The development of distributed technologies is expected to generate great value in an increasingly interconnected world. They could foster the transactions between actors that are geographically distant or have no particular confidence in each other. Any digital assets could be exchanged through these technologies, such as money, contracts, land titles, medical records, or even services and goods, on a peer-to-peer basis, and with fewer to non-existent intermediaries (Pólvora et al., 2020). Indeed, some sectors are already showing great interest in the adoption of the blockchain (Acciarini et al., 2020).

The project Blockchain for Industrial Transformations was developed by the European Commission with a focus on multi-stakeholder engagement and co-creation. The project focuses on the challenges and the opportunities for the development and uptake of Blockchain in European industrial and business contexts.

Data are furthermore provided by smart and connected devices, as well as smart and connected products. They gather and transmit data on processes, use, and environmental conditions, allowing for process optimization, predictive diagnostics, and in their most advanced stages the autonomous operation of products.

2.2.2. Servitization

Digital innovation has led to a servitization of industry. New opportunities have emerged for innovation in services, especially regarding the possibility to continuously interact with actual and potential customers. This is also possible for manufacturing firms, through the servitization of manufacturing, that means the opportunity to offer services to complement their products. Customer knowledge is thus more and more relevant and the use of technological devices to grasp data that could lead to such knowledge are sought continuously. In fact, retailers are investing heavily in data collection and data analytics capabilities, augmented and virtual reality, and IoT, among others, in order to enhance the consumer experience and optimize processes.

2.2.3. Faster Innovation Cycles

Digital technologies offer opportunities for accelerating innovation processes, ultimately reducing R&D costs and time-to-market. The cycles of development of new products are getting shorter and organizations have realized that the traditional governance models of the projects must speed up in order to align with the rapid changes of the markets. Five trends have been identified in one of the latest and most prominent analyses of OECD (Paunov & Planes-Satorra, 2019):

1. The cost and the time invested in designing, prototyping, and testing new products are significantly lower, thanks to new digitally enabled techniques, such as virtual simulation (enabled by visualization technologies like virtual reality and augmented reality) and 3D printing.
2. Final versions of the digital innovations are launched after testing in a real-life environment. Using versions although they are not in their definitive version, allows conducting real-life testing of the innovative products or services. Through direct interactions with customers, via automatized feedback or online surveys, these new technological opportunities have enhanced the attractiveness of test-and-learn approaches to new product development.
3. Also, for physical products, digital innovations allow launching regular upgrades of the intangible component of the products, so that innovation can happen at a faster pace and lower costs.
4. Manufacturing is more flexible, as digital technologies enable the production of small series at low cost. This means keeping the costs similar to the cost of mass production, while allowing higher customization of products, to respond to customers' requirements and serve niche markets. Production responds to orders, which automatically

pass through the production planning process to the machine control. The machine then reconfigures itself to process individual orders. 3D printing can represent a significant enabler technology within this context.
5. Pay-per-function has emerged as a way to customize products through software rather than hardware (Stolwijk & Punter, 2018). In this way, platforms such as marketplaces like eBay, Amazon, Etsy, Alibaba facilitate market expansion. In fact, customers can be reached regardless of their location, but competition pressures remain high due to the accelerating rate of introduction of new products and functionalities.

2.2.4. Open Collaboration and Digital Business Ecosystems

Faster innovation cycles are connected with more agile, collaborative, and open-ended innovation. The ICT department, which in the past was a silo, today is a hub, the nerve center on which the innovative efforts of the LOB (Line of Business) and external partners, which are now increasingly involved in the renewal processes, converge and from which».

The Digital Age has disrupted the innovation processes, and they have become more collaborative. They involve global networks of stakeholders, and the locus of innovation has shifted from single firms to business ecosystems. In such ecosystems, firms interconnect their business processes and interlink their product modules to architect new digital business models (N.V. Venkatraman et al., 2014).

Digital business innovations are not intra-organizational processes, but they rather happen in "multiorganizational platforms driven by interoperable technologies, intelligent data, and inputs from multiple firms in the ecosystem" (N.V. Venkatraman et al., 2014, p. 2). Thus, **digital business innovation platforms** are *"actions of a network of companies with complementary competencies to co-innovate new business models that are intrinsically based on information and technology functionality"*.

The networking imperative is at the core of the concept of **open innovation** (Chesbrough, 2006; Enkel et al., 2009):
"Open Innovation is a paradigm that assumes that firms can and should use external and internal ideas, and internal and external paths to market. Open Innovation combines internal and external ideas into architectures and systems whose requirements are defined by a business model. The business model utilizes both external and internal ideas to create value, while defining internal mechanisms to claim some portion of that value" (Chesbrough, 2003, p. 4).

Three core processes can be differentiated in open innovation (Enkel et al., 2009):

1) the *outside-in process*: enriching the company's knowledge base through the integration of suppliers, customers, and external knowledge sourcing;
2) the *inside-out process* refers to earning profits by bringing ideas to market, selling IP, and multiplying technology by transferring ideas to the outside environment;
3) the *coupled process* refers to co-creation with (mainly) complementary partners through alliances, cooperation, and joint ventures during which giving and taking are crucial for success.

Traditional firms may find embracing the open innovation paradigm very difficult. In fact, traditional industries considered knowledge as power to held tightly, whereas moving from closed to open innovation requires getting outside past corporate barriers.

Hierarchy, management, or property rights can be barriers to open innovation. Open innovation, on the contrary, needs flat organizations, collaboration, or employees that accept that they do not have all the knowledge.

The journey from Closed to Open Innovation requires a proper organizational change, and effective change management (Table 2.1). In particular, four main dimensions must be activated (Chiaroni et al., 2010):

a) inter-organizational networks,
b) organizational structures,
c) evaluation processes and
d) knowledge management systems.

Table 2.1. Comparison between closed and open innovation paradigms.

Closed Innovation	Open Innovation
Hire the best and the smartest. Most of the smart people in our field work with us	Recognize that lot of smart people work elsewhere and find ways to interface with them
To profit from R&D, we must discover, develop and ship ourselves	External R&D can create significant value; internal R&D is needed to claim some portion of that value
If we discover it, we will get it to market first	Building a better business model is better than getting to market first
Put them in special conditions	Open your networks to different talents
We should control our intellectual property (IP) so that our competitors don't profit from our ideas	We should profit from others' use of our IP, and we should buy others' IP whenever it advances our own business model
Delivered to passive consumers	Delivered to engaged consumers

Source: author's elaboration on inputs from Amaya Erro.

Implementing Open Innovation entails:

1. Use of Business Model as a cognitive device through which decisions about innovation are evaluated and taken;
2. Overcoming NIH (not invented here) and NSH (not sold here) syndromes (inertia);
3. Development of new organizational routines;
4. Continuous experimentation, adaptation, and learning.

Knowledge management is closely related to Open Innovation. Embracing an open approach fosters knowledge creation, absorption, and connection, which in turn enhances the efficiency of an open innovation strategy.

The development of a successful Knowledge Management System is likely to generate an open environment, presenting new opportunities for knowledge exploitation and exploration. In fact, intra- and inter-organizational innovation processes result from the capacity to share, combine, and create new knowledge in the current dynamic environment. KMS is the starting point for collaboration and knowledge exchange among internal departments while creating virtual spaces with external partners where participants can share information and knowledge through common platforms.

Digital Business Ecosystems (DBE) appear as the evolution of enterprise networks, that are enabled by digital technologies.

It is possible to identify a path within the company that, starting from the creation, reaches the sharing of knowledge. The current knowledge-oriented market favors, in fact, the business activity in the affirmation of KIBS (Knowledge Intensive Business Service) or companies operating in the role of mediators between creators and users of knowledge. In this way the actors, on the one hand, optimize knowledge and, on the other, increase the qualification and skills of the human resources employed. The optimization of knowledge that is created among users of a collaborative network can be achieved through:

- an increase in the heterogeneity of the knowledge exchanged (Dyer, Nobeoka, 2000; Kogut, 2000),
- a renewal of knowledge (Dyer, Nobeoka, 2000; Nooteboom, 2004),
- an implementation of innovation (Powell et al. 1996; Kogut, 2000; Ahuja, 2000).

Digital technologies can be used as tools to share and manage knowledge with other companies, and thus to seek opportunities for creating innovation through digital platforms. Innovation, as a collective model, is based on two key elements such as sharing knowledge and cooperation between the actors. Consequently, innovation is facilitated by the interaction between a multitude of "knowledge owners" such as large and small businesses, stakeholders, and policymakers. Within a relational knowledge network, virtuous mechanisms of collaboration between companies are identified and identified at an inter-organizational level.

Inter-organizational networks represent a rather old organizational method, attributable to the first forms of organized commercial exchange of the classical era. Their modern empowerment is given by the extensive use of digital technologies (mainly ICTs) which support an increased possibility of connectivity between businesses and economic agents. Currently, relational networks are increasingly used by businesses for business purposes through global relational technology networks. These connect operators, be they companies, policymakers, or stakeholders often very distant from each other. To ensure the success of the business activity within a relational network it is necessary to identify a virtuous mechanism of collaboration that allows companies to improve their performance and/or to develop new business opportunities. The reference is to inter-organizational collaboration intended as a tool available to economic operators for the acquisition of skills, overcoming economic and organizational constraints, and the development of new knowledge.

The importance that Business Social Networks assume for organizations, and the inter-organizational networks, explains the importance to be attributed to the methodologies and tools of Social Network Analysis (SNA), which allow photographing and measuring informal networks. Today SNA provides a new and consistent system of government to read real flows, to identify talents or experts, to recognize undervalued communities, to optimize processes based on informal networks.

In particular, the literature on SNA has flourished over the past decades and has provided conceptualizations, metrics, and tools appropriate to the organizational context that provide a key to understanding the networking phenomenon[3].

Concerning the network itself, important elements are:

- the size (number of nodes present in the network);
- the density (quantity of actually active relationships and robustness;
- the degree of cohesion;
- the degree of inclusiveness.

---

[3] This book is not the right place to fully review the literature on SNA. For a deeper discussion on the tools, the methodological underpinnings, the conceptual advancements in this field, we recommend referring to prominent authors, such as Wasserman, Faust, Borgatti, Freeman, Scott, just to name a few founding fathers of the discipline.

Regarding the ties (i.e. the relations) between nodes (or actors), important elements are:

- the nature of the relationships at the base of the network (problem-solving, circulation of information, personal ties, etc.);
- the degree of intensity;
- the frequency of the relationships;
- the symmetry/reciprocity.

Finally, as regards the nodes/actors, the following elements are highlighted:

- the characteristics of their network (ego-net);
- proximity (number of steps to access the other nodes);
- centrality in the network that can be measured in several ways (one example is the indegree/outdegree centrality that is measured through the number of ties incoming/outgoing in/from the node);

With particular reference to the social networks that develop in virtual environments (online social networks), it is interesting to underline the fact that most of them consist of three links (social rings as shown in Figure 2.1), namely:

1) a central core of densely connected actors;
2) a second link of weakly connected actors,
3) an outermost ring of disconnected nodes, which we could define isolated users.

Figure 2.1. Three rings of nodes in online social networks.

Source: author's elaboration.

Typically, the percentage of nodes in each ring in online communities is quite common, as isolates are more numerous than the densely connected users. The outer ring of the network contains nodes that have been attracted to the online community but have not yet connected and established relationships. This group is the most likely to leave the community or remain passive members, in any case making a null or marginal contribution to the community itself. In online social networks, the percentage of these isolates can exceed 60% of total users.

The intermediate ring of nodes has few links – typically actors that they already knew before joining the online community. They are not connected to the larger community – they have not yet developed a sense of belonging. The relations between these intermediate nodes could be managed also through other means of communications (for example direct connections offline) and do not need a particular online social network to survive. Even these actors could leave the network if they do not perceive the value of the online network, and most likely they would do so altogether.

Instead, the central core of the community is made up of densely connected actors (Figure 2.2). These actors are very involved and have formed an engaged group. Community leaders are part of this core group. The main nodes are usually less than 10% of most online groups but they are a powerful attraction for new users. These are the actors that can make the network successful because they perceive the positive network externalities from which they can benefit firsthand as the community grows. These may be considered the influencers in the community, and they actually give rise to other subnetworks of their own.

Figure 2.2. The central core of an online social network.

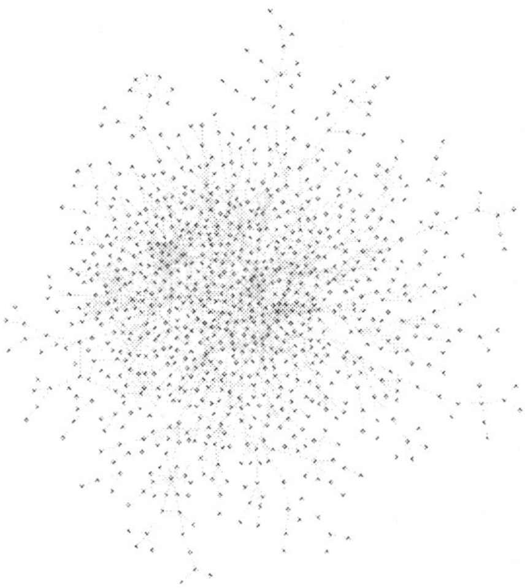

Source: author's elaboration.

> **Box 2.1.** The design thinking approach in new product development

Tim Brown, president and CEO of IDEO, defines Design Thinking as: *"a discipline that uses the designer's sensibility and methods to match people's needs with what is technologically feasible and what a viable business strategy can convert into customer value and market opportunity"*, Harvard Business Review, June 2008.

Today, design thinking permeates every step of bringing products to market. Companies like Airbnb, Facebook, Netflix, and Amazon have reshaped entire industries by employing design-forward practices that make them look almost clairvoyant as they release every new version of their product. Design thinking is a problem solving framework that allows companies to reach competitive advantage through creativity and design.

The process can be better seen as a system of three spaces that do not have to be undertaken sequentially rather than linked stages that have to be consequentially taken:

a) Inspiration: this phase starts with the briefing, in which a framework is given to the team in order to make them start. Once the briefing has been organized, the design team has to find out people's needs. The best way to do that is to go out and ask people what they are searching for.

b) Ideation: this space starts with a synthesis process. Afterwards, the team starts with the brainstorming process in which they may generate hundreds of ideas, and in which just one rule is given: to not judge other's ideas because everyone has to feel free to express him/herself. Just if this rule is observed the ideas will be free to flow and generate other ideas.

c) Implementation: the best ideas generated in the brainstorming process are turned to a concrete action plan. This is the prototyping phase.

Design Thinking drives thinkers to "four mental states": *Divergent thinking*: thinkers create different alternatives to the current situation; *Convergent thinking*, in which the team choose the best option created and apply analysis and synthesis. The team then *breaks the patterns down* and eventually they *reassemble* them. To go trough all the phases, managers should use ten tools in order to build the process in the best way and to reduce risks of failing (Liedtka & Ogilvie, 2011):

• Visualization: try to image every possibility in order to bring them to life

• Journey mapping: this tool helps companies to watch the world with the customer's eyes and to deeply understand their needs

• Value chain analysis: it is necessary to have in mind the value chain of the product or service in order to better support the process of value creation

• Mind mapping: it consists of drawing and writing the connection of ideas that come into the team members' brain

• Brainstorming: as I already mentioned before, it is the phase in which the team should generate new ideas

• Concept Development: drive the best ideas in a coherent solution that can be evaluated

• Assumption Testing: test the features of the product or service in order to understand if they will drive to success or to a fail

• Rapid Prototyping: transform the idea in a tangible prototype to test if it works and to test the customer satisfaction.

• Customer Co-creation: this is a very important phase as it is required to customers to participate in the product or service's creation. So, once they express their needs and the company can find the best way to satisfy them.

> • Learning Launch: creating an experiment that gives to the company the chance to test the product or service with real market data.
>
> Innovative design is a highly collaborative culture of continuous prototyping and iteration, and it's dependent on getting as many diverse viewpoints as possible, as early as possible. Diverse internal and external feedback has two major advantages. It takes into consideration more cases of product use, creating a more comprehensive view of the customer, and it helps product teams ship the right product the first time and focus on iteration – not "back to the drawing board" repetition.
>
> By using the designers' method, companies can create new ideas that can easily drive to innovation and test the customers' satisfaction in a shorter time. Of course, companies have to work hard to change the managers' mentality, in order to let them be more like "design thinkers" than "profit oriented employees". Managers must stop thinking to solve one problem at time and to climb the hierarchy and start to think as a group member with shared goals to achieve. In order to do that, business owners, first have to build the right strategy and change their behaviors, then to give them useful input and tools that lead the teams to achieve the goal.
>
> The perfect designer thinker, according to Tim Brown (2009), must have the following features: be optimistic, empathetic and collaborative. When a firm starts to develop the Design Thinking process, must evaluate the current employees and if they are not considered as "good thinkers" then the company should hire new thinkers, who have the right attitude.

Source: author's elaboration in collaboration with Benedetta Rossi.

2.3. Which Technology? What Are the Exponential Technologies?

With the massive diffusion of computers, back in the '70s the very popular Moore's law was formulated, stating that states that processor speeds, or overall processing power for computers, would double every two years. Although it has not been proven to be precise, this law indicates a forecast biannual exponential growth. The core of the argument is that the technology with the power of computing at its heart, grows exponentially, not linear. Recalling this exponential growth, exponential technology has been defined as "*innovations progressing at a pace with or exceeding Moore's Law*" that "*evidence a renaissance of innovation, invention, and discovery ... [and] have the potential to positively affect billions of lives*" (Hagel et al., 2013).

Exponential technologies can be defined also as *those innovations that continue to advance exponentially, with disruptive economic and lifestyle effects. Moreover, exponential technologies are those whose current price-performance makes it feasible to incorporate them into today's business and social problems in new and previously impossible ways* [4].

---

[4] https://xponentialworks.com/what-is-exponential-technology/.

The following paragraphs analyze in detail the characteristics of the most promising exponential technologies, and they illustrate their impact on business organizations, innovation, and on everyday life. A particular focus will be of course on knowledge creation, retrieving, and sharing provided by these technologies.

We believe also that exponential technologies have offer promising scenario to solve the big societal challenges. For example, the application of advanced data science and AI to the medical sector can be extremely useful to anticipate, or manage, medical disaster. Unfortunately, not only this is only at a very preliminary stage of development[5], it is also far beyond the scope of this book.

In the future, and other circumstances, it will be great to discuss the possibilities of exponential technologies to make an impact on society as a whole.

2.3.1. Big Bata [6]

It's all in the data! In 2006, the mathematician Clive Humby[7] speaks for the first time of data in terms of "new oil":

"It's valuable, but if unrefined it cannot really be used. It has to be changed into gas, plastic, chemicals, etc. to create a valuable entity that drives profitable activity; so data must be broken down, analyzed to have value".

Thus, the importance of data in the digital age is evident, as is evident the success of the companies that are "giants" of data: Alphabet (Google), Amazon, Apple, Facebook and Microsoft seem unstoppable and have a enormous power.

Data, therefore, constitute the basis of modern technology if collected, analyzed and processed and it is precisely this concept that is the key to digitization. Large volumes of data are analyzed and used daily by Data Analysts to develop new forms of knowledge that are aimed at representing reality in as much detail as possible, to exploit it to derive greater efficiency, process optimization and new product development. and services. However, a large amount of data cannot be easily analyzed with traditional tools such as spreadsheets or statistical software but requires a combination

---

[5] As we are writing, the world is undergoing the Covid-19 pandemic. It is unfortunately very clear that no AI or big data have been able to predict the flow of the pandemic, and to avoid general lockdown as the only means of containing the spread of the virus.

[6] This paragraph has been written based on (Pennacchini, 2019).

[7] http://www.humbyanddunn.com.

of more specific technologies and analysis methods in order to obtain useful and detailed information.

The high volume, the required speed and the variety examined in the use of today's data are the basis of the evolution of the concept of "Data" in "Big Data". This definition took hold in the early 2000s, when Doug Laney analyzed new Data Management solutions in the development of e-commerce, through the characteristics of volume, speed and variety, which are referred to as the 3 Vs of Big Data (Figure 2.3).

Figure 2.3. The 3Vs of Big Data.

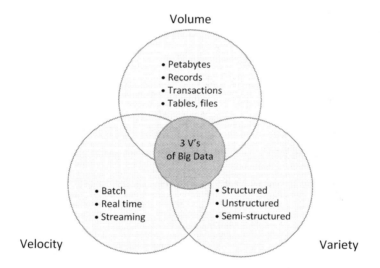

Source: author's elaboration based on (Zikopoulos et al., 2011).

By volume we mean the size of the data available, which has grown exponentially thanks to the popularity of the Internet (which makes the acquisition and sharing of data simple and immediate) and to the development of the ability to acquire and analyze the data that allows processing more and more and more diversified amounts of data.

The growth of the data volume requires a faster process speed of the same to make large quantities of data usable in real time or almost. The data, therefore, are produced with increasing frequency and speed and also need to be processed at the same rate.

Furthermore, the data's volume and speed also depend on the greater variety of data available: structured, deconstructed or semi-structured data must be made uniform through specific platforms to make them operational. The complexity, in fact, compared to the past, is a fundamental feature to fully understand Big Data: while in the past the data to be analyzed were mainly structured (mainly numeric or alphanumeric), with the advent of the Internet and Smartphones each person produces unstructured data (text, images, video, audio) that can be used to add value to the analysis of structured data.

Volume, variety, and speed are primary characteristics of Big Data, to which others such as value and truthfulness can be added. Big Data is analyzed with the ultimate goal of creating value in achieving a goal. It is therefore essential that the data are cleared in the collection, validation, and analysis, in order to process valid, reliable, and truthful Big Data. With the large-scale introduction of unstructured data, it is easier to come across unnecessary or incorrect information.

Managing a large amount of structured and unstructured data, therefore, helps the company to take strategic actions for the business, be it direct to management or customer analysis. The main problem remains the quantity and quality of data: the information in the databases proliferates, and, coming from sources that are not always reliable, they make the analysis and process of data complicated through standard management tools.

The path for effective use of Big Data in companies, therefore, is not yet obvious: in Human Resources, for example, using data relating to a professional path, skill, remuneration, involvement, performance, training, and so on must be the starting point to offer strategic support to the business but, once the analysis is finished, appropriate actions must be taken in order to exploit the potential of Big Data fully.

Therefore, it is necessary that these are analyzed in a "smart" way, using algorithms that can identify patterns and correlations between the data, which allow translating knowledge into concrete actions aimed at competitive advantage.

2.3.2. Business Intelligence

The term Business Intelligence (BI) is intended to describe the processes and tools through which Big Data is collected, analysed, and then used in order to elaborate strategic decisions for the company. Through the BI process, data is used more effectively and faster: BI platforms are developed by experts creating the possibility of integrating data from different sources, which are of different format or size, and will therefore be able to provide predictive analysis based on the collected data. This leads to identify the best strategies or the best business processes in real time. Easy-to-use platforms are also developed for "non-professionals," through company dashboards and performance indicators that give an immediate image of the activity carried out with Big Data.

BI activity takes place in three main phases:

1) data collection;
2) normalization of the collected data;
3) analysis of normalized data.

The first phase, data collection, is carried out by selecting the same from large databases where data of different nature are present, identifying those relevant for the company and the business. Often, the data collected is "Small Data," collected in company databases, including information, surveys, surveys or analysis of user behavior. In this way, it will create its database where the Business Intelligence Analyst will have selected the most interesting data for the company and crossed them with each other, thus providing aggregated information.

Once a database has been created, it is necessary to normalize the data since they are not homogeneous, of different nature and origin, of various sizes. Therefore, it is necessary to start by cleaning, which consists of identifying the most important and consistent data with what is sought in the analysis. The data are then validated and inserted into a single data warehouse, divided into different subsets called "data marts," which see the data shared by specific sectors or company variables. Here, the data are reorganized in a practical way for their use in subsequent analyzes.

The third phase consists of the data analysis process, i.e., Data Analytics. The analysis can be carried out through different models (such as Descriptive Analysis, Predictive Analysis, Prescriptive Analysis or Automated Analysis), which allow to analyze the company performance or user behavior, predict future developments or trends, propose strategic actions to be implemented, analyze the risks, optimize company performance and, not least, predict the skills that will be most needed.

Using Business Intelligence in the company, therefore, allows you to make strategic decisions that are guided by the analyzed data, that is, data-driven decisions, to improve performance and make decisions in faster times. Data management through BI is safer, by complying with the new European Data Collection and Management Regulation (GDPR, General Data Protection Regulation).

2.3.3. Cloud computing (by Lucia Marchegiani and Andrea Grieco)

Cloud Computing (or only Cloud) refers to a technology that provides on-demand processing services (such as applications, IT resources, processing power, storage, data centers) through a platform via the Internet with consumption-based pricing methods. A Cloud platform is, therefore, able to provide quick access to IT resources that are agile, fast, and inexpensive. In fact, the Cloud allows accessing the necessary services almost instantly, paying only on the basis of actual use thanks to the measurement of the service provided.

The resources present in the Cloud are therefore customized to be able to access them independently according to the needs that you have. Among these resources we find storage, networking, processing, and applications that enable managing and use data via the Internet, without the need for hardware infrastructures. The advantages of using the Cloud are manifold for companies: elasticity, cost savings in capital costs, speed, accessibility, global scalability, productivity increases, higher performance, reliability, and safety. Because of the numerous advantages, the Cloud is widespread in every person's daily life because it covers a wide range of services. For example, Cloud, web-based e-mail services such as Outlook and Gmail, or the storage space provided by Dropbox and Google Drive.

There are three business models of Cloud Computing that differ in the provision of services concerning the user choices (Figure 2.4):

i) The IaaS (Infrastructure as a Service) model, infrastructure distributed as a service, refers to the central IT components that can be "rented": physical or virtual servers, storage resources, networking, operating systems. These infrastructures are rented to the user by a cloud service provider on a "pay-per-use" basis. The use of IaaS presupposes a technical competence in the management of the same infrastructures. It is interesting, for example, for companies that want to create applications and control all the elements. An example of IaaS is EC2 (Elastic Compute Cloud) offered by Amazon Web Service;

ii) The PaaS (Platform as a Service) model, in addition to renting IaaS services, includes platforms that are configured as an environment in which the tools necessary to develop applications are found, including software, servers, operating systems, development tools or data management. In this way, developers can quickly and easily create Web-based applications, without the cost and complexity of the hardware, software, underlying infrastructure, servers and storage. An example of PaaS is the Google App Engine;

iii) The SaaS (Software as a Service) model provides software applications via the Internet on-demand and on a subscription basis. Generally, they are configured as an application or an interface on a Web browser. SaaS providers host an application and therefore make it immediately available to the user, without this being concerned with development, maintenance, updating. The Software as a Service is the most used model because anyone can use it, as it does not need to have specialized technical skills or competences. An example of SaaS is Netflix.

Figure 2.4. Models and characteristics of cloud computing.

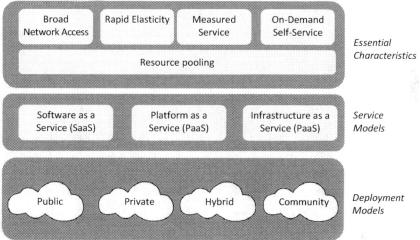

Source: wiki.cloudsecurityalliance.org, © 2020 Cloud Security Alliance – All Rights Reserved.

Moreover, Infrastructure as a Service (IaaS) model can be distinguished in three different types: public, private, and hybrid.

a. Public model is the most common. Its Cloud resources are owned by a third-party provider, it is provided via the Internet and it is used, for example, by e-mail or Office applications. In a public cloud, the applications of different customers are hosted in a shared environment. Public cloud business models enable significant economies of scale. These solutions are currently preferable for non- business-critical applications that relate only to a few core processes of an enterprise.

b. Private, where Cloud Computing services are used by a single organization that manages them in a private network, usually also including infrastructure. Generally, private clouds are used by government agencies, financial institutions, or medium-large companies to have more advanced control and security. Private clouds are often deployed when public clouds are deemed inappropriate or inadequate for the business's needs. For example, a public cloud might not provide the level of service availability or uptime that an organization needs. In other cases, the risk of hosting a mission-critical workload in the public cloud might exceed an organization's risk tolerance. There might be security or regulatory concerns related to the use of a multi-tenant environment. In these cases, an enterprise might opt to invest in a private cloud to realize the benefits of cloud computing while maintaining total control and ownership of its environment.

c. Hybrid, which combines the types of Public and Private Cloud to obtain the maximum benefits from both. It offers more flexibility given the possibility of transferring data and applications between public and private Clouds, optimizing the existing infrastructure. Hybrid Infrastructure as a Service models combine public and private cloud models. Non-critical functions can be outsourced with hybrid models. Enterprises that prefer hybrid models should remember that – at least to start with – this option is only suitable for simple applications that do not require complex databases or synchronization.

The reduction of transaction costs and the shift to operational expenses helps the organization to enter in a Cloud Technology value chain wherever they need because a Cloud architecture could be created at every level; starting from the migration of physical infrastructures to the simple delivery of SaaS instead of on-premises software to its employees. On the contrary, successful experiments with some SaaS, with small recurrent costs and near to none upfront costs, could easily convince the organization to shift on an allover cloud solution.

Another fascinating paradigm is Multicloud. A Multicloud solution uses multiple different public cloud services from multiple different providers. The different clouds are used to achieve best-of-breed results or to reduce vendor lock-in. Multicloud solutions address the necessities of different departments in an organization: Marketing and Sales, for instance, likely have different needs than Engineering teams. Multiple clouds also lower the risk of vendor lock-in for organizations on a single provider, nonetheless providing flexibility and, often, lower costs.

Another advantage is that Multicloud could efficiently address every aspect of the IT strategy of an organization. A Multicloud strategy usually begins with multiple clouds, usually thanks to the phenomenon of Shadow IT, that is the use of non-certified solutions in an organization. With the time these solutions could easily be added to organization-certified solutions and create Multicloud architectures if executives judge them more flexible and less expensive.

By using the Cloud, companies have the opportunity to avoid creating IT departments that deal with hardware and software, thus saving capital costs. The use of Big Data requires dedicated infrastructures to perform analyzes on such a vast amount and range of data. Furthermore, through the Cloud, data processing will be more efficient and more accessible, also thanks to its intrinsic elasticity: the platforms created in the Cloud, in fact, can be increased or reduced based on the data to be processed. The complexity of implementing Big Data solutions is then reduced based on the Cloud's automation, which does not require the development of additional components. Today, many companies are using the Cloud by integrating it with the use of Big Data. This reduces the infrastructure, provides more agility, speed and elasticity, and lowers the costs. Companies such as AirBnB and Uber are using the Cloud in combination with Big Data to increase competitiveness and improve performance, facilitating the sharing and data organization via the Cloud.

Box 2.2. Forbes case study

Forbes Media (Forbes) is a global media, branding, and technology company, with a focus on news and information about the business, investing, technology, entrepreneurship, leadership, and affluent lifestyles. The Forbes brand reaches more than 120 million people world-wide through its popular magazine and ForbesLive events, with 40 licensed local editions in 70 countries.

Forbes began working with Google using Google Analytics 360 and Google Ad Manager to optimize its digital marketing channel, and recently completing a migration of Forbes.com to Google Cloud.

An example of an insight from Analytics 360 was that Forbes users are increasingly visiting Forbes.com on mobile devices. Its migration to public cloud started with a SaaS delivered by Google

The company needed to move from physical data centers to a modern cloud platform and chose Google Cloud as the new foundation for Forbes.com, which consists of 50 different services that all had to be moved to the Cloud.

One of the reasons for selecting Google Cloud was the big selection of Managed Services that offer in a single a bundle both the service and the skills needed to run them. Using Managed Services Forbes' the development team released the application more than twice as fast and reclaim about 50 hours per week of the engineering team.

Forbes also uses Google's Artificial Intelligence and Machine Learning services that learn from 100 years of Forbes editorial and current market conditions to leverage the power of data by optimizing contents, analyze the sentiment, and giving better insights to the writers.

> Another Google SaaS used by Forbes is Google Data Studio that produces interactive dashboards and reports; at first, this solution used the manual joining of data from all over the organization, but nowadays, they are using Google Cloud BigQuery to do that.
> The collaboration between Google and Forbes then expanded also to productivity and collaboration SaaS, thanks to the rolling out of Google G Suite to its employees, and even to physical products with the use of Google Chromebooks in the meeting rooms.

Source: authors' elaboration based on https://cloud.google.com/customers/forbes/.

2.3.4. Internet of Things (of Everything) [8]

Kevin Ashton coined the term "Internet of Things" (IoT) in 1999 during his work at Procter & Gamble. It semantically means "a world-wide network of interconnected objects uniquely addressable, based on standard communication protocols". The IoT, therefore, is configured as an evolution of the use of the Net through the use of "things" that actively communicate with each other and with the Net itself.

However, a more formal definition could be:

"An open and comprehensive network of intelligent objects that have the capacity to auto- organize, share information, data, and resources, reacting and acting in the face of situations and changes in the environment.".

The objects connected to the Internet, more adequately defined as "smart objects," and the technologies that allow this connection transfer information and perform actions, thus interacting with the surrounding world.

Smart objects are characterized by specific functions: identification, connection, data processing, status diagnosis, location, and interaction with the surrounding environment. Connection and identification, among all, are essential features of intelligent objects. These must be equipped with unique identifiers in order to provide them with an "electronic identity" that makes them recognize each other and from the Internet. The most common forms of identification are radio frequency (RFID) and QR codes. Connection, then, is the necessary condition for making objects smart and, therefore, connected. Smart objects can mean devices, appliances, appliances, plants, systems, machinery and equipment, means of transport, materials.

The main strength of the IoT idea is its high impact on several aspects of everyday life and behavior of potential users. NIC Inc. highlights future opportunities that will arise, starting from the idea that 'popular demand combined with technology advances could drive widespread diffusion of an

---

[8] We are thankful to Alessio Balducci for the content of this paragraph.

Internet of Things that could, like the present Internet, contribute invaluably to economic development. The possible threats deriving from widespread adoption of such a technology are also stressed. Indeed, it is emphasized that 'to the extent that everyday objects become information security risks, the IoT could distribute those risks far more widely than the Internet has to date.

In the Internet of Things paradigm, many of the objects of common use will be included in the network in one form or another. This results in the generation of enormous amounts of data that have to be stored, processed, and presented in a seamless, efficient, and easily interpretable form.

For the Internet of Things vision to successfully emerge, the computing criterion will need to go beyond and evolve into connecting existing everyday objects and embedding intelligence into our environment. For technology to *disappear* from the consciousness of the user, the IoT demands:

(1) a shared understanding of the situation of its users and their appliances,
(2) software architectures and pervasive communication networks to process and convey the contextual information to where it is relevant,
(3) the analytics tools in the Internet of Things that aim for autonomous and smart behavior.

For the realization of a complete IoT vision, an efficient, secure, scalable, and market-oriented computing and storage resourcing are essential. Cloud computing is the most recent paradigm to emerge, which promises reliable services delivered through next-generation data centers that are based on virtualized storage technologies (Gubbi et al., 2013).

One of the most important outcomes of this emerging field is creating an unprecedented amount of data. The data have to be stored and used intelligently for smart monitoring and actuation. It is crucial to develop artificial intelligence algorithms that could be centralized or distributed based on the need. Non-linear, temporal machine learning methods based on evolutionary algorithms, genetic algorithms, neural networks, and other artificial intelligence techniques are necessary to achieve automated decision making. Furthermore, they are usually very well-suited for IoT applications.

The real competitive advantage lays on the ability of the firm to apply effectively existing and new knowledge to create new products and processes (Thrassou et al., 2012). Thus, knowledge management regards the identification and leveraging of knowledge to foster innovation processes (Del Giudice & Della Peruta, 2016; Santoro et al., 2018).

The emerging phenomenon of the IoT, where network connectivity enables individuals and organizations from different sectors to gather and exchange data, suggests that firms from different manufacturing and service sectors should invest in new ICTs and develop KMS.

With the development and implementation of the IoT, several issues arise, and they must be dealt with.

1) Addressing and networking issues. The IoT will include an incredibly high number of nodes, each of which will produce content that should be retrievable by any authorized user regardless of her/his position. This requires effective addressing policies.
2) IoT extreme vulnerability. Its components spend most of the time unattended, and thus, it is easy to attack them physically. Most of the communications are wireless, which makes eavesdropping extremely simple. Low capabilities characterize most of the IoT components, in terms of both energy and computing resources (this is especially the case for passive components). Thus, they cannot implement complex schemes supporting security.
3) Privacy. In the traditional Internet problems of privacy arise mostly for Internet users (individuals playing an active role). In the IoT scenarios, privacy problems arise even for people not using any IoT service. The privacy should be protected by ensuring that individuals can control which of their data is being collected, who is collecting such data, and when this is happening. Furthermore, the personal data collected should be used only with the aim of supporting authorized services by authorized service providers, and, finally, the above data should be stored until it is strictly needed only.

In order to ensure that the personal data collected is used only to support authorized services by authorized providers, solutions have been proposed that usually rely on a system called privacy broker. The proxy interacts with the user on the one side and with the services on the other. Accordingly, it guarantees that the provider obtains only the information about the user, which is strictly needed.

Finally, it is necessary to mention digital forgetting as this has been recognized as an essential issue only recently. Thanks to technological development, the cost of storage is becoming cheaper and cheaper, so as this cost decreases, the amount of data that can be memorized increases. Accordingly, there is the need to create solutions that periodically delete information that is of no use for the purpose it was generated. So, the new software tools that will be developed in the future should support such forgetting functionalities (Atzori et al., 2010).

IoT should be considered as part of the overall Internet of the future, which is likely to be dramatically different from the Internet we use today. It is clear that the current Internet paradigm, which supports and has been built around host-to-host communications, is now a limiting factor for the current use of the Internet.

From a business point of view, the IoT represents an opportunity for both cost reduction and increased business efficiency.

With respect to knowledge management, the IoT is a plus that, in addition to efficient business knowledge management, can enable faster transmission of information within the company and accelerate business knowledge growth. The possibility to have tools in constant communication with each other and their ability to collect and process information from themselves is an advantage when this system can assist employees' work but also a threat when this could become a substitute for them.

Finally, it is not possible to overlook the many problems mentioned above. Implementing an unsafe structure in a company would put the entire business at risk, and therefore, rather than creating a competitive advantage would lead to a destruction of value.

The IoT is still under development, and we still cannot fully understand the possible applications, let alone its destructive potential.

2.3.5. Artificial Intelligence (AI) [9]

The origin of Artificial Intelligence dates back to 1943, when researchers McCulloch and Pitt introduced the first artificial neuron, which was followed by Hebb's work, which analyzes the connection between artificial neurons and the human brain in 1949. Thanks to the article Computing Machinery and Intelligence, written in 1950 by Turing (from which the well-known Turing test was derived), the first theories on machine intelligence began to spread. In 1956, a conference was held in Dartmouth College in which the major exponents of computer science participated: it is here that the mathematician McCarthy proposes the term "*Artificial Intelligence*" and that programs already capable of carrying out logical reasoning are presented, including the program "Logic Theorist", developed by Newell and Simon, able to prove some mathematical theorems. In 1958, then, Rosenblatt proposed the first neural network model, the Perceptor, which, however, had limited computational capabilities and was dependent on the choice of inputs and algorithms used.

Years of great ferment of ideas and interesting theoretical developments followed (including advances on neural networks in the sixties and the

---

[9] We acknowledge the contribution to this paragraph brought by Sara Pennacchini.

birth of "expert systems", that is, based on knowledge, in the seventies) but characterized by the limited calculation tools available. Universities and IT companies (first of all IBM), however, continue to focus on AI research and development, and, in those years, Lisp was born, the first programming language. It is thanks to Lisp that, from the second half of the sixties, the tendency to search for solutions closer to man began to appear, going beyond the solution of mathematical theorems; this is also thanks to the development of GPUs, which reduce the training time of the networks.

In the 1980s, AI found practical applications, especially in American and Japanese industrial companies and more powerful optimization algorithms developed: the first AI in the industrial sector was R1, developed to configure orders for new computers. It was during the 1990s that neural networks were perfected, new calculation procedures developed and the construction of expert systems improved. The famous chess game in which Deep Blue, IBM's calculator, managed to beat the reigning world champion, confirmed the progress of the algorithms that allowed learning of neural networks. Recently, "neuromorphic chips" have been developed to emulate the sensory and cognitive functions of the human brain. Today, the advancements in the field of Artificial Intelligence are countless, favored by the development of new technologies: the availability of a large amount of data allows the construction of increasingly powerful neural networks, the possibility of processing these Big Data makes it possible to extract additional information with Data Analytics, the Cloud provided the necessary elasticity for design with lower costs.

Artificial Intelligence is a branch of Computer Science that allows the design and programming of hardware and software systems with characteristics considered typically human (understanding, reasoning, learning, and interaction) that allow it to perform actions, carry out activities, or solve problems. The human requirements with which an Artificial Intelligence is endowed allow it to think humanly and rationally and then act similarly, humanly and rationally. These purely human actions carried out by an AI allow the scientific community to classify it into two dominant paradigms, which describe its learning methods:

- Weak Artificial Intelligence identifies systems that are capable of emulating man's cognitive abilities. Therefore, the machines would be able to perform the most varied actions without being aware of the activities carried out.
- Strong artificial intelligence is made up of systems that independently develop their own intelligence, without emulating man. Proponents of this theory, therefore, believe that machines are capable of developing "conscious intelligence.".

The functioning of Artificial Intelligence mainly consists of four different functions: understanding, reasoning, learning, and interaction. These functions can be achieved through the process of ever new, ever more numerous and increasingly sophisticated algorithms that allow AI to make decisions or learn from experience. The explication of these functions, thanks to the technological maturity reached, has allowed the AI to leave the laboratories and settle in every area of daily life.

The segments that use Artificial Intelligence are varied, and each has benefited from its use. In the sales sector, thanks to the use of expert systems, complex commercial proposals are configured that would require specialists for each sector or activity in which one must act. In Marketing, AI advances more and more in the management of the relationship with users, working in real-time on data such as behavior, habits, needs and providing improvements in the user experience, in assistance and in the development of business strategies, with the aim, for example, of persuading users to take a specific action or purchase a specific product. In the health sector. AI has helped improve the diagnosis or treatment of rare diseases, intervene in complex operations, provide support for staff or help people with disabilities through vocal or motor systems. Another area in which AI comes in handy is finance, where there are fraud prevention or risk management applications, anticipating fraudulent activities. In the industry, then, Artificial Intelligence plays a central role in the optimization of Supply Chain Management, in the distribution or in the management of orders.

2.4. Diffusion of (Digital) Innovations

The relevance of networks has started to become evident already in the Information Economy and is of utmost evidence in the Digital Age.

In the management field, networks are used to depict a typical service provision, where many components are required. Given that clients demand services that are composed of different complementary components, network elements are complementary to each other. Especially with the emerging and consolidation of the Information Economy, networks have become more and more critical. Each of the network components may have close substitutes, so to offer different configurations of the same services, according to the providers' industrial interrelations.

Truthfully up until the '70s, networks were analyzed under the assumption that a single firm owned its components. Later on, under antitrust pressures, economies of scope drove a considerable amount of research.

Here, the assumption was that an efficiency gain could be realized if joint operations were established among complementary components of the networks. Under these premises, and considering the other characteristics of the Information Economy, it becomes clear that complementarities play a crucial role in defining the quality of the information service, provided by a network of actors. Such a concept will be deeper analyzed in the following chapters when the resources and competences framework is exposed.

When it comes to considering the demand-side networks, network effects are their primary consequences (Weitzel, 2004). Such effects result in an increasing benefit or network value when the network is growing. In economic terms, network effects make it so that the utility of a participant to a network increases when the number of participants increases (Figure 2.5).

Figure 2.5. General network effects.

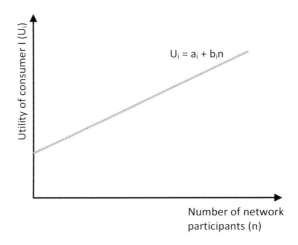

Source: author's elaboration based on Weitzel, 2004.

This is true when no costs are associated with the network growth, and the network shows inexhaustible positive effects. On the contrary, when those circumstances are taken into account, different developments of network costs and benefits are possible. Several contributions have analyzed such interplays between costs and benefits (see for example, Weitzel, 2004). These studies fall beyond the scope of this book, so they will not be further recalled here. Nevertheless, what is important to underline are the implications regarding coordination and efficiency concerns that link profit-maximizing to social optimization. Complementary to this contribution is the intuition of Katz and

Shapiro (Katz & Shapiro, 1985), who introduced the distinction between direct and indirect effects. The first ones refer to the increasing value of being part of a network according to network's size. Direct physical effects come from exchanging information with a higher number of participants to the network. Indirect effects are related to the likelihood that complementary products or services are offered when the network size increases. In this way, interdependencies are exploited in the consumption of complementary goods (Teece, 1986). I will come back later on this distinction because direct and indirect effects seem to drive the decision to adopt a new technology in different ways.

The existence of positive network effects, which imply a positive correlation between the number of users of a network good and its utility, legitimate the existence of standards. In particular, standardization issues arise concerning which standard should be correctly chosen over the others, and with regards to the process of adoption of the standard. Nevertheless, a commonplace among researchers in the Information and Network Economy says that the good thing about standards is that there are so many of them. The real problem about standards seems to be how to standardize them (Besen and Farrell, 1994; Weitzel, 2004). More in particular, the standardization problem refers to the lack of coordination among agents, being them part of the suppliers or the users (Besen and Farrell, 1994). Initially, with the consolidation of the industrial economy, standards were sought to reduce the heterogeneity among product offerings and realize economies of scale. With this respect, the most often cited example of standardization is the railway gauge of 4 feet and 8 ½ inches. The latter was set as a standard for all railroads by the British Parliament in the Gauge Act of 1846 (Kindleberger, 1983). With the uprising dematerialization of industries, a so-called transition occurred, from Alfred Marshall's World to the Increasing-Returns World (Arthur, 1996). This meant to abandon massive production plans, with "commodities heavy on resources, light on know-how," in favor of service offerings characterized by increasing returns. To admit increasing returns would then lead to admitting multiple market equilibria outcome, and possibly huge profits. Thus, information-based industries are characterized by demand-side economies of scale, which provide room for network positive externalities, and on the other side, stimulate the birth of standards. Especially with the take-off of Information and Communication Technologies, standardization issues gained momentum (Arthur, 1989).

Standards may be de jure, when a regulation Authority sets them by law, like in the case of the above-mentioned British railway gauge. On the contrary, standards may arise as de facto, when a new technology emerges as a superior above the existing ones. In this way, it is the number of its adopters that decree its setting as a standard. With respect to the Information Economy, the existence of networks, and of strong positive feedback, which have been enlightened in paragraph 0, make it so that the Information-based industries are tippy. In Shapiro and Varian's words.

"[…] when two or more firms compete for a market where there is strong positive feedback, only one may emerge as a winner. Economists say that such a market is tippy, meaning that it can tip in favor of one player or another" (Shapiro & Varian, 1999, p. 176).

Therefore, when a standard emerges, it dominates the market. Consequently, it is part of a firm's strategy to try to set its technology as a standard. In such game for standards, firms can either fight each other engaging in a war for standards, or they can decide to agree on one standard turning inter-technological competition into intra-technological competition, or even co-opetition (Damsgaard, 2002; Damsgaard & Marchegiani, 2004; Nalebuff et al., 1996).

From the perspective of strategic innovation management, it is worth mentioning that two phenomena play a crucial role in replacing one standard with another: the excess inertia and excess momentum (Farrell and Saloner, 1986).

The first occurs when the adoption of possibly superior technology is delayed due to the high risk of being the first adopters. The importance of compatibility and positive network externalities could prevent the adoption of new technology, even though it might offer superior performances.

At odds, the term excess momentum describes a situation where the adoption of new technology happens suddenly, at the early stage of its appearance on the market. This may be driven by a sponsoring firm's pricing strategy, which could attract new adopters with low prices. Also, a bandwagon effect is triggered. This fits with a vendor strategy of predatory pre-announcement.

In both situations, a game theoretical approach could help understand the coordination problem, which is beyond the decision to simultaneously switch to a new standard (Shy, 2002). Nevertheless, such a theoretical approach falls short in encompassing both the demand-side and the supply-side of the Information-based industries. With almost the same limitations, the traditional theoretical streams about innovation management generally use a micro-perspective focus, referring to either a single firm behavior, such as pricing strategies, entry decisions, and sponsoring. Alternatively, they instead use a macro-perspective focus to analyze the decision to form consortia for the settlement of a common standard to agree upon and leverage lock-in effects (Farrell & Klemperer, 2007).

The knowledge-based economy would simply not exist if innovations in information processing and communication technologies had not been continuously developed, introduced into the market, and accepted by users. Accordingly, to talk about the organizational configurations that better innovate would be incomplete without having a basic understanding of the market mechanisms, which rule the diffusion of the innovation among users. Coherently, the following paragraphs are dedicated to frame theoretical support about the Diffusion of Innovations (DoIs) within the markets.

At first glance, it is possible to identify two theoretical trends in the study of innovations diffusion (Attewell, 1992; Rogers, 2010):

1) the first one concentrates on the metaphor of diffusion as a communication and influence process. Accordingly, the potential technology users get to know about its existence and are persuaded to adopt it because of the communication with those who have already adopted it. This implies that the dynamics of adoption mirror the dynamics of communication among the members of a community. The focus of such a trend of studies is, therefore, mainly directed on the role of individuals within the community and the role of the communication networks among individuals.
2) The second theoretical trend focuses on economics and regards diffusion mainly in terms of costs and benefits: the higher the costs, the lower the diffusion rate; the higher the profit of innovation, the faster its adoption (Mansfield, 1968).

In his seminal contribution to innovative dynamics analysis, Schumpeter (Schumpeter, 1934) individuated three phases in the innovative process: invention, innovation, and diffusion. The Author, however, does not explicitly deal with the diffusion phase, and he considers it as residual concerning the other two. Furthermore, by considering the content of the innovation (i.e., the new technology) as a black box, this approach neglects to consider the diffusion of innovation as a possible source of innovation itself. During the diffusion phase, indeed, the innovation could be modified or improved as far as more people adopt and use it. The Schumpeterian approach influenced scholars in industrial economics for several decades, and only in the late 1960s did new streams of thinking emerge. The common characteristic of those "new" approaches is that they consider the innovation as embedded in the social and economic context. For that reason they have been labeled as "contextual approaches". In this view, the role of adopting agents is crucial for the innovation improvement and spread.

The premises of many diffusion models are marked by their intellectual history, which began outside of economics during the 1950s. Geographers, sociologists, and anthropologists proposed these models when studying the diffusion of agricultural innovations, illnesses, or generically cultural innovations (Rogers, 2010). The primary assumption underlying their models was that the innovation is always better than existing alternatives. The slow or unbalanced rate of diffusion is due to the lack of information in the social system about the existence or the performance of a given innovation. The necessary and sufficient condition for innovations widespread is thus the diffusion of the relevant information. According to the most common diffusion models, the relevant information about innovation comes from former adopters instead of from innovation suppliers. Thus, the innovation is diffused mainly through imitation processes. Due to their similarity with contagious disease transmission, those diffusion models are often referred to as "epidemic models."

Bass (Bass, 1969) tested this approach on early sales data for eleven consumer durables. He showed that the model had a good fit for the sales curves (presumed to represent first time purchases or adoptions) for each of the eleven product categories in his study. Further evaluative studies of the Bass model have provided strong empirical support for the structural soundness of the model in a variety of different circumstances, from the diffusion of an educational innovation in the US over a 11 years, to VCR markets in Europe and the United States and cocoa-spraying chemicals among Nigerian farmers over 25 years. The Bass model also holds true for the TLC market, in forecasting the diffusion of mobile services (Marchegiani, 2012). All these studies reported a very high explanatory power of the Bass model (R^2 always over 0,9) (Wright & Esslemont, 1994).

The Bass model has also been successful in forecasting the number of adoptions at the peak of the sales curve using early sales data and estimating long term diffusion patterns. Companies that have used the model include Eastman Kodak, RCA, IBM, Sears, and AT&T.

At a practical level, the Bass model can be used to forecast the long-term sales pattern of a product when one of the following situations happens:

a. The product has recently been introduced, and sales have been observed for a few periods.
b. The product has not yet been introduced, but it resembles another product in the market with known sales history.

The basic idea of the model is that the probability that initial purchase of a new product will be made at time t given no purchase has yet been made is a linear function of the proportion of the population that has already purchased it. Thus:

Bass Model (1994) $f(t) / 1 - F(t) = p + qF(t)$ (1)

where:

f(t) is the unconditional probability of purchase at time t,
F(t) is the accumulated probability of purchase up to time t,
hence f(t) /1 − F(t) is the likelihood of purchase at time t given no purchase has been made before.

The coefficients p and q are constant, where p is called "the coefficient of innovation", or external influence. It refers to the probability of initial purchase independent of the influence of previous buyers, under the effects of because of mass media coverage or other external factors. On the other side, q is called "the coefficient of imitation", or internal influence. It refers to the pressure on imitators from previous buyers, through, for example the mechanism of word-of-mouth.

The Bass model's strength lies in its simplicity allowing managers to use it as a plain managerial tool for market analysis and demand forecasting of new technologies. In fact, it is used to describe, and even predict the number of purchases of innovative durable goods under some circumstances. On the other hand, the original model has been accused of being oversimplistic. Consequently, according to the contingent application of the model, other authors have made many further adjustments. In particular, the Generalized Bass model is one of the most important sophistication of the original formulation. It takes into account other marketing variables, such as pricing and advertising, and takes the following form:

Generalized Bass Model (1994) $f(t)/(1 - 150 F(t)) = [p + q F(t)] \times (t)$ (2)

where:
t = adoption time;
$f(t)$ = probability function of t;
F(t) = cumulative probability function of t;
p = coefficient of innovation;
q = coefficient of imitation;
x(t) = operators' marketing effort.

Both the simpler and the generalized Bass models result in an S-shaped curve, which provides a visual representation of the increase in adopters of new technology. Typically, the curve slopes slowly upwards until it reaches a take-off point, where the rate of adoption dramatically increases. Later on, the rate of adoption decreases, and the curve becomes stationary. Figure 2.6 shows a typical graph of the standard Bass curve (with the average values of p and q of 0.03 and 0.38, respectively).

Figure 2.6. The Bass model.

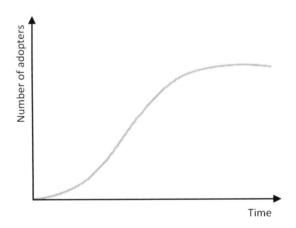

Source: author's elaboration.

Later on, Rogers proposed a diffusion model that was to become widespread (Rogers, 2010).

An innovation, according to the Author, is *"an idea, practice, or object that is perceived as new by an individual or other unit of adoption"* (Rogers, 1995, p. 11).

The newness of innovation is thus a subjective concept that strongly depends on the perception of the individuals in the social systems where the innovation spreads. Rogers further argues that innovation can be described through five characteristics:

1) relative advantage: the degree to which an innovation is perceived as better than the idea that it supersedes;
2) compatibility: the degree to which an innovation is perceived as being consistent with existing values, past experience, and needs of potential adopters;
3) complexity: the degree to which an innovation is perceived as challenging to understand and use;

4) trialability: the degree to which an innovation may be experimented with on a limited basis;
5) observability: the degree to which the results of an innovation are visible to others.

He defines diffusion as a «*process by which an innovation is communicated through certain channels over time among the members of a social system*» (Rogers, 2010, p. 5). The four main elements of this concept are thus the (i) innovation, (ii) communication channels, (iii) time, (iv) social system.

From the definitions of Diffusion and Innovation, Rogers proposes a theoretical model based on four elements – the innovation, communication channels, time and social system – identifiable in any dissemination research, and an Innovation Decision process divided into several stages, that the individual or organization has to overcome in order to reach the definitive degree of adoption of an innovation.

He claims that the diffusion of innovations over time can be represented by a S-shaped curve: at the beginning, only a few agents adopt a specific innovation, then a sensible increase in the number of adopting actors takes place after which a deceleration in the adoption rate follows, and the curve grows at a decreasing rate. Economists explain the S-curve pattern in terms of a balance between supply and demand: the upsurge in the diffusion would be caused by the decrease of innovation costs, which would increase demand and, therefore, diffusion.

Time is a crucial element of this theory since its basis is that adoption is completed over time. It consists of three dimensions, the innovation decision-making process, the mental process by which an individual or an organization makes a decision, the categories of adopters, depending on how close they are to adopting innovation, and the rate of adoption within the social system, depending on the time elapsed.

The establishment of different categories of users is considered the most significant contribution of Rogers' theory. According to this Author, individuals do not adopt an innovation at the same time. According to the time needed for it, five categories are established: the innovators, the first adopters, the early majority, the majority lagging behind, and the traditional ones. Each category responds to a series of personal, socio-economic, and educational characteristics of the users that configure them as a distinct group. Innovators, they import the idea from outside and incorporate it into the system. The first adopters, traditionally accepting innovation and the strategies used for its dissemination before the majority, maintain leadership positions among their colleagues and have a certain weight in local decision-making. The early majority play an essential role in broadcasting. It is skilled at maintaining informal channels of communication but differs from previous categories in that it needs more time to adopt an innovation. The majority lags behind, adopting the new ideas due to pressures of the environment, therefore it needs a greater motivation. For the traditional ones, the reference point is the past, and they act with reservations about adoption and the role of intermediaries. The last dimension of time, the pace of adoption is defined as the relative speed with which the members of a social system adopt an innovation. It is measured by the number of individuals adopting an idea in a given time, a numerical indicator that affects the curve of adoption of an innovation.

Communication channels are the third element of the theory of diffusion. A distinction is made between interpersonal channels and international channels or mass media (media, periodicals). Theory shows that innovation spreads more rapidly through informal channels. The final element of the theory of diffusion is the social system, understood as the norms, the structure, and the intermediaries in the diffusion. The Rogers model is initially designed for decision-making in a centralized structure, where there is control of decisions on innovation to be taken from the highest level and where there is a low level of adaptation to the user.

The role of intermediaries is to convince innovation to be adopted and make the necessary changes to suit users and the system. Rogers recognizes importance to leaders' opinion, who possess a sufficient status that gives credibility to the other users, and to change agents, who work proactively to spread innovation, create demand, persuade, and support decision making. The literature emphasizes the role of the change agent as an external member of the group and a high technical qualification.

What is more interesting is to connect such knowledge about the demand-side with other studies, which have been indeed focused on the supply-side. In this way, a brighter light may be cast on the digital age and its rules, as it applies to the management of firms, which work in information-based contexts (Meade & Islam, 2006).

Applying the theory of **critical mass** (Olson, 2009) to the diffusion of interactive technologies, some authors have shown that it is necessary to modify the traditional S-curve to consider the peculiarities of such means of communication (e-mail, instant messaging, social networks). In fact, interactive technologies should be expected to have a pronounced critical mass in their adoption rate. While the rate of adoption for every innovation may display somewhat of a critical mass effect, for interactive innovation, the critical mass is particularly crucial (Grajek & Kretschmer, 2012; Mahler & Rogers, 1999). For such means, the adoption becomes progressively more convenient as others adopt them.

Prospective adopters perceive more value as the adopter pool grows, so the utility of an interactive innovation depends on the size of the user community. Contrariwise, in the early stage, such means of communication must face discontinuities since it is only possible to communicate with those who have already adopted them. This pattern affects the rate of diffusion: the S-shaped curve ordinarily occurs because positive messages are spread interpersonally from satisfied adopters in a system to potential adopters who are thus persuaded to adopt. In comparison with the process of diffusion for non-interactive innovations, an interactive innovation initially diffuses more slowly until a critical mass of adopters is reached. The perceived number of other adopters influences not only the utility of the innovation to all future potential adopters but also increases the utility of the innovation for all past adopters. This backward flow of increased utility of the innovation presumably leads all past adopters to spread even more positive perceptions about the innovation to others in the system.

The term critical mass comes originally from nuclear physics, where it referred to the amount of radioactive material needed for a pile to "go critical" in a self-sustaining reaction. The critical mass is defined as the minimal number of adopters of an interactive innovation for the further rate of adoption to be self-sustaining (Mahajan et al., 2000). It is the formal term that addresses the "chicken and egg" drawback beyond the adoption decisions. An adopter-to-be would not actualize her interest until a sufficiently high number of already users is granted. On the other side, such a number is not reached until potential users decide actually to adopt.

Whether or not such a critical mass problem is involved in the diffusion of innovation depends on the innovation's degree of interactivity. The number of users is more important when the adoption of innovation requires interaction with other users.

The Chasm model explains how the diffusion of innovations is a two-steps process. Firstly, the smartest and most innovative segments adopt it. Afterward, they put pressure on the other segments, thus making them adopt the innovation in their turn. This implies that the early adopters allow the take-off, boosting the diffusion process and the crossing of the chasm. In Figure 2.7, the number of new adopters is shown during time (axis x). As shown, it is only after the adoption of a few innovators that the early adopters and the early majority decide to adopt the innovation. Unfortunately, this is not as simple as one might wish. Due to the so-called chasm, innovation adoption could also never involve the early adoption, thus making the innovative products or services never reach the mass market. When the chasm is not crossed, either the innovation remains a niche service or simply dies.

Figure 2.7. The Chasm Model.

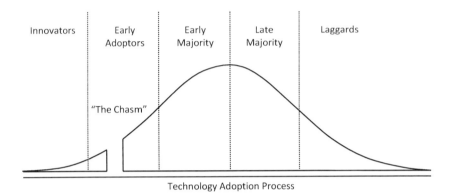

Source: author's elaboration based on Moore, 1995.

Since the information industries are hardly suitable as niche markets, it is fair to assume that crossing the chasm is a must in these contexts. This may also provide a valid explanation to the likelihood that oligopolies or even monopolies may arise within information-based industries.

In addition to that, it is foremost important to highlight the network approach to innovation diffusion. With the increasing spread of complex and networked innovative digital technologies, networks become crucial in sustaining and boosting the adoption of new technology. Lyytinen and Damsgaard (Lyytinen & Damsgaard, 2001) have stressed the relevance of a network approach while studying complex and interactive innovations. In the case of simple and relatively stable innovations, researchers have traditionally focused their attention on two units of analysis: individual adopters and adopter populations. Moreover, these units of analysis are fixed for the whole analysis and over time. In the case of complex and interactive innovations, this choice of analysis units alone is not sufficient. However, it can help to obtaining interesting insights into how individual adopters react or behave in relation to available complex technologies (Damsgaard & Lyytinen, 1998).

Specifically, a network- approach is needed when the adoption of innovation involves two or more independent adopters and often requires the involvement and/or the availability of several other actors in the adoption process. This need relies both upon the structure of the competitive environment that involves a different kind of actors (consumers, companies, institutions, and service providers) and on a set of mechanisms that are activated by the spread of interactive innovations. Arthur (Arthur, 1989) highlights this point by introducing the concept of "attractiveness" of an innovation. Generally, technology becomes more attractive for the users when it is diffused, and others adopt it, the more it becomes "trendy."

A high level of attractiveness induced by adoption, which Arthur (1989) defines as "increasing returns of adoption" (p. 590), may originate from diverse sources. However, five of them are more relevant:

- *Learning by using*. The more people adopt a specific technology, the more it is used, and the more it is learned about it. Consequently, such technology is continuously developed and improved. Mobile apps are also good examples, as the higher the number of users, the higher the awareness of the app and all its features. A double-loop learning actually emerges, as users learn how to leverage the app functionality. It is also the app developers that can learn how to improve those functionalities by observing how the users adopt the app.
- *Network externalities* (Katz and Shapiro, 1985). Technology often offers the possibility to "keep pace" with the other adopters of the same technology, therefore, to belong to the users' network, as it has happened in the case of VHS technology for videotape reproduction against Betamax technology, and later Blu Ray. The more users there are, the more it is possible that a user benefits from the higher availability and variety of products compatible with such technology (for instance, video recorders and video cassettes). This is also true in the video gaming industry, and in all the multi-sided markets (see Chapter One).
- *Scale economies in production*. When technology is incorporated in a product, such as the Polaroid technology, the cost of the product decreases to the number of produced items. Consequently, the technology becomes more convenient as its diffusion increases.
- *Increasing information returns*. When technology diffuses broadly, it benefits from being known and understood. For an adopter who is risk-averse, to adopt such type of technology is more attractive. For instance, the operating system Unix probably offers better performance than Microsoft Windows; however the latter has the advantage of being known and diffused so that in the mind of the new adopter it will be easier to use.

- *Technological interrelations.* When technology diffuses, a series of sub-technologies or products that are a part of the technology's infrastructure or that support the users in its use are also diffused. For instance, with the diffusion of technologies that produce gasoline, a whole industry of oil refineries, petrol stations, and car components associated with gasoline have broadened their diffusion. Also, in the sharing-economy paradigm, the diffusion of Airbnb has fostered the development of interrelated apps and services.

Furthermore, many economic contexts are characterized by the presence of network externalities, which impact on the utility associated with a product when other consumers use the same product. Some examples are provided by the telephone, the mobile phone, the fax, and the Internet connection, in which the higher the number of consumers adopting them, the higher their intrinsic value. Network externalities of innovation are, in Rogers' terms, an essential aspect of relative advantage because they create utility for the adopter as other adopters increasingly adopt it.

The externalities are direct when an increase in the number of adopters raises the value of possessing it (e.g., telephone, but also apps like Whatsapp or social media like Facebook or Instagram), whilst indirect externalities exist when an increase in the number of adopters provides higher incentives for complementary services or products (e.g., information services, m-commerce).

Externalities are related to innovation, from a twofold perspective. 1) The first aspect lies in the relation between the number of adopters and the perceived utility of the innovation. 2) This implies the need for shared standards, or open architectures, which are often necessary for the development of a sector. As far as the mobile telephony is concerned, operators generally tend to defend their own customer base and close their wallets. Nevertheless, cases of big success were born from the sharing of a standard (GSM above all, and later 3G, 4G, and possibly 5G).

The diffusion of innovations models is strictly related to the models that discuss the acceptance and adoption of new technologies by users, which will be discussed later in the chapter (par. 2.5.2).

Box 2.3. Diffusion of Innovation, the case of Apple

Apple revolutionized personal technology with the launch of the Macintosh in 1984. Today, Apple is a leader in innovation with iPhone, iPad, Mac, Apple Watch, and Apple TV. Apple's four software platforms – iOS, macOS, watchOS, and tvOS – all offer the same experience on all Apple devices- and allow users to do even more with revolutionary services like the App Store, Apple Music, Apple Pay, and iCloud. The company claims that *"over 100,000 Apple employees are dedicated to creating the best products and leaving a better world than we found"* (Apple, 2019).

Rogers' model can be adapted to the case of Apple, with respect to the release of new version of the Iphone, in terms of the five attributes: *i)* relative advantage; *ii)* compatibility; *iii)* complexity; *iv)* trialability; *v)* observability.

The relative advantage refers to the fact that Apple succeeds in differentiating its electronics either in terms of a higher degree of innovation or leveraging the design and the aesthetic dimension of the products. Thus, Apple aims at obtaining the relative advantage over its competitors, which is usually expressed in economic profitability or the granting of status.

Compatibility is a secure attribute of Apple's innovations since for example if a user of these products wants to renew her device, there is no doubt that she will continue to acquire the new models of the company because her past experience has shown her that the innovations introduced are fully compatible with her set of electronic equipment. So, when it comes to making a purchasing decision, innovation becomes less and less uncertain.

On the other hand, the attribute of complexity is a key factor for potential Apple adopters because the operating system of mobile devices is completely different from those that people mostly use, that does not mean it is hard to understand or use, but generally the reason why people do not to purchase an Apple product is that they do not understand their operating system.

The testing capability of Apple's new technologies is high, because all of its stores have the devices available to potential users, which can interact with the innovations proposed each year by the company, in addition to having staff who is in charge of explaining and deepening the capabilities and uses of the products.

Finally, visibility is the last attribute that favors Apple sales because the results of the innovations are easily observed and communicated to others.

"We have closed a fantastic 2019 fiscal year, with our highest revenues so far in the fourth quarter, thanks to accelerated growth in services, wearable devices and iPad capabilities", said Tim Cook, CEO of Apple. *"Customers and experts are delighted with the new generation of the iPhone, today's release of the new AirPods Pro with noise cancellation and the expected launch of AppleTV+, which is only two days away. It all adds up to our best range of products and services to date, so we can't wait to see what Christmas brings us"*. The company invests hugely in its communication channels because the innovations spread quickly and effectively so that customers can acquire the new technologies of the iPhone, which is reflected in the high revenues of the quarter.

Based on the Apple example, it seems that the correct diffusion of innovation, hand in hand with the great technological and digital transformation that the brand has had in recent decades, have been the main tool of differentiation from its competitors in the industry.

Source: author's elaboration in collaboration with Verònica Contardo Giadach.

It is worth mentioning that this competitive advantage of the diffusion of innovation and technological development can be seen in various brands that nowadays lead various markets, such as Microsoft, Tesla, Amazon, among others. This responds positively to the hypothesis that the great masters of the future will be organizations capable of creating, communicating, and spreading innovations over time.

Certainly, the innovative development will continue and produce great inventions in the future. It is also necessary to understand the methods of diffusion, so that the change can reach more people, creating communication networks in shorter times in the most efficient ways, as time and its dimensions are another key factor in Rogers' theory. By strengthening the areas mentioned above, it will be possible to lead and gain sustainable advantages.

2.5. All that Glitters Is not (Technological) Gold!

The organizational and managerial academic literature has long investigated the relationship between organizations and technology. One of the most prolific and prominent streams of research has focused on the dual nature of ICT in Information Systems (W.J. Orlikowski & Robey, 1991). Information Systems refer to both the technological and sociological elements. In fact, technologies that enable data storage and information flows must also be studied with respect to how they are used and perceived by the people within the organizations. Thus, information systems are seen as socio-technical complex systems (W.J. Orlikowski, 2002). The sociomateriality perspective allows taking into account both dimensions (Kallinikos et al., 2012; Leonardi & Barley, 2010; W.J. Orlikowski & Scott, 2008).

Also, with the affirmation of the digital age, digital technology could not make any impact if it was not for the humans who, individually and collectively, are generating a series of changes and often contradictory implications. As an ongoing product of our own making, the digital age "*reflects our collective energies and efforts, interests and innovations, visions and values, whether these are deliberate or inadvertent, intended or unintended*" (W. J. Orlikowski & Iacono, 2000).

The dual nature of digital technologies clarifies that:

1. ICTs are artifacts: material products of programmers, technicians, engineers, managers, developers, hackers, etc. Users appropriate these artifacts and adapt them to their needs and requirements through an enactment process that gives them meaning.
2. ICT mediate essential organizational processes: the availability and quality of data and information greatly influence the processes of "sense-making," "decision making," and "knowing." The influence of ICTs is not direct; it rather depends on how people appropriate it and what use they make of it. It is the way in which ICTs are used, and not

ICTs per se, that conditions the practices, routines and theory of action used by organizational actors. This conception of ICTs is called technology in use, a sort of theory in use of how to use ICTs.
3. ICTs are located: the interaction between ICT and behavior is located within a pre-existing social context made up of declared and in use action theories, power structures, rules, and shared meanings. This context influences how people decide to use ICTs.
4. ICTs can change the context: with the use of ICTs, behaviors are implemented, which can both reinforce the existing context and modify it.

Individuals, groups, different organizational units choose how to use ICT to strengthen or modify the routines and practices with which they carry out the processes of "sense-making," "decision making," and "knowing" that make up the theory of action in use.

2.5.1. Information Systems in Organizations

The use of technologies allows the individual to increase her information processing capacity, as this is outsourced and transferred outside her brain.

The computational capacity of individuals remains unchanged because neurocognitive blocks limit it, but technologies replace it in processing and memory procedures, as in writing. In any case, it is not possible to increase the individual's capacity for interpretation and knowledge: the amount of information that he can process to produce knowledge remains the same.

This holds particularly true as Artificial Intelligence is substituting manpower in tasks that are becoming more and more complex.

Nonetheless, Information Systems cannot wholly replace managerial roles. It is interesting to discuss how IS relates to managerial roles at different levels in organizations. With respect to intermediate managerial tasks the greater availability of information and the reduction in the cost of processing it may contribute to the disappearance of the intermediate managerial line. This could be due to the fact that the top management, through suitable IS, directly controls the activities previously delegated to the intermediate line. At odds, it may also be the case that the automation of operational activities achieved through the IS gives greater importance to the intermediate managerial line, to which responsibility for the control and achievement of the objectives has been delegated.

Midway managers, in this way, analyze and control data and strengthen their power. This seems to be the case, for example, of the marketing department (see Box 2.3).

IS leads to the automation of operational tasks, and digital technologies could lead to hyper-automation. IS allows replacing human labor in tasks aimed at solving structured problems (**automate effect**). Moreover, IS allows increasing the number of SOP (Standard Operating Procedures) to be adopted in response to different problems (**high variety**). The IS also collects and processes information relating to the activities carried out (**informed effect**). Therefore, both a shift of employees from some jobs to others and a change in the jobs themselves materialize.

Tasks that are de-specialized are no longer focused on the solution of structured problems; rather tasks are enriched and dedicated to the solution of various and delicate problems (**job enrichment**). IS also allows for a job consolidation, through which multiple tasks, previously assigned to separate tasks, are entrusted to one person (**job enlargment**).

With respect to teams and group work facilitation, the rapid and temporary aggregation of different tasks in workgroups is facilitated using digitally-based IS. Task forces, project groups, and quality circles are facilitated, and overlapping tasks can be introduced. These technological solutions also facilitate the use of organizational forms called "electronic matrices" and the mobility of people between different groups engaged in different projects.

In particular, Group Decision Support Systems (GDSS) have a significant effect on teamwork. They can increase the number of participants in the group with an increase in their productivity. Collaboration and creativity increase, also thanks to the anonymity guaranteed by the GDSS. Feedback and the circulation of ideas in groups and between groups increase.

GDSS, on the other side, introduce difficulties induced by the Group Decision Support System (GDSS) on teamwork. In fact, they are of little use in conflict situations. They do not satisfy participants' need for affiliation, reducing commitment and motivation. They do not value individual contributions to group decision-making processes, demotivating the most brilliant participants. Due to anonymity, they can facilitate free-rider opportunistic behavior. Thus, they are not adequate means in conditions of high ambiguity, where instead, direct interpersonal relationships work better.

IS of Groupware may indeed support Virtual Teams, which are groups of people who work together remotely and at different times on the same project or product. The more and more sophisticated use of digital GW allows to: increase the connections and contacts of each participant (asynchronous nature of messages); increase the number of groups a worker can join; reduce the role differences. However, the Virtual Teams have been shown to take longer to decisions making processes; to reach a lower level of affiliation and members' motivation.

Both at the intra-organizational and inter-organizational levels, digital technologies support the formation and development of virtual communities (VC). They are an evolution of communities of practice, which are made up of individuals who do not know each other, but who find the environment on the internet to interact and share the same interests. They can be distinguished in VCs:

- of relationship: based on the need to dialogue on topics of common interest (chat lines, forums, and newsgroups);
- of interest: based on the need to access secure information sources;
- of consumers: made up of people who exchange information on the products and services purchased;
- professional: made up of people who change professional experiences.

The power of Virtual Communities lies on the theory of the strength of weak ties (Brown & Konrad, 2001; Granovetter, 1983; Hansen, 1999). Strong ties are established between people who share the same information. To get more information, people establish weak links with less similar people who do not know each other well. Weak ties are characterized by sporadic contacts, without emotional involvement. They are useful because they are more numerous and therefore, the probability of receiving an answer is higher. They allow activating the contributions of more experienced people.

Information Systems, as said at the beginning of the chapter, are dependent on their technological component but also, and mostly, by their applications in the social context in which they are embedded (for example, the company). Thus, the IS theory identifies the interrelation between IS and organizational structure. Taking into account the perspective on the dynamic aspect of the structure, it is possible to distinguish between the infrastructure, the sociostructure, and the superstructure (Fombrun, 1986). This is useful to analyze the impact of IS on each one of them (Mats Alvesson, 2004).

A) The **infrastructure** consists of the activities and interdependencies that bind the technical and the economic dimension.

B) The **sociostructure** highlights how the different actors who are responsible for the activities interact (political dimension).

C) The **superstructure** highlights how values and culture oversee the essential processes of an organizational actor (symbolic dimension).

A) As far as the infrastructure is concerned, the benefits deriving from the introduction of the IS will be limited if there is no change in the way the activities that make up the infrastructure are carried out and coordinated (N. Venkatraman, 1994). It is possible to distinguish between five levels of infrastructure transformation:

a) Local automation, in which IS automates individual procedures or activities and which are adopted within individual organizational units. It is based on IS which introduce business practice standards. The inclusion of these IS does not cause major changes, but can generate interesting benefits: reduction of costs, increase in the speed of response to customer requests.

b) Internal integration. A more systematic approach is adopted that integrates IS that regulates the activities carried out by different organizational units. It does not reflect on how the activities are carried out, but common platforms are developed to make different IS dialogue. The success of these interventions depends on the ability to activate horizontal relationship mechanisms that guide and support the workflow of automated activities.

c) Business Process Reengineering (BPR), through which IS is used as a lever to modify the infrastructure and redesign its processes profoundly. The BPR methodology requires that a new vision of how a process should be organized and developed. Process refers to a systematic series of activities aimed at achieving a goal. The processes are composed of interdependent activities which, starting from defined inputs, achieve a precise output aimed at specific customers, internal or external. The introduction of IS help rethink and optimize processes to improve their speed of execution, the level of service, the quality offered. The same sequential structure of the activities can be redesigned, identifying the flows to be performed in parallel and eliminating unnecessary and redundant activities. The IS facilitates the control of the processes and integrates separate organizational units. The use of BPR is frequent with the introduction of ERP systems. The risk of failure is, however, significant. Digital technologies in BPR allows to:

– standardize unstructured processes;
– eliminate communication difficulties between organizational units;
– reduce or replace human labor in a process;
– apply analytical methods of managing and controlling a process;
– increase the available information relating to a process;
– change the sequence of activities.

d) Business Network Redesign. The impact of IS is also exercised in the inter-organizational field and changes the relationships between companies in a network with the following potential benefits: *i)* Transaction processing: the exchange of data and information between companies is improved; *ii)* Inventory movement: warehouse and inventory management is moved from one company to another; *iii)* Process linkage: interdependent processes carried out within different organizations are integrated; *iv)* Knowledge leverage: professional resources belonging to different organizations are connected.

e) Business Scope Redefinition. The introduction of IS produces a rethinking of the nature of the business and the corporate mission in two ways: *i)* expansion of the core business; *ii)* shifting and refocusing of the core business. Corporate venturing is also facilitated.

B) Regarding the impact of IS on the sociostructure, it is of utmost importance to highlight the resistance to change that may hinder the adoption and usage of digital technologies. Resistance to change refers to emotional reactions that can translate into hostile actions and behaviors, such as aggression and sabotage of the technology, the introduction of cognitive mechanisms of attribution and projection, blaming the technology for any failure; the new IS can as well be ignored while continuing to use the old systems.

The resistance to change has individual as well as collective factors.
Individual factors comprise:
- habit (theories of action in use);
- insecurity and social uncertainty: roles and power relations become unclear, restructuring and downsizing are feared;
- fear of the unknown: new sense-making and learning processes to be developed are feared.

Collective factors include:
-- structural and group inertia: it is difficult to change the social context within which individual behaviors have value;
- threat to power relations.

C) With respect to IS and superstructure, it is useful to recall the theory of the technology in use. IS can be interpreted as cultural artifacts, i.e., symbolic and material manifestations and expressions of the corporate culture. The organizational culture can influence (mediate) how a technology is adopted, inserted, and diffused. The analysis of the technology in use allows the interpretation of the corporate culture, as it can represent a reification.

The concept of drift (Ciborra et al., 2000) explains how IS are often used in an unexpected and different way from that suggested by the designers. The drift or drift process is defined as a slight or significant difference between the role and functions attributed to the technology in use, and those imagined and planned by the designers or by the top management. The drift depends on:
- the degree of plasticity and flexibility of IS;
- crafting, i.e., a sort of do-it-yourself behavior implemented by users.

Also, the relation between IS and superstructure is influenced by technological frames (Henfridsson et al., 2014; W.J. Orlikowski & Gash, 1994).

Technological frames are the product of the assumptions, expectations and knowledge that members of an organization use to understand the role, nature, and consequences of technology. The technological frames depend on the different corporate subcultures and the national background culture. The presence of multiple subcultures that create different technological frames can be an obstacle to digital technological innovations.

2.5.2. Technology Acceptance Models

Many different streams of research have flourished around the problem of technology acceptance and adoption, and several models have been structured in order to understand the foundations of the prospective users' reaction towards a novel technology. One of the technology acceptance mainstream models is the Technology Acceptance Model (TAM) initially conceived by Fred Davis in 1989 (Money & Turner, 2004).

The Technology Acceptance Model (TAM) is an intention-based model aiming to explain of the determinants of technology acceptance, capable of explaining user behaviour across a broad range of end-user computing technologies and user populations (Davis, 1989). Since its introduction TAM has enjoyed increasingly wide approval and has proven to be a reasonably accurate predictor of both users' intentions to use an information technology and their system usage. The TAM is derived from the Theory of Reasoned Action (TRA) developed by Fishbein and Ajzen in 1975 (Fishbein & Ajzen, 1975) tailored to explain and predict a broad range of people behaviours based on situation specific combinations of personal beliefs and attitudes with the fundamental premise that individuals will adopt a certain behaviour if they believe that it will lead to positive outcomes. TAM belongs to the line of thinking encompassed in the so-called variance approach, mainly focused on determining antecedents of adoption and usage of new technologies (Money & Turner, 2004). In its original version by Davis, the Technology Acceptance Model presents five main components: Perceived Usefulness (PU), Perceived Ease Of Use (PEOU), Behavioral Intention to use (BI), Attitude toward using (AT) and Actual usage (U) (Davis, 1989; Legris et al., 2003).

A prospective user's overall attitude toward using a given system is hypothesized to be a significant determinant of whether the user herself actually uses it. The attitude, in turn, is a function of the two beliefs expressed by the Perceived Usefulness PU and the Perceived Ease Of Use PEOU: the former is defined as the degree to which an individual believes that the usage of a particular system can improve his work performances; on the other hand, the ease of use is defined as the degree to which an individual believes that using a particular system would be free of physical and mental efforts. The hypothesis stated by Davis claims that the PEOU has a direct and relevant effect on the PU, while the opposite is not valid, meaning that the PU is not hypothesized to have an impact on the PEOU. Furthermore, PEOU and PU are influenced by external variables, including system design features, user characteristics, task characteristics.

Figure 2.8. The Technology Acceptance Model (TAM).

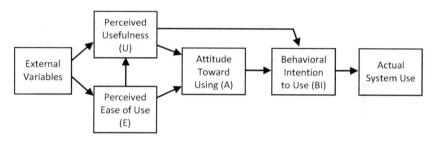

Source: author's elaboration based on (Davis, 1989).

Consequently, those external variables directly influence PU and PEOU and indirectly influence Attitude AT toward use. PU and PEOU are usually measured by a four-items measurement scale derived by the six items identified by Davis. Starting by the original model, the Technology Acceptance Model has evolved, and many scholars developed it applying some amendments. Overall, it can be defined as a widely accepted model.

Nevertheless, the Technology Acceptance Model presents some limits. The most relevant one is related to the concept of technology within the context where it is embedded. The TAM considers information systems as an independent issue from the organizational dynamics in which they are enclosed. Though research in innovation and change management field suggests that technological implementation is strictly related to the organizational environment that will have a substantial impact on the outcomes. According to Orlikowski and Hofman the effectiveness of any change process relies on the interdependence between the technology, the organizational context, and the change model used to manage the change (W. Orlikowski & Hoffman, 1997). This supports the suggestion that it may be challenging to increase the predictive capacity of TAM if it is not integrated into a broader model that includes organizational and social factors (Legris et al., 2003; Money & Turner, 2004).

In 2003, the Unified Theory of Acceptance and Use of Technology (UTAUT) was proposed based on the results of a study that developed and validated a new research model with seven constructs (Venkatesh et al.,

2003). The model includes four key determinants of use and four moderators of individual use behavior (Figure 2.9). The UTAUT seminal study suggests that performance expectations, efforts, and social influences predict intentions, which consequently predict usage behavior. Gender, age, experience, and the perception of voluntary changes are the moderating factors for intentions.

The eight original models and theories of individual acceptance that are summarized by Venkatesh in 2003 include Theory of Reasoned Action (TRA), TAM, Motivational Model (MM), Theory of Planned Behavior (TPB), Model Combining the Technology Acceptance Model and Theory of Planned Behavior, Model of pc utilization, Innovation Diffusion Theory and Social Cognitive Theory.

Figure 2.9. The UTAT model.

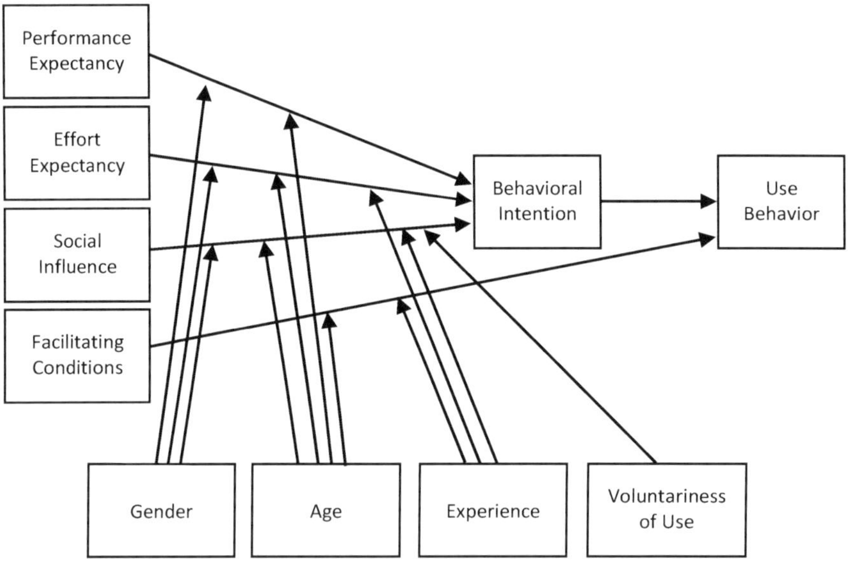

Source: author's elaboration based on (Venkatesh et al., 2003).

The construct derives from eight different user acceptance models, as follows:

1. Performance expectations are the degree to which an individual believes that using a system improves her performance.
2. Expectations related to efforts are the degree of simplicity associated with using a system.
3. The attitudes towards use are the degree to which an individual believes that she should use that system.

4. Social influences are the degree to which an individual perceives that others believe she should use the system.
5. The facilitated conditions are the degree to which an individual believes that the organizational and technical infrastructures exist to support the use of a system.
6. Self-efficacy is the degree to which an individual judges her ability to use a particular system to perform the task.
7. Anxiety represents the degree of emotional reactions associated with the use of a particular system.

The key determinants identified in the UTAUT can shift in importance depending on the environment. Although the UTAUT is one of the few models that try to incorporate the concept of awareness or voluntariness for the use of new technology, it considers it only in a binary variable classifying it at the top or bottom.

The technology acceptance models are very closely related to the diffusion of innovations. As seen previously in the chapter, the diffusion of innovations is the process by which an innovation communicates through specific channels over time among the members of a social system. It is a particular type of communication, as messages are concerned about new ideas. Communication is a process in which participants create and share information among themselves to reach a mutual understanding (Rogers and Kincaid, 1981). Following this assumption, **Social Cognitive Theory (SCT)** acknowledges the complex nature of behavior intention, which is influenced by the reciprocal interaction between the environment in which an individual operates and their behavior (Bandura, 1988, 2001). Social cognitive theory is built upon the foundations of individual and group psychological behavior, and is also referred to as social learning theory (Bandura & Walters, 1977). Social cognitive theory is a widely accepted model of individual behavior as it examines the reasons why individuals adopt certain behaviors. It has been used to understand the adoption of technological innovation in several contexts (Chan & others, 2004; Ratten & Ratten, 2007). It proposes that behavior is evaluated through an individual's expectation of the outcome of their behavior, the expectation of their direct experience and can be mediated through the observations of others (LaRose & Eastin, 2004). Thus, the major premise of social cognitive theory is that individuals can reciprocally influence their actions, and this may lead to the emergence of leaders who prominently influence others (Mccormick & Martinko, 2004). This has become particularly important to understand with the explosion of social media and the social media discourse. In fact, a new field of research has emerged that analyses how the discourse on social media (Twitter, as an example) can influence the attitude and the behavior towards a new technology (Acciarini et al., 2020; Bolici et al., 2019).

2.5.3. IS and Change Management

In general, investments in information systems are characterized by a significant impact on the corporate organizational system within which they are made. It should not be forgotten, in fact, that any system supporting the exchange of relevant information within the company organization must be understood as a tool that the members of the organization are called to use in various capacities. From this point of view, therefore, considering that the organizational unit includes social subjects called to interact with information media, it is clear that the impact of these systems on the organization itself cannot be overlooked.

In particular, this impact is articulated along three fundamental lines:

a) Job design;
b) Training and development;
c) Value creation.

As regards the job design and the training and development, both comprise a series of operational activities, aimed at guiding the introduction and use of the information system. These are, therefore, activities that can be defined as operational.

As already mentioned, the implementation of new Information Systems inevitably provokes a series of reactions in the organizational context. On the other hand, this also implies that the organizational change, once the need is felt, can be achieved through the development and introduction of certain IT solutions. In other words, successful implementations require careful change management (Laudon & Laudon, 2009). It has been shown that information technologies can allow for changes, but the mere existence of these technologies does not mean that these changes must necessarily occur. This increases the importance of the control and management of organizational change following the introduction and use of information systems. A useful conceptualization of the organizational change management following the introduction of information systems considers two fundamental directions of change: depth and rapidity (Pendlebury et al., 1998).

The perspective adopted in the model identifies a positive correlation between information change and organizational change. In fact, following the guidelines indicated, the higher the depth of change in IT, the higher the depth of organizational change required. In a specular way, the higher the speed with which the information system is subject to changes, the higher the speed with which the entire organization must make a change.

In particular, the depth of the change indicates the degree to which the nature of the company is influenced. In this perspective, superficial or incremental changes can be identified, where an improvement activity takes place, which involves existing structures and traditional processes are used. On the contrary, there is talk of radical or profound change in cases where the existing IT architecture is radically changed, the entire organization is involved. It has a significant impact on traditional processes, giving rise to the need to adapt professional skills.

The direction of the rapidity of change, on the other hand, identifies the time within which the change must take place. This variable is increasingly important, as the timeliness of the change could be decisive for achieving the desired competitive advantage.

In the original formulation of the matrix, high rapidity and high depth of change would be addressed as *Organizational Development*. The rapid technological innovations continuously appearing in the Digital Age clearly require that change management occurs at the entire organization and very rapidly. This leads to a real transformation, which is called digital transformation. The latter will be extensively discussed in the next chapter.

Figure 2.10. The depth and rapidity of change.

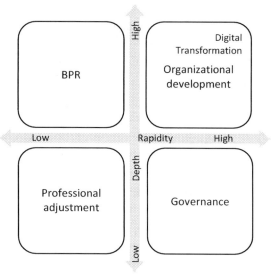

Source: author's elaboration based on (Pendlebury et al., 1998).

Chapter 3
KNOWLEDGE AND (DIGITAL) LEARNING ORGANIZATIONS

SUMMARY: 3.1. Digital Transformation. – 3.1.1. The Hype of Digital Transformation. – 3.1.2. Digitization, Digitalization, and Digital Transformation. 3.1.3. Chief Digital Officer, who? – 3.2. Organizational Learning and Learning Organizations. – 3.2.1. Organizational Learning. – 3.2.2. Learning Organizations. – 3.2.3. Learning through Experience. – 3.2.4. Knowledge intensive firms. – 3.2.5. Agile Organizations. – 3.3. Digital Technologies for Human Resources Management. – 3.3.1. Managing the Knowledge Workers, Revisited. Cognitive Computing and Machine Learning. – 3.3.2. Digital Workplaces. – 3.3.3. Flexible Working, Smart Working?

3.1. Digital Transformation

Speculation about knowledge, knowledge-based organizations, and knowledge workers should be cautiously pondered. In fact, a wealth of information and the diffusion of managerial practice related to knowledge management in contemporary firms do not necessarily lead to better performances, better working environments, and ultimately to competitive advantage. In some types of work, for example call centers or the so-called job on-call type of work arrangement, workers are still made to deal with hierarchy and knowledge, although being at the core of the working processes; this is far from being considered a means of empowerment for the workforce. In most of the cases, though, firms that embrace the knowledge-based approach adopt flatter, decentralized structures and organize their work processes in more flexible, fluid, and networked arrangements.

"Digital transformation" has become widely used to mean the transformational or disruptive implications of digital technologies for businesses, in terms of

- new business models,
- new types of products/services,
- new types of customer experiences

(e.g., Boulton, 2018; Boutetiere and Reich, 2018).

More broadly, digital transformation requires that existing companies need to radically transform themselves to succeed in the digital age (McAfee & Brynjolfsson, 2017; Nambisan et al., 2019; V. Venkatraman, 2017). It is thus of paramount importance to deeply understand the breadth of change that digital transformation requires, and how digital transformation differ from digitization and digitalization.

3.1.1. The Hype of Digital Transformation

Using a query on Scopus to analyze the trend in academic publications on digital transformation, 22,896 records include the keyword "digitalANDtransformation" in the period 2000-2019.

Figure 3.1. Trend in academic publications on digital transformation (2000-2019).

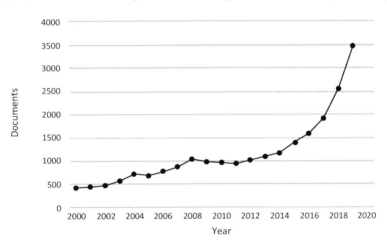

Source: author's elaboration on Scopus, as of May 15, 2020.

Figure 3.1 clearly shows the recent hype in academic writing, as a rapid acceleration of the number of publications started in 2016, following the publication of seminal articles e.g., (Hess et al., 2016; Horlacher & Hess, 2016; Matt et al., 2015).

The bulk of the academic publications on the subject fall in the subject area of Computer Science (26%) and Engineering (22.7%), while the contributions in Business, Management, and Social Sciences account for only roughly 10% altogether (Figure 3.2). This means that, while the companies are thriving to embrace the Digital Transformation with a new strategic mindset, the theoretical contributions are still mostly focused on the technological underpinnings of such transformation. It must be said, though, that technologies do play a fundamental role in the digital transformation. Thus it is not surprising that most of the studies fall in these areas.

Figure 3.2. Publications on digital transformation by subject area (2000-2019).

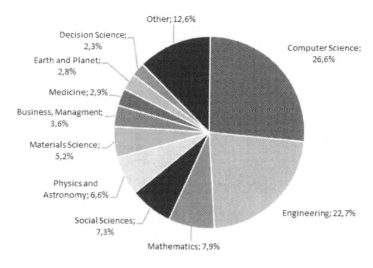

Source: author's elaboration on Scopus, as of May 15, 2020.

Figure 3.3. Publications on digital transformation by country (top 15 countries, 2000-2019).

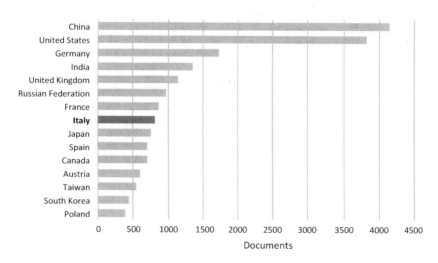

Source: author's elaboration on Scopus, as of May 15, 2020.

It is also interesting to notice that the vast majority of the articles are published by researchers affiliated with either Chinese or American institutions (Figure 3.3). On the other side, European affiliations would be more comparable to those of China and the US, if the single countries could add up at the continental level.

The recurring themes debated in the articles revolve around the strategic scope of the digital transformation, which should not be considered only a technological-driven organizational change, but rather a complete strategic turnaround, to reimagine the concept of a business. This transformation must be coherent with a clear digital strategy supported by leaders who foster a culture able to change and invent the new (Kane et al., 2015).

Considering also the grey literature and the posts on business media, which has abounded in the last five years or so, what is mostly debated is that the term "transformation" is adequately used to address an organizational revolution, which is far more than a "simple" organizational change. Such transformation requires that the company embraces a new paradigm that spins around the adoption and exploitation of digital technologies for internal purposes, such as processes redefinition and knowledge management, as well as external objectives, such as communication and advertisement. New digital technologies, like social networks, data analytics, advanced manufacturing, to name a few, are the means through which a company can foster significant business improvements. The ICT revolution needs complementary factors to cause positive impact on productivity and growth (Paganetto, 2017). Certainly, human capital is one of the most important factors that must be developed through a well-managed organizational change.

3.1.2. Digitization, Digitalization, and Digital Transformation

Having become hot topics in literature and in practice, the buzzwords *digitization*, *digitalization*, and *digital transformation* should be first of all defined to clear the confusion about them. Although they are strictly related, they are not same and it is imperative to understand the differences and the managerial implications that each of them brings about.

Digitization means creating digital (bits and bytes) versions of analog/physical things such as paper documents, microfilm images, photographs, sounds, and more. It often becomes a synonym of automation: use digital data, extracted from physical carriers, to automate business processes and workflows. It is impossible to digitize a whole process, but it is advantageous to automate the process by digitizing information.

Digitalization refers to the changes that business operations, business functions, and business models undergo by leveraging digital technologies.

Digitalization thus implies a broader use and context of digitized data, which are contextualized in the specific organization. Through digitalization, digitized data can be turned into intelligence and actionable knowledge.

An example refers to the development of new digital communication channels to have more direct and more straightforward interactions with customers and optimize existing business processes (Pagani & Pardo, 2017).

Digitalization requires the organizational system's engagement so that all activities undergo an incremental adoption of digital technologies, and a process of sensemaking is fostered throughout the organization at all levels.

The complexity of digitalization has become evident as companies have begun to understand that simply converting analog content into digital content does not imply immediate business positive outcomes. Instead, the digitalization process needs to be conceived as a radical organizational change, which puts knowledge at the core, and knowledge management as a diffuse managerial practice (see Table 3.1).

Table 3.1. Digitization vs. digitalization.

	Digitization	Digitalization
Definition	Encoding analog data and information from analog into a digital format	Altering and optimizing existing business processes by leveraging digital technologies, in order to increase efficiency and coordination between different processes, and ultimately improve the customer experience
Examples	Encoding an image into a digital file; converting a paper document into a text file; feeding a digital checklist or a shared calendar	Implementing data analytics by leveraging Internet-based communication channels with customers, that feed process optimization; collecting real time data from distributed sensors to calibrate processes and communication
Organizational implications	Individual team, unit, or function reaches a shared understanding on what needs to be digitized and automated, and how	Cross-functional integration and communication are needed; knowledge management system that allows shared sensemaking of the adoption of digital technologies

Source: author's elaboration.

Digitization and digitalization are strongly correlated, yet they are very different things and the one does not necessarily imply the other. This is even more true concerning digital transformation.

Through digital transformation, entire business models can be reshaped or replaced. Giving this overarching scope, it is essential that DT strategies are aligned with other strategies, both at the company and the business levels. Indeed, DT strategies cut across the whole organization. The concept of IT alignment for transforming organizations is not new (Henderson & Venkatraman, 1999). It is widely accepted that successful IT strategies are those that are aligned with the company strategy and the organizational solutions (Giustiniano, 2005). As digital transformation is also reshaping supply-chain, as well as coopetition among firms (V. Venkatraman, 2017), the concept of IT alignment, enlarged to include the broader array of digital technologies, has become even more pertinent.

The **Digital Transformation Framework** (Matt et al., 2015) links the elements of the DT strategies common to companies regardless of their industry, size, or technology maturity stage (Figure 3.4).

Figure 3.4. The Digital Transformation Framework.

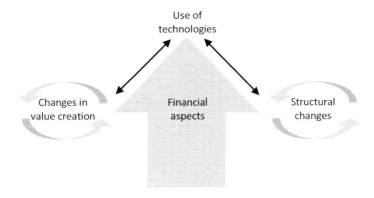

Source: author's elaboration on (Matt et al., 2015).

First of all, the *use of technologies* represents the firm's technological readiness, i.e,. its attitude towards new digital technologies and its capability to leverage them for organizational purposes. Strategic options include either becoming a technological leader or adopting existing standards to fulfill business operations.

The use of new technologies then leads to changes in *value creation*. DT strategies impact value chains, which could lead to expand and enrich the current products and services portfolio or build different technological and product-related competences and change the business scope, for example, serving additional markets or new customer segments.

Structural changes are required to fully leverage the opportunities created by different technologies in use and different forms of value creation. Structural changes refer to variations in a firm's organizational setup, especially concerning the placement of the new digital activities within the corporate structures. If changes are substantial, it may well be the case for creating a separate subsidiary.

Of course, the *financial aspects* must be taken into good account. The firm's ability to finance a DT and companies with financial distress may lack obvious ways to finance a transformation.

Moreover, digital technologies fuel new forms of innovation and entrepreneurial initiatives that cross traditional industry/sectoral boundaries and embrace networks, ecosystems and communities and integrate digital and non-digital assets (Nambisan et al., 2019).

All this considered, it is also crucial that new leadership emerges to drive organizations through the multifaceted challenges of digital transformation.

3.1.3. Chief Digital Officer, who?

The Chief Digital Officer is emerging as a crucial role in driving the Digital Transformation (Horlacher & Hess, 2016).

At the dawn of the Digital Age, companies relied on Chief Information Officers as the technologists who were deemed as experts in charge of digital innovation. As digital technologies became more and more invasive in business, and also private lives, it also became evident that the competencies held by CIOs did not fully fit the requirements of the Digital Transformation paradigm. Companies have hoped that their CIOs would be able to expand their roles, and devote less time to managing IT services and more time delivering broader business value (Weill & Woerner, 2013). This was, however, a flawed expectation, as CIOs did not have the right mindset and competency to lead the whole organization in such a big transformation. Indeed, CIOs are, by definition, pure technologists with managerial skills, while the digital transformation requires business strategists as leaders. At odds with CIOs, CDOs do not have functional IT responsibility, and mostly they do not have profit and loss responsibility either. Further, their overall corporate perspective is broader than CIOs' (Singh & Hess, 2017).

Digital Transformation is, by definition, cross-functional, and it involves multiple functional areas, from marketing to information systems, to R&D and operations management. To avoid DT implementation in silos, a CDO would act as a leader who connects all the functional areas and optimizes cross-fertilization opportunities (Verhoef et al., 2019).

In a qualitative study on the role performed by CDOs in selected case studies, Horlacher and Hess (Horlacher & Hess, 2016) provide a beneficial discussion of what CDOs do in organizations. First of all, they define the CDOs as **digital evangelists** in their organizations. More specifically, not only do the CDOs set the tone of the digital strategy, they also detect and drive the changes across the whole organization that are necessary to implement the digital transformation. They are, in fact, **change agents** and **change catalysts**. This also requires that the organization adopt a coherent corporate culture and a set of shared value that may be lacking. Therefore, CDOs also act as spokespersons to persuade the whole workforce across the organization, at cross-departmental and cross-functional level. In order to do so, CDOs must possess excellent communication skills and the ability to foster a cohesive digital vision. CDOs are leaders in the digital journey of the organizations, as DT requires the alignment of the functional executives to overcome the organizational silos problem and seek the necessary strong coordination among all organizational areas. As an organizational silos approach would lead functional or departmental executives to focus on their own objectives and those of their specific organizational units, this would be problematic in implementing a DT, which is cross-functional by definition. CDOs need to work not only cross-functionally but also cross-disciplinarily. This requires a diverse set of competencies so that CDOs can understand the different aspects of a business, such as business models, processes, technologies, and customer needs.

The CDOs are usually in charge of recruiting the new digital talents and identifying the training needs of the existing workforce, who need to be motivated to face the DT challenges and required changes.

3.2. Organizational Learning and Learning Organizations

Digital transformation, if properly managed, can boost the ability to create new knowledge at the organizational level continuously. Thus, the concept of learning organizations and organizational learning are more and more critical in the Digital Age.

3.2.1. Organizational Learning

What is learning? As early as the 5th century BC, Confucius, the great Chinese philosopher, put forward the importance of learning, as he stated that everyone should benefit from learning.

One of the issues in innovative organizing in knowledge-based contexts is related to the necessity to convey individuals' knowledge within the organization and how the companies subsequently manage it. Organizational learning is defined as *"a change in the organization that occurs as the organization acquires experience"* (Argote & Miron-Spektor, 2011, p. 1124).

From an epistemological perspective, knowledge can be distinguished between "tacit" and "explicit" knowledge (Duguid, 2012; Polanyi, 1966). **Tacit knowledge** is the kind of personal knowledge that is hard to formalize and communicate; it is deeply rooted in action, commitment, and involvement in a specific context. **Explicit knowledge** or codified knowledge refers to knowledge that is transmittable in formal, systematic language. Tacit and explicit knowledge engage in a continuous dialogue within an organization, and their interaction recreates new concepts and ideas (Nonaka, 1994). Being "continuous activity of knowing," sharing tacit knowledge resembles an "analog" process in which individuals build mutual understanding. At odds, explicit knowledge can be considered "digital" as it is discretely captured and codified in records or knowledge repositories.

From an ontological perspective, knowledge can be studied with respect to the interaction between individuals that share and develop knowledge-building communities of interaction, which contribute to the amplification and development of new knowledge.

To make middle-up-down management more efficient, it is necessary to provide the organization with a strategic ability to acquire, create, exploit, and accumulate new knowledge continuously and repeatedly in a circular process. Nonaka, in earlier collective work (Nonaka et al., 1992), has described a dynamic cycle of knowledge under the concept of a "hypertext organization," a structural base for that process. The model has been refined in later contributions (Nonaka, 1994; Nonaka & Takeuchi, 1995b), and it has been adapted to the field of knowledge management (e.g., Maier, 2005).

The hypertext organization can be seen as a multilayered organization, made up of three layers:

a) knowledge-base layer: this is the bottom which embraces tacit knowledge, associated with organizational culture and procedures, as well as explicit knowledge in the form of documents, databases, etc.;
b) business-system layer, where a normal routine operation is carried out by a formal, hierarchical organization;
c) project team layer, where multiple self-organizing project teams create knowledge.

Figure 3.5. Nonaka's hypertext organization.

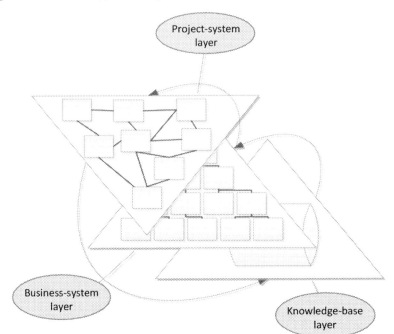

Source: author's elaboration based on (Nonaka, 1994; Nonaka et al., 1992).

In Nonaka's hypertext model, the creation of organizational knowledge is conceptualized as a continuous dynamic cycle of knowledge and information flowing through the three layers.

Three concepts increase the commitment and creativity of single individuals within the organization: a) intention, b) autonomy and, c) fluctuation. Intention is concerned with how individuals form their approach to the world and try to make sense of their environment. With autonomy, the organization may increase the possibility of introducing unexpected opportunities by allowing people to act autonomously. Fluctuation says that chaos or discontinuity can generate new patterns of interaction between individuals and their environment.

According to Nonaka's model, four modes lead to the creation of knowledge: 1) socialization; 2) externalization; 3) combination, and; 4) internalization. We emphasize the role of socialization and externalization as they are a mix between tacit and explicit knowledge.

The assumption that knowledge is created through conversion between tacit and explicit knowledge allowed us to postulate four different modes of knowledge creation.

a) Socialization is the process of creating tacit knowledge through shared experience. From tacit to tacit knowledge is a mode of knowledge conversion that enables us to convert tacit knowledge through interaction between individuals by observation, imitation, and practice like on-the-job training.
b) Combination is the process of creating explicit knowledge from explicit knowledge, using social processes to combine different bodies of explicit knowledge held by individuals.
c) Externalization is the conversion of tacit knowledge in explicit knowledge.
d) Internalization is the conversion of explicit knowledge into tacit knowledge, and "action" is deeply related to this process.

Organizational knowledge creation, as distinct from individual knowledge creation, occurs when all four modes of knowledge creation are managed to form a "spiral". The triggers that induce the shift between different modes of knowledge conversion in an organization are team-dialogue/metaphors-coordination and experimentation. The interactions between tacit/explicit knowledge tend to become more abundant in scale and faster in speed as more actors in and around the organization become involved. We can draw this process as an upward spiral, starting at the individual level, moving up to the collective level, and then to the organizational level.

Self-organizing teams represent one way to implement the management of organizational knowledge creation. Individual members come from a variety of functional departments and collaborate with others to create a new concept. So, this kind of team has two functions: facilitating the building of mutual trust among members and sharing implicit perspectives through continuous dialogue with members. One enabling factor is "creative chaos" that could be generated naturally when the organization faces a real crisis due to changes in technologies or market needs. However, it could also be intentionally generated when leaders try to evoke a sense of crisis among employees by proposing challenging goals.

Another factor is "redundancy", which means an overlapping company information, business activities, and management responsibilities. To some managers, the term has a negative connotation, although it makes the interchange between hierarchy and non-hierarchy more effective in problem-solving and knowledge creation.

Because of its importance, there are many ways to build redundancy into the organization: one is to divide the product development team into competing groups that develop different approaches to the same project and then confront each other over the advantages and disadvantages of their proposals; another way is a strategic rotation between different areas of technology and between functions. This helps employees understand the business from a multiplicity of perspectives. The management models of organizational knowledge creation have been a fundamental point of our analysis. Here we want to summarize the main features of the three models: top-down, bottom-up, and middle-up-down management.

In the top-down model, top managers create information, seen as commanders: they create basic managerial concepts in terms of objectives and means, and then middle managers decide how to realize the concepts. On the contrary, in the bottom-up model, those who create information are middle and lower managers while top managers remain sponsors for individual employees.

A completely different approach is that of the middle-up-down model, based on the principles of creative chaos and redundancy: here there's a cooperative relationship between top, middle, and lower managers, and no one has the exclusive responsibility for creating new knowledge: every employee who works in association with middle managers can create knowledge. In this model, top managers only provide visions for direction and the deadline by which the visions should be realized while preparing the ground for a self-organizing team headed by middle management. The primary role of middle managers is to serve as team leaders who are at the intersection of the vertical and horizontal flows of information in the company. Managers who create organizational knowledge are seen as catalysts.

Scholars of organizational learning have pointed out three phenomena that are of utmost interest:

a) experiential learning;
b) superstitious learning;
c) vicarious learning.

Organizational learning is seen as **experiential learning** (see also par. 0), as it is defined as routine-based, history-dependent system that adapts incrementally to experience.

Superstitious learning is defined as *"a situation in which the subjective experience of learning is compelling, but the connections between actions and outcomes are misspecified"* (Levitt & March, 1988, p. 325). This type of learning is actually detrimental to organizations, as it may induce routine behavior in individuals starting from the false perception of causal links between decisions and outcomes. Indeed, superstitious learning causes inferences that may be at the origin of routinized behaviors, and organizational routines may, in these cases, represent organizational pathologies instead of positive elements for the organizational development (Zollo, 2009).

Moreover, in these cases learning from experience would be detrimental as it would cause lousy learning outcomes stemming from the wrong inference of causal links between decisions and outcomes.

Vicarious learning refers to the process of learning from the experience of others through interaction and observations. Organizations learn from other organizations by imitating successful practices (Argote, 2011). Organizations tend to imitate or avoid specific actions or practices based on their perceived impact when they do not possess sufficient information from their own experience. In these cases, organizations' decision-makers leverage vicarious learning to reduce uncertainty, and they imitate others' actions to interpret their situations. Nevertheless, this may bring about suboptimal results, as imitations happen on the basis of what is perceived as successful practices. Indeed, decision-makers' evaluations are biased, and attention is limited. Hence, they are selective in their observation and imitation of other organizations (Baum et al., 2000).

3.2.2. Learning Organizations

Organizational learning determines and is favoured in learning organizations. **Learning Organizations** (LO) are those organizations that ease the learning of all their members, and that have organizational mechanisms that allow their own transformation over time (Pedler & Aspinwall, 1999). Spontaneous learning opportunities arise in all organizations, linked to the exchange of experiences that develop from the organizational routines and the resolution of daily management problems. It is necessary that individual learning is put into practice, transformed into organizational culture, and institutionalized within transferable forms of knowledge. Indeed, the organization must acquire the traits of a learning organization. This organization learns as it is capable of encouraging the continuous learning of its members at all levels and of facilitating the processes for the circulation of organizational knowledge.

Several definitions of Learning Organizations have been proposed, such as:

- A LO is an organization which facilitates the learning of all its members and continuously transforms itself (Pedler et al., 1989; Pedler & Aspinwall, 1999);
- LO are places where people continually expand their capacity to create the desired results, where new and expansive patterns of thinking are nurtured [...] and where people are continually learning how to learn together (Senge, 2006);

- A LO is an organization skilled at creating, acquiring, and transferring knowledge, and at modifying its behavior to reflect new knowledge and insights (Garvin, 2003).

The concept of organizations that can learn *collectively* is indeed not a new one. It is possible to find one of the first seminal contributions on this subject (Argyris & Schön, 1997). More recent contributions added details on the description and understanding of what makes an organization a learning one (e.g. (Argote, 2011; Argote & Todorova, 2007; Wang & Ahmed, 2003). Generally speaking, it is an organization that is exceptionally good at

- Creating knowledge;
- Acquiring knowledge;
- Interpreting knowledge;
- Transferring knowledge;
- Retaining knowledge.

The activities that characterize a learning organization are:

- problem-solving based on scientific methods;
- the systematic search for new knowledge through continuous improvement programs and non-repeatable demonstration projects;
- reflections on successes and failures in order to generate learning from previous experiences;
- continuous benchmarking on industry best practices;
- knowledge sharing (or knowledge sharing) in the organization.

The abundance of literature on the subject is justified by the fact that putting learning organization into practice is extremely difficult (Friedman et al., 2005; Garvin, 2003) and it requires that structural, cultural, and IS, as well as HR management, are balanced and coherent with each other (Figure 3.6).

Figure 3.6. Characteristics of Learning Organizations.

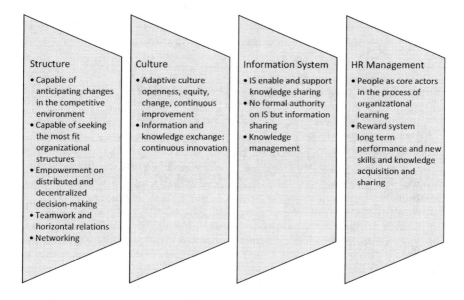

Source: author's elaboration.

3.2.3. Learning through Experience

One of the various quotations attributed to the great Leonardo Da Vinci goes, "*La Sapienza è figliuola della sperienza*" meaning that wisdom descends from experience. Indeed, in the academic literature on knowledge and knowledge management, the experience is considered a primary source of knowledge.

Several works focus on the company's ability to retain knowledge and the impact of the knowledge loss risk. The concept of absorptive capacity (Cohen & Levintal, 1990), which concerns the ability to acquire new knowledge and apply it quickly within the company as well as to have access to external knowledge and recombine it with that already held internally, has been applied to process outsourcing decisions (Marchegiani et al., 2012), or in general to restructuring (Bergh and Ngah-Kiing Lim, 2008). The associated vision on the exploitation of absorption capacity is based on the idea that learning is cumulative and that its performance increases when the learning objective is linked to what is known. This vision also implies that the company can take advantage of the information acquired and the related learning process. The absorptive capacity is influenced by the level of previous knowledge, the repetition of, and the exposure to similar events (e.g. Zahra and George, 2002).

Box 3.1 provides an application of concepts such as experience-based learning, superstitious learning, and vicarious learning in a particular strategic choice. This exercise is useful to understand how these types of learning happen in organizational contexts in real business situations.

Box 3.1. Learning opportunities in divestment processes

In divestiture strategic choices, experience is a determinant of choice between spin off and sell off, with effects on the profitability of the company (Bergh and Lim, 2008). The experience related to previous transactions has a different impact, in the case of sell offs and spin offs. In the first case, there is a positive effect. Specifically, as the number of sell offs increases, the probability of resorting to sell off again as a strategic choice increases. In this sense, the greatest benefits can be attributed to the sell off compared to the spin off for various reasons. The sell off is, in fact, a transaction characterized by greater complexity because it involves different actors, often external to the company and consists of several phases. This greater complexity favors the benefits of repeated actions. The beneficial effect of the experience is not only reflected in a greater propensity to replicate the same strategic choices, but has a positive effect on the financial performance of the company (Bergh and Lim, 2008).

For the spin off operations, the same authors have verified a positive effect of the previous experience, but limited to the closest transactions. These data are compatible with short-term learning, linked to improvised organizational choices. Spin offs, in fact, occur less frequently than sell offs (Bruner, 2004), involve activities already known within the organization and are often managed by management from the parent company (Seward and Walsh, 1996). Again the learning process affects the parent's performance. In fact, while recent spin-offs have a positive impact on the decision to resort to other spin-offs with incremental effects on the ability to create value, the more distant spin-off experiences have a negative impact on performance over time. A dynamic vision of the divestment process becomes increasingly relevant to explain not only its decision, but also the method of implementation.

There are different learning dynamics that can be activated through the accumulation of divestment experience.

1. **Experience-based learning.** The ability of companies to learn how to manage divestment operations translates into greater efficiency in selecting and eliminating internal inefficiencies and managing the complexity of divestment operations. Organizational learning theory suggests that decision makers can acquire this competence through autonomous learning (Dutton and Thomas, 1984), first level learning (first order learning, Adler and Clark, 1991), or learning by doing (Zollo and Winter, 2002). Therefore, learning is generated by the knowledge that develops thanks to the repetition of actions by the organizational agents. In the case of divestment operations, this translates into the repetition of the tasks necessary to complete the phases described in the previous paragraph, and therefore the identification of the targets to be divested, the evaluation of the assets, the negotiation of the contractual terms, and the unpacking (Unbundling) of resources. In general, managers acquire the knowledge necessary to generate effective procedures, to avoid unnecessary procedures and therefore improve the entire process. However, situations of excessive security could arise,

as they increase knowledge and skills. Since such operations, as already mentioned, are expensive and affected by high complexity at multiple levels, there is a risk that the accumulation of knowledge leads managers to underestimate the operation itself and the need to maintain adequate communication at all levels. Already in other works, such as that carried out by Gopinath and Becker in 2000, it is highlighted how correct communication directly impacts the perception of procedural justice and therefore increases the commitment of workers.

2. **Superstitious learning.** In general, in extraordinary operations, such as acquisitions or alliances, experiential learning should be further qualified. In fact, in order for an experience effect to be generated, decision-makers must be able to identify the causal link between strategic decisions or the actions taken and the effects in terms of performance obtained (Zollo and Winter, 2002). The accumulated experience could generate negative effects if it is not possible to correctly identify the causal link between decisions, actions taken and performance. This identification is particularly problematic when divestment operations are conducted in heterogeneous sectors while it is simpler if it is activities related to one's core business that are divested. In general, the learning curve theory proposes that organizational learning is positively influenced by the accumulated experience. The moderating effect that previous experience can have on the results of divestment operations depends largely on the type and composition of this past experience. A general heterogeneity of the experience accumulated through divestments in different sectors, rather than generating positive effects, activates processes of random ambiguity and can even generate negative learning effects.

3. **Inter-organizational and vicarious learning.** The learning effect not only depends on the experience accumulated internally, but it is important to also consider external sources of knowledge. In particular, companies that do not have a sufficient knowledge base often turn to external experts and consultants, or observe the behavior of other companies. The use of external consultants in the management of sell-off transactions allow companies to accumulate experience more effectively and increase their absorptive capacity. This is due to a double virtuous mechanism: a) external consultants have specialized knowledge, which is reactivated from time to time with the various customers, and can draw on a large network of knowledge; b) sources of external knowledge facilitate organizational learning through knowledge clarification mechanisms, such as coding and definition of support guidelines for the different phases of the divestment process.

Source: author's elaboration based on (Peruffo et al., 2018).

3.2.4. Knowledge Intensive Firms

An essential concept in the Digital Age is that of Knowledge Intensive Firms (KIFs). A KIF is a firm where the majority or even the whole of the workforce consists of knowledge workers. First of all, it is necessary to define who the knowledge worker is. S/he facilitates the learning of knowledge and its sharing within the organization; s/he is a person whose goals are clear to be attained, who provides the tools to be used and the guidelines that must be followed and s/he is responsible in large part of the decision of how and when to carry out the necessary activities.

Autonomy is one of the most important characteristics of Knowledge Workers: the nature of the work is characterized by creativity and problem solving that demands it. Knowledge workers decide how and when to initiate, plan, organize and coordinate the work's tasks; they expect autonomy, and the management is not in a position to deny them. Perhaps its role is to provide the condition to facilitate knowledge work.

Co-location is another relevant characteristic: more often than not knowledge workers work remotely from the firm's location. This is the case of a consultancy firm: the client's firm could offer permanent employment to knowledge workers who produce good results. Here, the management's role is to facilitate coordination and integration across the team without direct action. Knowledge workers are also known as «Gold Collar Workers»: they are highly skilled knowledge workers, traditionally classified as white collar but have become so essential that they warrant a new classification; management has to pay attention to them.

The expression Knowledge Intensive Firms can be used for different kinds of companies operating across different sectors. Alvesson (M. Alvesson, 2001) describes KIFs as *"companies where most work can be said to be of an intellectual nature and where well-educated, qualified employees form the major part of the work-force."*.

It is possible to identify three generic types of KIFs:

1) client-based. These firms are organized along with partnership with recognized codes of practice and defined "UP or OUT" career paths, usually characterized by a hierarchical structure, for example, law and accountancy firms;
2) output-based. These are some large management consultancy firms. These firms are organized like the traditional service firms, but they tend to be output rather than client-based;
3) problem-solving. These firms are team-based and these teams can solve very complex problems and find new solutions, for example advertising agencies or software development firms.

Although they seem to overlap, client-based and output-based are different in their targets: in the former, the final objective is the client's satisfaction, while in the latter the output is more important than the client, and the aggregate result is more important than the client satisfaction. Many KIFs tend to adopt an organic organizational structure and organize flexibly around teams. Mintzberg (1979) identified five archetypal structural forms, and he suggested that when innovation and creativity were a conscious strategy, the **Adhocracy** was the most appropriate organizational configuration. The adhocracy does not follow classic management principles but tends to spontaneity, flexibility and creativity, in which the individuals are free to show their talent under different business needs.

This kind of organizational configuration is almost the complete opposite of bureaucracy. First of all, adhocracy is characterized by a minimal hierarchy compared with the multiple-level hierarchy of bureaucracy. As previously said, in the adhocracy the work processes are self-organized around teams and not in functional groups; there isn't a direct control of the management but there is a normative control characterized by self-management. Unlike in the bureaucracy, where decision making is centralized, in the *ad-hoc* organizations, the decision making process is very decentralized; this flexible organization is a highly organic form where there are few or no formal rules, policies and procedures and where the coordination is achieved through mutual adjustment rather than through explicit rules and procedures like in the bureaucracy.

The main task of the management of this type of firm is to attract and retain knowledge workers and promote innovation and creativity. This difficult task is a continuous mediation because the managers must try to remove the obstacles and support the knowledge work and knowledge workers. It is like a struggle between structural constraints and cultural conditions.

As far as the structural constraints are concerned, the development of organizational «best practice» must be considered. When an **informal routine** becomes part of the organizational culture, it curbs innovation because the boost to create is less and stagnancy is very easy. Moreover, the monitoring of time plays a crucial role in KIFs. When time spent working is carefully controlled, such as in advertising agencies, the control can often reduce innovative behaviors and the development of new routines. Where this is a common practice, knowledge workers often reduce time searching for or creating new knowledge; as previously said, they demand autonomy, and the management is not in a position to deny it. Sometimes the manager needs to control the time, and limit the work of this kind of employee.

Also, **growth** can be a problem with KIFs. Paradoxically enough, when the company grows, even the formalization and the hierarchy grows. However, a formal and hierarchical organization is not a right solution for these kinds of firms. Mintzberg himself suggests that the adhocracy is a typical organization of young, start-up companies, and many other authors agree with him that this organizational configuration is impossible to sustain in the long term. A possible solution might be "spinning out," a strategy which consists of creating new business units as soon the firm reaches a particular size. In this way, the new business units might work as in the past (maybe organizing as an adhocracy) and the "original firm" can grow without any problem.

This highly informal approach can often be problematic to sustain in the long run. While structural conditions are important preconditions facilitating knowledge work tasks, the cultural conditions primarily promote responsible autonomy and a workforce that can be trusted to work in the firm's interest, that is, working autonomously but working very hard and to the best of their abilities.

The **leaders** of KIFs have to acknowledge that diversity across the workforce is considered to be a significant facilitator of innovation; they are often faced with the requirement to employ and manage a highly diverse workforce. A form of management grounded in culture or normative control is the most appropriate approach to adopt within these organizational environments so the suggestion is to develop a corporate culture in which workers will identify with it; in this way it can internalize the organizational ideology and the knowledge worker will behave in the interest of the firm.

According to many authors, the main task of leaders in any organization is to develop a **strong organizational culture**. There is a strong organizational culture when it is shared across the firm, and it makes reliable firms through integration and enhanced productivity. In other words, the interest of the firm should overlap with the interest of its employees. A robust **system of values** spreads across the whole organization over time, and it serves to influence the behaviors of the old and new employees. The way the leaders of firms can create a strong organizational culture is explained by Schein's seminal work (Schein, 1988), who identifies three distinct levels in organizational culture:

- artifacts: they are all the aspects immediately observable like symbols, dress code, rituals;
- values: the strategy, the mission, the goals and the philosophy posted by the top management;
- assumptions: they are the most important ones, the deep convictions, the firm's guidelines.

In this vein, the task of the leaders is to guide the organizations under these assumptions. First of all, they must recognize these assumptions, and they must manage and transfer them over time. For example, if the sharing of knowledge is a value for the company, they should reward those employees who have worked even if they were not part of that particular project. In this way, workers perceive that action as something to do and will quickly replicate it. The core organizational values will become shared values across the workforce leading to performance and productivity improvements.

Knowledge workers are highly skilled workers with a range of values and beliefs and it's not certain that knowledge workers in KIFs will subsume their identity and their values to those of the firm. The integration perspective on culture assumes certain structural preconditions such as a well-defined hierarchy and highly centralized decision making, but these are often not apparent within the KIFs. The **fragmentation** perspective suggests that culture is a metaphor, not a variable, and it is *something an organization is and not something an organization has*. This perspective acknowledges ambiguity because individuals might experience a lack of clarity or have multiple beliefs in the organization.

Leaders must accept the fragmentation rather than integration predominate. By promoting an organizational ethos rather than trying reinforcing a core value system, knowledge workers perceive the firm as a "good" place. Timothy Koogle, the founder of Yahoo, promoted the idea that employees should communicate freely with others and join in any decision that needs to be made because it was considered essential.

3.2.5. Agile Organizations [1]

The Digital Transformation shares some epistemological and managerial foundations with the concept of agility and agile organizations. Introduced in the field of Project Management, the agile concept has soon been extended to the whole organizational field. At the beginning of the 21st century, the new Agile Software Development (ASD) methodology was introduced, a set of software development methods based on common principles. These principles are rooted in the "Manifesto for Agile Software Development," also called "Agile Manifesto," published in 2001 (Beck et al., 2001). The basic principle of the Agile method is the continuous interaction with stakeholders, whose satisfaction is crucial for the success of the project and the development of the organization.

Agility is defined as the ability to adapt quickly and deliberately to the change of context and the change of requests and needs of the end customer while controlling the risks. At odds with traditional waterfall approaches, the agile methods offer a less structured approach focused on the objective of delivering to the customer, shortly and frequently (early deliv-

---

[1] The author acknowledges the input provided to this paragraph by Matteo Pagnani.

ery/frequent delivery), functional and quality software/product. The process is not planned entirely from the beginning, rather objectives are set for short development cycles. One functionality at a time is developed, so that customers can give continuous feedback and eventually propose changes in between, in an emerging way.

Change is the main driving force of agility, defined as the ability of an organization to respond immediately to market changes and customer requests. Agility increases an organization's ability to offer high-quality products and services by contributing to organizational efficiency. An agile organization integrates organizational processes and individuals with high technology, developing high-quality products and services, thus improving organizational competitiveness. It also helps to reduce production costs, increase its market share, meet customer needs, introduce new products, evaluate and estimate activities without added value. Thus, the Organizational Agility has proved to be a successful strategy in competitive markets, with rapid changes in customer needs and a particular need for potential skills to deal with the changes and uncertainty characteristic of a dynamic environment (Maruping et al., 2009).

A prominent example is the case of Netflix. More than 20 years ago, it started based on a business model that included DVD sales and rental by mail. It then switched to video on demand, and it has been able ever since to renew its business model continuously. Since 2011 it has started a successful strategy of producing film and series that now generates a huge amount of revenues. Being able to renew so many times and so relentlessly is a perfect example of agility. From an organizational point of view, successful organizations have been able to create start-ups within the scale of multinational companies, so that the company could foster agility and scale up at the level of the whole organization.

Also, Agile recognizes the importance of delegating and empowering self-managing teams, thus increasing employees' motivation (Highsmith & Highsmith, 2002). Agile incorporates a different culture because it brings with it the focus on quality; it subverts the push logic with the pull logic; it introduces transparency based on bottom-up intelligence, self-management, and continuous change. Unlike on formal hierarchical levels, Agile focuses on the skills and beliefs of people at all levels, including managers.

Practices promoted by agile methods include:

- the formation of small, cross-functional and self-organized development teams;
- iterative and incremental development, adaptive planning;

- direct and continuous customer involvement in the development process.

These methodologies aim at increasing the productivity and efficiency of the self-managing team, through the design of projects as incremental stages. These stages are called "sprints". Each sprint corresponds to a new feature, and customer satisfaction is verified, which shows the work done up to that point. An itcrative (and interactive) system that easily changes the project, reduces production costs and, above all, avoids unnecessary efforts and a possible failure of the project. Each iteration is a small project in its own right and must contain all necessary to release a small increase in the functionality of the software: planning, analysis of requirements, implementation, testing, and documentation. Even if the result of each iteration does not have sufficient functionality to be considered complete, it must be published. In the succession of iterations, it must get closer and closer to the customer's requests. At the end of each iteration, the team must re-evaluate the project priorities. Agile methods prefer real-time communication, preferably face-to-face, rather than written documentation, as well as open and interactive discussion, reducing the use of traditional channels such as e-mail/telephone and promoting the use of visual tools such as post-it notes, flip charts, and white board. However, in cases where this is not feasible, current technologies and infrastructures can help improve and facilitate the interactive exchange of information, preferring those that also allow visual interaction, such as the webcam.

People and their interactions founding elements of the Agile philosophy, as described in the Agile Manifesto:

1. Individuals and interactions rather than processes and tools: the relationships and communication between the actors of a software project are the best resources of the project. This principle is based on attention to choosing the right resources to be involved in the project actively participating in the creation of value, and independently managing problems and critical issues (problem solving).
2. Working software rather than exhaustive documentation: new versions of the software must be released at frequent intervals. The code must be kept simple and technically advanced, reducing the documentation to the bare minimum
3. Collaboration with the client rather than contract negotiation: direct collaboration offers better results than contractual relationships. This implies high levels of stakeholder engagement: users, experts, and sponsors must always be present throughout the life of the project, both in the initial stages, to provide detailed specifications to be

developed, and during the development of the project, for the necessary clarifications and / or any changes that should be required.
4. Responding to change rather than following a plan: therefore, the development team should be ready, at any time, to change the work priorities in compliance with the final objective. A clear focus is on value: creating value through the reduction of so-called "waste," that is, the superfluous, and recycling; limiting the essentials to the documentation, which does not mean, however, not drawing it up or attributing little consideration to it.

The Agile process follows the following criteria:

1. Short development cycles that are reasonably predictable: all teams should deliver every four weeks (or shorter). That is, therefore, the duration of each assignment or "iteration," during which the team can work undisturbed. After each iteration (or "sprint"), new customer requests may be added.
2. Small, efficient teams: a team should be composed of about seven members. Teams are fully responsible for achieving a result and should integrate their different knowledge bases primarily based on face-to-face communication. The development work within each team should include a "core loop," which involves planning, design, testing, and a final delivery check.
3. Close contacts with customers: a team should plan regular contacts with customers (internal or external), for example, about the presentation of a demo, to check if the requirements have been interpreted correctly, or if something is missing.
4. Engage in a planning game: this refers to a simple exercise conducted when a team receives a new assignment. Each member receives a form in which he writes a number from 1-10 to evaluate the assignment's difficulty. If the member ratings are similar enough and the assignment is rated, for example, as a 5, it would appear to be well understood and feasible, and the game can then be ended. However, if their views are very different, further rounds of explanation, , and voting will be needed. A game should take an hour or two to complete.
5. Daily stand-up meetings: each day should begin with a 15-minute meeting, where each member lists what they did the day before, what they will do during the day, and what problems they anticipate. Non-team members, such as program managers and line managers, may also be present at these meetings. However, speaking during the meeting is not allowed.

6. Testing programming and programming in pairs: nothing that cannot be tested should be designed. This requires close collaboration between those responsible for the test and the designers. Pairing programming is another means of promoting collaboration. A person can be busy programming and, at the same time, have access to the experience of another member sitting next to him. This can be a means of providing greater problem-solving skills or a way for apprentices to learn from more experienced ones.
7. Retrospective reflection. After each iteration, the team will have to meet for 1 or 2 hours to reflect on issues such as *"what have we done well, what have we learned, what should we change as we do the next iteration, and what is still a problem?"* The outcome of the discussion must not be put on paper, assuming that the team has a stable membership and will not forget the lessons learned since they will immediately work in a new iteration.

These criteria are at the core of the agile knowledge and learning processes. An important feature of the agile approach is to learn from failures. Indeed, failures are seen as an essential condition for learning. Nowadays, it seems that it is even easier to switch to an agile methodology in smaller companies because they tend to have less codified organizational structures, fewer process layers, and less hierarchical levels. The feedback loop is by nature very short, customers are in direct contact with those who develop the product, and, in general, there is much more willing to fill multiple roles.

At the core of the Agile methodology is the requirement for individuals and organizations to keep innovation and learning as a priority (Highsmith & Highsmith, 2002). Within the Scrum, team members coordinate their work, and the so-called "Scrum Master" tends to solve problems if they arise. Teams are put under pressure, needed to work on improvements, to nurture additional process skills, to respond to tool planning changes, and to open up to new systems. Thus, the attitude towards learning and self-management, as well as the ability to generate innovative ideas, are essential elements of Agile (Plonka, 1997).

Agile Learning leaders should possess five types of agility (Cashman, 2013):

a) *Mental agility*, the ability to analyze and criticize in depth the circumstances, relationships, and solicitations. The agile learning leader is at ease with the complexity, and (s)he can provide timely answers by conveying her/his application immediately according to the versatility of the "connecting the dots" attitude.

b) *Change agility*, the ability to have courage in experimentation, to be intellectually adventurous, and to always dare.

c) *People agility* expressed through interaction, communication, and inclusion capacity, through negotiation skills in situations of stress and conflict, through the ability to grow and enhance, to act as a delegating teacher so that the collaborators grow independently.
d) *Results agility* belongs to those who "testify" with the results, enacting their behavior, ethics, culture, dedication, as opposed to those who proclaim words without putting them in practice. This leader gives imprinting to the organization. Her/his style is recognized as a guide, inspiration, and orientation, not only as a method, to obtain only operational results, but as the ultimate purpose of the organization.
e) *Self-Awareness* means being reflective and understanding one's own capabilities and personal impact on others.

This methodology involves higher cognitive demands, promoting new knowledge, and supporting the development of a unique set of organizational skills (Sherehiy et al., 2007).

Nonetheless, recent studies show that the learning processes in agile organizations remain at the team-level. A close investigation of the micromechanisms involved in the learning processes at the self-managing team level; reveals substantial flaws in agile methods' capacity to foster organizational learning (Annosi et al., 2020). In fact, managers can actively influence the significance of team priorities and how they respond to the organizational goal of learning. Agile does not automatically enable. Agile organizations are complex systems; they are influenced and constrained by a network of stakeholders and routines that may introduce conflicting needs and opposing perspectives. Leaders should apply flexibility-injecting structures in existing organizational structures, such as additional stakeholders and goals for agile teams, to strike the right balance between flexibility and efficiency.

3.3. Digital technologies for Human Resources Management [2]

Digital Transformation is thoroughly modifying the Department of Organization and Human Resources management, In fact, the term "Digital HR Transformation" has been proposed to define new roles, approaches, skills and enabling technologies that must be put at the service of HR in order to

---

[2] We are grateful to Sara Pennacchini and Pietro Pratense for their valuable input to this paragraph.

convey a proper Digital Transformation also in personnel management. Only in this way, will it be possible to make the processes more agile and to use new tools that enhance the person, a key concept in the Digital Transformation.

Therefore, the digitization of Human Resources Management is at the basis of the ongoing renewal, which is why the demand for new enabling technologies for the HR function is always on the rise.

Privacy is a big issue in the use of digital technologies in personnel management. The lack of data protection may put the security of workers' personal information at risk. Resorting to social networks or the Internet in the search for personal data, for example, for hiring, makes the worker vulnerable if the data is misused, invading his privacy to obtain private information. It is not difficult for this to happen because of the use made of Social Networks, by entering information on the Internet that can be used by anyone. Therefore, there is a need for personal data to be protected by a more advanced security system, limiting the use of employee data. On the other side, information security will not be affected by changes in the storage of information. The development of Cloud Computing, in fact, increasingly focuses on data security, considering it of central importance for the management of sensitive personnel data.

Box 3.2. Focus on the HR-tech market in Italy

According to the 2nd Observatory on the HR Tech Market in Italy, presented in January 2019 by Intervieweb and Talent Garden, the turnover generated by the HR Tech Companies in Italy is more than one billion euros, thus going to duplicate the turnover found in the 2018 Observatory (the estimated turnover of the HR Tech vendors analyzed in 2018 amounts to 500 million euros). With a focus on Italy, the Report mapped 90% of the HR Tech players operating in Italy or 103 companies that turn to the Italian market for human resources technologies. The companies analyzed by the Report are "HR Tech Companies," i.e., companies that offer technological solutions (software and hardware) for the digital management of HR.

The HR Tech sector is overgrowing on the global market, as well as the investments in HR Tech: «2018 was the year in which investments made in HR Tech companies by Venture Capital (VC) funds exceeded four billions of dollars, a figure equal to 4 times the investments of 2017. Compared to the previous year, however, it should be noted that, although the investments have grown, the percentage of companies that have collected investments has decreased. This indicates that HR Tech companies are not yet so receptive to investments as to generate significant growth in turnover. The signs for the future, despite this, are very positive, in the direction of rapid but lasting growth, given the continuous use of technologies in organizations.

The growth of the Digital HR sector must be seen in two different directions: vertically, as the number of players increases, and horizontally, thanks to the birth of new technologies for the management of Human Resources.

As regards the vertical dimension, i.e., the number of players, most of them are concentrated mainly in Northern Italy; where 81% of the companies are present (in particular in Milan we find 44% of the companies and in Turin the 14%), in Central Italy, on the other hand, there are fewer players as 15% of the companies are allocated to it. In the South and Islands, the percentage drops significantly, finding only 2% of HR Tech companies.

As for the size of the companies that produce new technologies for Human Resources, it is to be noted that of the 103 companies analyzed by the report, 73% of them are small and micro enterprises; and 18% are medium-sized while only 9% of the companies surveyed are large. Compared to 2018, however, the number of large companies has doubled, a sign that the growing interest in HR technologies involves larger players given the importance of the sector's growth on the market.

The HR Tech sector is young and, for the most part, recently established: 57% of the companies analyzed by the report, in fact, were born from 2013 onwards and of these as many as 40% see the light between 2017 and 2018. It should also be noted, like most HR Tech companies, that it is a start-up.

What are the benefits brought to the end users of the HR Tech solutions, or the HR themselves? The HR Tech Italia 2019 Report examines the benefits found by the customers of the players analyzed. Among the benefits found, these stand out the most: "faster and more efficient" (71 companies), "simplify the work of HR" (54 companies) and "generate and collect data to make decisions" (51 companies).

The expanding Italian HR Tech market should also be analyzed on the basis of the market niches it represents: 51.46% of companies operate in "Human Capital Management", 40.78% in "Talent Acquisition," and 77% in "Talent Management." The micro areas of application of the new technologies for Human Resources have helped to integrate and automate the typical HR functions in companies, going on to automate the basic processes of personnel management. In particular, in the sample of the 103 companies in the Report, the areas of greatest application are "Job Board" (which develop 13.5% of the companies), followed by "Personnel Management" (12.6%) and "Training" (11.6%). Compared to the Report of the previous year, moreover, it should be underlined how the presence of players in the fields of AI, Machine Learning and HR Analytics has increased, a sign that growth is in the direction of new interesting developments as regards data processing and automation.

Source: author's elaboration on the basis of (Pennacchini, 2019).

BIG DATA

First of all, Big Data is redefining some important HR practices and revolutionizing the competencies of HR specialists. A central task of Human Resources in competitive environments is the recruitment of talents. In this sense, the use of Big Data provides a significant competitive advantage since it compensates for the information asymmetry deriving from the description provided by the candidates themselves. The deviation of the information would not allow companies to acquire the information necessary to evaluate a candidate in the best way. The use of Big Data, in this regard, provides a competitive advantage for companies, which can use the Internet in order to find more information. Through social networks, for example, it is possible to get a more detailed image of the candidate. Furthermore, the use of online Recruitment platforms allows the company to be put in contact with the most qualified candidates for the job sought. LinkedIn, in this regard, represents a good example. Born in 2003, the leader of professional social networks has the mission of "connecting professionals from all over the world to help them be more productive and achieve their professional goals." With the use of Big Data, however, also the ability emerges to capture data and information from multiple sources, thus being able to refine the search for talent. LinkedIn Talent Insights, an application developed by LinkedIn pushes this trend forward: it analyzes the data that is available on the platform and provides companies with access to its database, improving recruitment strategies and making decisions on the selection of candidates more efficiently. Providing information on the market, sector, geographical area of reference, activities and skills require helps improve the entire recruitment process by accessing real-time data.

With the use of Big Data, another area that is rapidly developing is Talent Training. Access to the information necessary for the development of knowledge and skills is immediate through Internet access. Above all, many companies are developing professional training courses directly via the platform, software, or online. These programs, allowing to analyze the needs of individual resources, are therefore customizable, consequently improving the effectiveness of training. The course's progress, the tests carried out, and the feedback received also allow the manager to keep the new skills and competences acquired by the employees under control.

Big Data can assist the employee assessment, avoiding subjective results. The assessment methods benefit by Big Data that provide new tools and methods for analyzing the results. The Assessment is a phase that is acquiring more and more value in HR Management, especially since it is useful for identifying the skills of resources both during the selection phase, and for mapping the staff already working for the company.

Big Data can be used to focus on both qualitative and quantitative terms of the performance systems, going to influence, for example, wage differences and therefore making the system as a whole a process based on individual employees, which are assessed individually on the results obtained. In this way, going to analyze the daily data of the resources, the salaries are automatically calculated based on the work done and the objectives achieved, improving work efficiency.

Furthermore, work interests, growth desires, experience, and professional performance of the employee are taken into consideration by making a quantitative analysis of information through Big Data, making it easier to understand the interests of employees and providing better assistance in Career Management. In fact, fully understanding the interests and desires of employees is the basis for providing them with a personalized orientation for their career, reducing turnover, and making the company more competitive. A satisfied employee with the possibility of professional growth will be more productive and involved in company processes.

As for Big Data, in short, they can undoubtedly bring benefits to HR, managing and analyzing vast quantities and varieties of data almost in real-time. However, their use is not fully functional, as it is not easy to implement traditional and structured data with unstructured data, which also require specific professional skills in management. With the progress in the use of Big Data, new professional figures are required, such as Data Analysts, Data Scientists, and Business Data Analysts, who use new methods of analysis and process of unstructured data, which could not be worked with traditional methods.

PEOPLE ANALYTICS

Human Resources Management is benefiting a lot from the emerging functionalities of Data Intelligence. **Human Resources Analytics (also called People Analytics**) refers to the use of Data Intelligence tools designed by integrating qualitative elements with quantitative data, developed with statistical and mathematical models, in order to make the data analysis activity evolve from simple a posteriori evaluation, projection, and forecasting of present and future events. In this way, HR managers can use employee data, transforming it into valuable information for the company. Analyzing and aggregating information through analysis systems and BI allows transforming data into information. BI analysis and processes lead to the creation of a flow of information that allows evaluating the company's progress, make decisions through a data-driven approach, and have an overview of the main business phenomena. Using People Analytics makes the company innovative and more organized. It allows acting both on the personal data front and on the organizational structure, going to act on productivity and competitiveness.

CLOUD COMPUTING

One of the most significant advantages of using the Cloud for HRM is the centralization of information: the conservation and recovery of the information make the organization more accessible and transform the company.

The Recruitment process becomes faster, making the visualization of the candidates' data and the feedback following tests or interviews immediate. Cloud-based technology can fill the communication gap between manager and staff, making, for example, the performance assessment and the most immediate feedback through a platform dedicated to continuous Assessment. Communication, therefore, plays a significant role and influences well-being and the human resources' satisfaction.

Furthermore, Engagement will be positively affected by greater communication, leading to the development of innovation. Through the Cloud, it will be easier to have access to new technologies, new applications, or software that will lead to the development of new ideas and business projects. Cloud technology can then eliminate the heavy workload caused by paper documents: all information will be stored digitally on a Cloud server and can be consulted at any time and in any place. In this regard, the HR managers of companies with branch offices will have the opportunity to have access to data in any place, leveling the differences between the offices and making sure that every aspect of personnel management is centralized, making Human Resources closer to key business processes.

IoT

IoT technology has become an essential driver for improving performance in the workplace because intelligent objects monitor, measure, and provide important quantitative data that can be processed and studied to develop optimized strategic decisions. Indeed, it has become increasingly necessary to monitor the productivity of resources in terms of data that can be analyzed for the benefit of the productivity of the individual, well-being in the workplace, and the competitiveness of the company. By integrating traditional management systems with IoT-oriented systems, in fact, data can be revealed that allow workflows optimization. Incorporating the IoT into a business strategy, therefore, is configured as a fundamental step to bring Digital Transformation into the company.

With the ultimate goal of increasing productivity, IoT sensors measure and monitor different aspects of work experience: movements, behaviors, emotions, and physical well-being are quantified through the use of intelligent data processing tools such as smartwatches or fitness trackers. The data processed by these sensors are then incorporated into the databases and used in Analytics, Cloud Computing, or in real-time intelligent technology.

Smartphones and tablets are the handiest and most famous examples of intelligent objects. Of central importance in this process, they allow the use of applications that can monitor the progress of daily activities: health, sleep-wake cycle, diet, psycho-physical well-being, behaviors. Fundamentally, these tools, also aid in developing the sociability of the resource within the company: social networks and company chats, used thanks to intranets, allow better communication between employees, teams, and management. The use of these devices also promotes Smartworking dynamics and the development of innovative working environments: large open spaces, where a fixed workstation is not required, promoting communication, concentration, and creativity.

AI

The impact of Artificial Intelligence on Human Resources Management is pervasive in many areas. First of all, Recruitment, then Training, Performance Evaluation, Compensation, Employee Potential Evaluation, Mobility, and Career Development.

Nonetheless, the Recruiting process can never be fully automated, the human component that will be assisted and facilitated in the selection of personnel by the AI will always remain present, in order to analyze information faster and smarter. Notably, AI cannot replace the purely "human" aspects of personnel selection, such as the relationships that are established with candidates, seeing hidden potential or measuring interpersonal skills. This means that the AI will not be able to replace the parts of the Recruitment work that require personal, or emotional involvement.

Even in the field of Training, AI plays a preponderant role. In business training, for example, AI primary purpose is to simplify the training experience (both for those who administer it and for those who use it) and to make it as personalized and engaging as possible. In this way, in addition to creating intelligent environments, the company can maintain greater control of staff training, optimizing the work-flow, and allowing those responsible for training to focus on activities that generate more value, that is, creating more effective and engaging training content. Given that the AI will be able to automate most of the complex, repetitive and error-prone manual jobs, better results can be obtained in less time, based on the fundamental concepts of training i.e., involvement and personalization. The e-learning platforms are also able to learn the needs of those who are using them, making the experience of training increasingly effective.

Another emerging trend is to monitor and evaluate the performance of both workers and the company with Artificial Intelligence, essential for understanding when to intervene to increase productivity. The performances are monitored through AI systems, the data relating to the activities carried out or the objectives achieved are analyzed and processed by integrating them with the data relating to employees and brought to the attention of managers who can, through ad hoc interfaces and dashboards, always have the performance of its employees is under control.

In addition to monitoring employee performance, the performance of the entire company can be monitored through Artificial Intelligence. All the data available on the company is analyzed and used to map company performance and thus further able to improve productivity and become more competitive.

The trend, therefore, is to use more and more Machine Learning tools for Performance Management and make assumptions through predictive algorithms. The Performance Management process, therefore, needs to change, becoming more agile and personalized.

3.3.1. Managing the Knowledge Workers, Revisited. Cognitive Computing and Machine Learning

The Digital Transformation requires a redefinition of the concept of knowledge workers and their management. In fact, on one side ,new generations joining the workforce are more familiar with digital technologies. On the other side, managers must acknowledge the impact of cognitive computing and machine learning on the organizational learning processes.

As far as the new generations of workers are concerned, they can be referred to as the "Digital Natives." These are people who were born in the late '90s and are familiar with digital technologies since they were born. The attitude to use such technologies have made them very different from their predecessors, the so-called "Digital Immigrants." Digital Natives are characterized by acquiring information faster and show multitasking capabilities and parallel process. The Digital Immigrants, in fact, are sometimes reluctant with the use of new technologies, and the skills they learn, slowly, do not match well their previous experiences or behaviors. This may cause an intra-organizational digital divide, which must not be underestimated. In fact, if Digital Natives are more acquainted with digital innovations, the Digital Immigrants are the business experts and have accumulated tacit knowledge about the organization, the business, and the market logics. Indeed, finding ways to have the two groups collaborating can help to foster a fruitful knowledge sharing and knowledge acquisition.

The spread of Artificial Intelligence imposes a redefinition of the core concepts of knowledge management. In fact, not only human learning processes need to be understood and managed towards the organizational objectives; managers must also take into account the learning processes of non-human actors. Cognitive Computing and Machine Learning are concepts that knowledge managers must not neglect.

Cognitive Computing tools can reproduce the functioning of the human brain, being able to learn autonomously, reason, and process data, providing non-binary indications. The more data available, the more these tools will be able to learn and process them in greater depth. Cognitive Computing, therefore, allows materializing the models of reasoning and learning of Artificial Intelligence, through the processing of unstructured data in information useful and understandable to humans, in "human" language and actions.

Machine Learning, a Cognitive Computing tool, performs mathematical and computational operations on algorithms that allow it to learn in an adaptive way. This means that Machine Learning allows machines to learn from experience by improving their performance in performing tasks or actions. By giving him examples of inputs and outputs to be used as indications to complete the requested action (supervised learning), letting the machine work without giving indications if not the result it must obtain (unsupervised learning) or "rewarding" it when it reaches certain objectives set (learning by reinforcement), this will be able to learn without having been programmed to do so (or without being told what to do step by step).

The functioning of Machine Learning, therefore, is linked to data management and learning techniques, which make us distinguish three types of Machine Learning:

- Model Prediction, a tool that enable answering questions relating to future events through the construction of predictive models and algorithms;
- Deep Learning, a set of techniques that is based on artificial neural networks organized in different layers, in order to be able to process the vast amount of data available to them layer by layer. The system, therefore, learns to carry out tasks independently;
- Online Learning, based on data processing techniques in which the latter become available sequentially. There is no pre-learning, but the decisions are made by the machine as the data becomes available.

Machine Learning finds application in many areas, more or less every day: Internet search engines, voice recognition, fraud prevention systems, recommendation systems, self-driving cars, voice assistants are only a few examples of the numerous possibilities of application of Machine Learning.

> **Box 3.3.** The Docebo case study
>
> Docebo, an eLearning platform on Cloud used by over 1400 organizations worldwide, states that using Artificial Intelligence makes the "learning experience automated and personalized, transforming training into a competitive advantage." According to Docebo, there are five ways in which AI will redefine corporate training:
> 1) t will be possible to answer users' questions in real time, offering continuous consultancy;
> 2) users will be able to interact with an AI assistant thanks to its natural language processing capability;
> 3) training will become faster and more efficient without sacrificing quality;
> 4) users will have new personalized training opportunities thanks to the possibility of discovering innovative content;
> 5) the creation of content will increase thanks to the possibility of processing huge amounts of data.

Source: author's elaboration on the basis of Sara Pennacchini. (More information available at https://www.docebo.com/it/chi-siamo-docebo-piattaforma-elearning/).

3.3.2. Digital Workplaces

Organizations have been seeking collaborative layouts for decades, and work layouts that could boost creativity and innovation are at the core of several streams of research in the Organization Design discipline.

Knowledge-intensive firms (KIFs) require office layouts that favor the nature of the work, which is based on the centrality of knowledge assets. Thus, not only the individual worker should be provided with a physical space that is suitable to boost her mindfulness, but it is also important that workers are collocated in physical spaces where knowledge sharing is favored.

Office layouts have a long history, tracing as far back as the Renaissance when the centrality of man and his intellectual capabilities led to the initial idea of desks and studios that were able to foster enlightenment and idea generation. Nevertheless, the concept of office spaces, as buildings dedicated to work, dates back to the XIXth century. In the XXth century, a clear affirmation of working districts, especially the financial districts, led to the development of skyscrapers as a block of offices developed vertically to exploit the physical space better.

Simultaneously, with the growth of manufacturing and big factories, the layout of the working spaces began to differentiate between the so-called blue collars and the white collars. The former refers to the working class, whereas the white collars are those workers who leverage their intellectual ability and perform tasks related to the management and control of the factories. From a layout point of view, though, both the blue-collars and the white-collars, except for the managers and the executives, were located in physical spaces that were very consistent with the Scientific Management Principles. Workers, no matter what, had to pursue efficiency in every aspect. Hence, at the manufacturing level, huge conveyor belts were assembled, whereas at the intellectual work level, workers were placed in pools. Cubicles were reserved for each office worker.

Only in the second half of the 20th century, the advancement of organizational theories based on motivations and human relations led to the development of more inclusive office layouts. This sort of revolution caused the organization of open offices, with the emergence of shared working spaces that could favor human relations and interactions among coworkers. Towards the end of the 20th century, terms like *"third places"* or *"great good places"* have been coined, to refer to intermediate places between the domestic home, the *"first place"* and the productive workplace, the *"second place"* (Oldenburg, 1989), such as cafes, bars, and bookstores. These places have started to be considered "homes away from home […] where unrelated people relate" (Oldenburg, 1999, p. 1) in an "inclusively sociable atmosphere" (Oldenburg, 1999, p. 14) that offers the basis of a community. This neat separation between first places – homes, second places – offices, and third places – social activities was apparent in Oldenburg's conception. Indeed, this has completely changed in recent years, when the separation between spheres of domestic, productive and social activity has widened significantly (Fonner & Stache, 2012; M. Gold & Mustafa, 2013).

This revolution has never come to an end, and nowadays it has been reinforced through technological innovations. The availability of Information and Communication Technologies, and the possibility that they allow working remotely, have emphasized the ephemeral role of space in working contexts (Gandini, 2015). Nomadism has become a keyword for intellectual workers. Indeed, the centrality of knowledge as a core strategic asset has transformed office workers into knowledge workers. Given these premises, it is evident that organization design, human resources management, and even strategic management cannot discard the importance of working configuration as a contextual variable that drives workers' motivation, well-being, and productivity.

The emergence of **coworking spaces** adds even more interest to the subject of working configuration and raises interesting questions both from a theoretical and a practical point of view. Coworking spaces are growing worldwide at astonishing rates (Global Coworking Survey, 2018, Deskmag). They combine the need to cope with financial restraints with the opportunity of leveraging technological solutions to design workspaces that are coherent with the contemporary megatrends.

In particular, these needs are typically linked by start-up business (Mind

Knowledge and (digital) learning organizations **141**

the Bridge, CrESIT, 2011). They are characterized by new business, few financial assets, and flexible organization, tremendous knowledge contents, and a lean business model (Osterwalder & Pigneur, 2010).

In Figure 3.7, coworking is compared with other spatial working arrangements in a graph with respect to time (horizontal dimension) and the focal activities (vertical dimension). The focal activities span from "discovery-play" to "learning" and "work." In reality, many spaces are hybrid and fall in between the different categories or change in nature over time (Waters-Lynch et al., 2016).

Figure 3.7. Evolution of workplaces over time per focal activity.

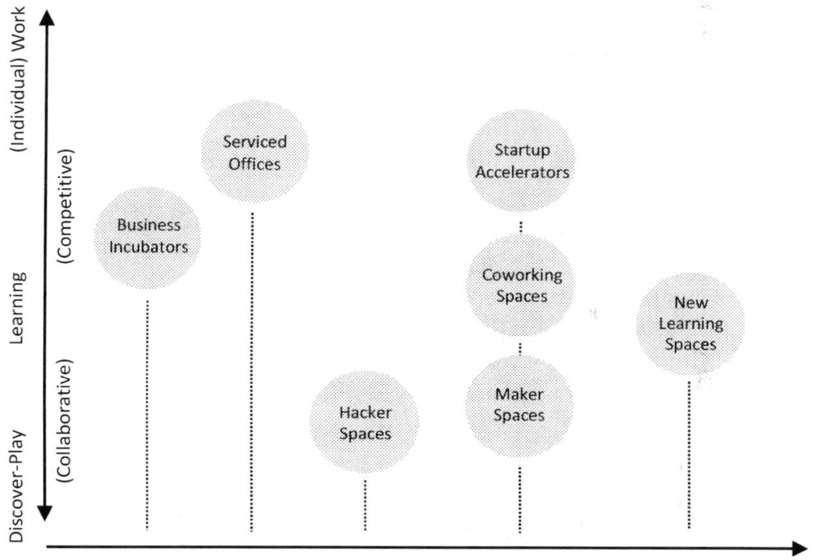

Source: adapted from (Waters-Lynch et al., 2016).

Coworking spaces resemble the serviced office industry, where customers pay a fee for access to space and amenities. However, the following three distinctive features (Waters-Lynch et al. 2016) characterize Coworking spaces as hybrid organizations:

i) The profiles of the pioneer coworkers: The early coworkers (between 2005 and 2008) were mainly freelance creative knowledge workers. They sought to overcome the social isolation that was associated with working from home or public places, such as cafes and libraries. Thus, Coworking spaces were characterized by informality,

such as informal dress code, language, and sociality, that imprinted the organizational culture of the newly born enterprises.
ii) The centrality of social interactions: Coworking spaces are usually referred to as a *membership community* (Sundsted et al., 2009), where social interactions are fostered and emphasized.
iii) The aesthetic design of the spaces that combine nonroutine, creative work and playful, open, and transparent workplaces.

Due to these characteristics, Coworking spaces can be considered hybrid or intermediary organizational arrangements, in which economic actors that engage in different forms of collaboration are co-located.

Inter-firm collaboration is thus intrinsic in the Coworking spaces, as colocation leads to the emergence of a highly collaborative community of freelancers, entrepreneurs, and professionals (Waters-Lynch et al. 2016). These forms of collaboration could be defined as an intermediate or hybrid organizational form (Capdevila, 2015).

Coworking spaces are not only places where professionals and other workers can work (other than the offices and their private places), they also actually serve as **collaborative spaces**. From this perspective, they are places that foster collaboration, knowledge exchange, and innovation.

On one side, the coexistence of several innovative firms within a physical space could boost creativity and innovation. On the other side, organizational challenges must be faced. At a macro-level, firms that are based in the coworking space aim at firm-level innovative outcomes and performance, while they build inter-organizational relationships with other firms in the same space. This raises questions about the design, social networking, and the knowledge management approach of organizations.

At a micro-level, individuals feel like members of a single firm and, simultaneously, of the broader coworking community. This paves the way for an interesting debate on organizational behavior, and how workers learn within this hybrid, knowledge-intensive context.

From a community standpoint, positive externalities and spillovers can boost innovation. This opens up new avenues of research in the innovation management field.

Coworking allows collaborative activities that favor, or even create, the emergence of new professions (Figure 3.8). This seems to be a response to the need to bring a new productive vitality to urban centers, deprived of their traditional activities, resulting in the redevelopment and conversion of real estate spaces and the functional regeneration of urban reality, in particular those of a smaller size.

From this perspective, coworking can contribute to social well-being as it is proposed as a place that represents a logistical solution and stimulates the development of complex social phenomena. Furthermore, the social function is carried out by respecting the characteristics of the business fabric of the area and by promoting the development of sustainable activities that can contribute to the development of an intelligent city model. The central role of higher education institutions makes it a point of reference for the area that pushes the property to foster learning opportunities and social relationships that stimulate creativity and innovation.

Figure 3.8. Categories of coworking users.

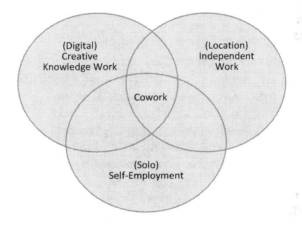

Source: author's elaboration based on (Waters-Lynch et al., 2016).

Box 3.4. The TAG case study

TAG is a global network of digital innovators, a physical Coworking space for digital ecosystems to meet, work, learn, and collaborate (Talent Garden 2017). It offers a variety of facilities well beyond Coworking spaces, such as training courses and events across Europe. The Coworking spaces are designed to enable the community to work, collaborate, connect, and reach their goals. Campuses are open 24/7 and offer workstations, meeting rooms, training classrooms, and relaxation areas. TAG is the largest physical platform in Europe for digital talent. In fact, TAG heavily focuses on talent, and it offers a journey toward growth and success. TAG claims to offer Passion Coworking Spaces, thus highlighting the community dimension, and stressing the importance of the ecosystem for the growth of the digital start-ups.

Among the campuses spread throughout Europe, Talent Garden Rome, located in an old Post premise, has been conceived as a unique innovation ecosystem where start-up and digital talent can find the tools they need to turn their ideas into reality and grow their business by joining a network. TAG is present in five nations and affirmed

> as the largest aggregator and natural accelerator of European talent. Not just a place but a platform where there will be more than 100 digital innovators, a TAG Innovation School – a school that will train professionals in the new digital and innovation professions, and more than 100 events that will be organized during the year to connect innovators with businesses and the realties of the territory. Within the Coworking space, the business incubation of Digital Magics is offered, which provides the training programs organized by TAG Innovation School and many events dedicated to innovation.

Source: author's elaboration.

3.3.3. Flexible Working, Smart Working?

As seen before, the concept of agility or flexibility has become part of the language used in contemporary organizations, referring not only to the ability to adapt easily in the face of exogenous changes, but also to the ability to adopt organizational solutions that enable this adaptation. The Digital Transformation requires profound organizational adaptations, while enabling new ways of designing, and implementing work.

Flexible ways of working have become increasingly known and adopted. New ways of working are characterized by organizational flexibility and the use of technological instruments to work remotely (Demerouti et al., 2014). By remote working, national legislations generally intend to work from home, while in some cases referring to the so-called "mobile" work, that is carried out in places such as coworking spaces, bars or hotels. The international comparison of the definition of flexible work in national legislations does not show any universally accepted definition. However, the definitions change based on the workplace, the intensity in the use of technological tools and the distribution of work time between offices and other places chosen by the worker as the location to provide their work.

The recent pandemic, as discussed in Chapter One, has forcibly extended these flexible ways of working for quite a long period. New flexible work arrangements can be defined as "new managerial philosophy founded on giving people back flexibility and autonomy in the choice of spaces, time, and tools to be used in the face of greater accountability"(Corso & Crespi, 2016).

The terminology used in the Italian regulatory framework that has recently been introduced offers interesting points of discussion. Previously, Italian legislation referred to "agile work," emphasizing the worker's autonomy in achieving the objective of corporate performance in an agile way. The Law, introduced in 2017 (D.L. 81/2017), uses the term Smart-working, emphasizing the smart skills of the employee, which are versatility, efficiency, and creativity. The organizational model relating to SW could, where applied effectively and efficiently, bring significant advantages and opportunities to organizations that adopt it both in terms of productivity and achievement of objectives and in terms of worker welfare and quality of life. However, in organizational practice, the fulfillment of these promises of work-life balance and greater worker involvement is not automatic. As with other organizational innovations, the practice could deviate from the norm in that it achieves a necessary translation of the norm itself and adaptas to the specific organizational context, which could lead to unexpected and not always positive results.

Remote work is concentrated in highly qualified job categories such as technicians, managers or professionals. These professional figures are thought to already have the degree of autonomy necessary to perform the work outside the company premises.

One of the concerns, linked to the introduction of remote work within the productive organizations, is that of a reduction of the work commitment due to physical absence in the offices. However, the research carried out on remote workers shows the opposite, at least in terms of hours worked: remote workers work 48 hours more weekly than other employed workers (Corso and Crespi, 2018).

At the European level, the "Europe 2020" strategy links work-life balance to gender equality, inviting the Member States to promote new forms of reconciliation of working time and lifetime and to increase gender equality. The ILO-Eurofound study offers a complete overview of the phenomenon of mobile ICT / Telecommuting work (Messenger, 2018). On the other hand, teleworking has existed since the 1970s, when teleworking developed in the information industry in the U.S.A. state of California. ICT-based mobile work emerged later, as smaller and lighter wireless devices such as laptops and cell phones enabled employees to work not only from home but also from anywhere.

In parallel with technological advances, flexible working time agreements have been adopted in recent decades, guided both by the needs of companies for more flexible production and by the desire of workers to be able to better balance their work with other personal commitments, often related to family duties. Planning flexibility allows workers to modify their work schedules using a variety of formalized policies. Flextime, for example, allows employees flexibility in arranging daily working hours in a range of acceptable options (Baltes et al., 1999). Employees with flextime options can choose when to start and end the working day, as long as they are physically in the company premises during specific hours, usually from 9 or 10 until 2 or 3 in the afternoon. Another example of flexibility is the compressed workweek, which allows people to work their weekly hours in fewer days than the "standard" five-day workweek.

Governments from various countries have promoted and/or regulated ICT telework or mobile work, in order to improve work-life balance and company performance, as well as to promote many other objectives, such as business continuity; in times of crisis and the inclusion of specific groups in the labor market (such as older workers, women with young children and people with disabilities).

The flexibility of location allows workers to choose where to carry out their work. One way to offer employees flexibility is to telework or work remotely from their traditional workplaces (generally from their homes), part-time or full-time. Another option is called a virtual office, space where employees are given the portable means to do their job and the freedom to choose which workplace would be best suited to meet business and personal/family needs (Hill et al., 2001). The literature identifies several flexible working practices, such as:

a) **Flexible working**. The concept of "Flexible Working" is often identified as a form of work that balances the company's competitive needs and the employee's private needs. Flexibility can be referred to as the number of hours worked daily, i.e., variable entry and/or exit times, compressed weeks, part-time work, shared work, or project work; it can be space flexibility, i.e., mobile working, work from home, work in other organizations, work in coworking or hub; it can be flexibility in employment contracts such as a freelance, group of associates or other alternative contractual forms.

b) **Telework**. Born in the U.S.A. in the mid-70s and developed thanks to IT technologies, telework is one of the first forms of organizational flexibility that contributed to the decentralization of work activities. In the "European Framework Agreement on Telework" it is defined as a "form of organization and/or execution of a job, using information technologies, in the context of a contract/relationship, in which the work, which could also be carried out at the employer's headquarters, takes place far from the local ones on a regular basis." Telework is characterized by strict rules regarding times, places, and technological tools used which reproduce the same organizational structure present in the workplace (office). The work carried out remotely is based on the use of telematic communication systems, normally for a fixed term, and was born with the aim of increasing productivity and work flexibility. Telework also has positive impacts on the environment because it reduces the use of means of transport and therefore the amount of carbon dioxide present in the atmosphere. The main feature of this organizational form of work is relocation: the work can be done anywhere. Not being configured as a specific contractual form, the legal qualification of teleworking depends on the context in which the employment relationship is configured. In fact, it is a working method that can refer to both a subordinate and an autonomous employment relationship. In subordinate relationships, in which the teleworking method is more widespread, the "mobile teleworking" consists in delegating to the worker times and ways of carrying out, and setting a deadline for the realization and delivery of the final result with or without intermediate checks. In the Telework report, the employer implicitly agrees to lose part of his control by trusting in the greater value of the performance of the employees.

Remote control of teleworkers is possible, subject to authorization, and, if motivated, exclusively for reasons of safety, production, organization or protection of company assets. The new forms of remote control, born with the spread of flexible forms of work, involve the use of work tools, as means for the supervision operated by the employer on the results produced by the employee. The use of work tools, in order to control what the employee does, does not require prior authorization, as this is implicit in the worker accepting the use of digital devices to carry out his assignment. The theme of the application of control, on the work of the teleworker is regulated by the contractual parties by agreement, to protect the employee. The worker's option to take part in the Telework project is voluntary and reversible.

c) **Agile Working** reflects the "Agile Project Management" approach that has been discussed earlier (see par. 3.2.5). Flexibility refers mainly to time and place but also includes the activities and staff employed. As the agile teams are inter-functional, the components, in fact, cover different roles and have various skills, functions and professional backgrounds, agile working requires the revision of hierarchical organizations and the full autonomy of the teams in planning and evaluating their projects.

d) **Home Working**, which restrictively means working from home. It is made possible by technology that allows the worker to be always connected. Working from home allows workers to organize their work and family life commitments in full autonomy, optimizing the company's time and costs. It is an increasingly requested and appreciated way of working by women workers, especially mothers. The "Home Working," if not consciously managed, leads to negative consequences, such as an overload of domestic tasks delegated to those who, between the spouses, remain to work at home, which imposes the need to precisely redefine the boundaries between work and life. Another negative consequence of working from home could be the risk of always being at work, continuously connected, and constantly under pressure due to the absence of direct supervision by the manager and the total freedom granted to the worker in managing his/her tasks. The flexible work approach could involve frenetic rhythms, and the worker must learn to manage them by arranging adequate daily time intervals to disconnect from the work tools. Indeed, home workers should set regular and constant hours devoted to their job and keep away all potential sources of distraction, in order to better face their commitments; define the boundaries between work and private life and learn to respect them; learn to take small breaks from the work process, and define a comfortable area of the house that is exclusively dedicated to work.

e) **Smart Working** is closely linked to Agile Working, but more complete: it is an organizational approach that has the aim of combining autonomy, flexibility, and collaboration through the use of new technologies. It expresses the working approach that integrates organizational behavior and culture, technologies, and workspaces. Smart Working indicates a work environment that eliminates the old concepts of a workstation that is no longer stable but dynamic subject to what is needed at that moment.

The adjective "smart" indicates advanced forms of work organization in which the smart worker is put in a position to operate on complex work processes, interacting at a cooperative distance with his colleagues and being evaluated, not through a sort of piecework of the evaded practices, but rather on the achievement of results (Mattalucci, 2014). Working "smart" means being versatile, efficient, updated, creative, and always connected. Smart Working combines autonomy (as in Home Work), flexibility (as in Flexible Work), and collaboration (as in Agile Work) through the use of technologies.

Chapter 4
KM AND DIGITAL TRANSFORMATION IN CONTEXTS

Summary: 4.1. Introduction. – 4.2. Operations & industry 4.0: Navantia and Shell. – 4.3. HR-TECH: IBM, Generali, Company X. – 4.3.1. Artificial intelligence. – 4.3.2. People analytics. – 4.3.3. Impact on Employees' motivation. – 4.4. Marketing and Sales. – 4.5. Supply chain and Logistics. – 4.6. IoT. – 4.7. When Innovations are Disruptive: The Evolution of the TLC Sector.

4.1. Introduction

Some examples of business in the Digital Age taken from real cases have been scattered throughout the previous chapters. This Chapter is aimed at reporting more detailed examples of organizations that have embraced the Digital Transformation. More specifically, each paragraph displays examples of how digital technologies can impact specific business processes or functions. As shown in the previous chapters, digital transformation embeds digitalization and digitization, and requires a profound organizational change. Not always companies understand that such organizational change must occur for digital strategies to be effective. So, the boxes also discuss the strategic and organizational implications of such implementations.

The last part of the chapter is specifically dedicated to the evolution of the telecommunication industry. Not surprisingly, radical digital innovations have disrupted the TLC industry in the last fifteen years, business models have been revolutionized, and traditional companies have had to reposition in the digital market. Thus, it makes the perfect case to test the evolutions of the theoretical concepts and the managerial implications of the Knowledge-based Economy that rules the Digital Age, which have been discussed so far in this book.

Finally, this chapter also deepens the discourse about networks and knowledge management. The last paragraph discusses the results of a study on knowledge management practices and their impact on the intra-organizational network.

4.2. Operations & industry 4.0: Navantia and Shell

> **Box 4.1.** The Navantia case study
>
> Created in 2005 after the merge of different shipyard companies, **Navantia** is a Spanish state-owned shipbuilding company. It's the largest builder of civilian and military ships in Spain, the fifth in Europe, and the ninth in the world. It's the first to experiment a new industry model that takes the name of "Shipyard 4.0" or, aka "Digital Shipyard", or "Marine 4.0". It consists of a new technology platform that improves ship construction using digital technologies.
> In order to establish this primacy, Navantia has partnered with Accenture, whowill help the Spanish company in their journey towards digital transformation, including digital technologies and competencies. The aim of the new platform is to improve business management systems and it is associated with Industry 4.0. They both aim at reducing costs and increasing productivity using the most innovative technologies available, while looking for a way to lower the impact on the ecosystem.[1]
> Emission reduction is one of the major drivers of the project. Emissions pose major threats not only to businesses but also on the climate. In fact, the International Maritime Organization (IMO) aims to reduce the average carbon intensity and emissions from shipping by at least 50% in 2050.[2]
> In order to quickly progress in the ship development and design, but also optimizing the electrical consumption, the navigation system, and implementing new services on-board, the Shipyard 4.0 model has implemented twelve main technologies from Industry 4.0:[3]
> - Additive manufacturing;
> - Artificial intelligence;
> - Autonomous vehicles;
> - Big data and analytics;
> - Cybersecurity;
> - Health, safety, and environment;
> - New materials;
> - Robotic process automation;
> - Secure cloud;
> - Ubiquitous connectivity and the Internet of Things (IoT);
> - Virtual and augmented reality;
> - Virtual modeling and simulation.
>
> The benefits of implementing a digitalization strategy are not easy to calculate as they are centered on saving time in building and control processes or on the potentiality of future improvements. However, what Navantia wants to achieve is the reduction of

---

[1] https://www.navantia.es/en/navantia-4-0/shipyard-4-0/.

[2] https://www.abb-conversations.com/2019/05/how-industry-4-0-can-work-for-the-marine-and-shipbuilding-sectors/.

[3] https://tep946.uca.es/noticia/shipyard-4-0-concept-features-3d-printing-digital-twins-advanced-technologies-for-shipbuilding-in-spain-and-australia/.

ships construction's heavy expenses as well as the number of materials required in the process: thanks to 3D printers the goal may not be as impossible as it seems. Shipyard 4.0 is about developing new functionalities and digital benefits, in order to create a more inclusive approach for both clients and builders as well as using data to obtain precious information that will surely improve the customer's experience and the manufacturing processes. These technologies, however, require a great expertise on digital technologies and the issues that revolve around data are not easy to overcome.

Source: author's elaboration in collaboration with Pietro Pratense.

Box 4.2. The Shell case study

Royal Dutch Shell PLC, known as **Shell**, is one the most important and largest oil and gas companies in the world. Shell has always been a driver of innovation, like in 1960, when the company worked on the "Remotely Operated Vehicle" a robot that could operate underwater with the aim to revolutionise the exploration and production of petroleum [4].

In 2018, the company announced a collaboration with **Microsoft Corp.** to bring digital transformation and innovation inside the firm, increasing not only worldwide efficiency of their drilling and extraction capacity, but also enhancing people effectiveness, productivity and collaboration, with a special focus on safety for both customers and the workers.

In order to bring digital innovation, Shell is focused on establishing their leadership in the market, as well as in the IoT and AI. In fact, a combination of the C3 IoT and Microsoft Azure will be necessary to construct the Shell AI Platform. [5]

A solid digital platform will not only help the company in addressing future challenges, but it will also promote and support the delivery of cleaner energy using technology, one of the major pillars of the Industry 4.0 model. [6]

There are two major improvements in using this technology: the development of the Shell Geodesic and the new cloud-based system on Azure.

Shell Geodesic has the aim to improve the accuracy and control on the drilling process in order to reach different and the deepest layers of rock. The major aspect is the machine learning algorithm that makes decisions and predictions in real time, having a drilling simulator featured in the process.

The cloud-based system of Azure uses the camera footage to identify dangerous situations inside the gas station and prevent them immediately. The interaction between the deep learning network and the IoT speed will increase the capacity of detection and prediction of future disasters, alerting the employees. One example is the use of cigarettes at the gas station, the system will automatically shut down to avoid explosions. [7]

Source: author's elaboration in collaboration with Pietro Pratense.

[4] https://aoghs.org/offshore-history/offshore-robot/.

[5] https://blogs.microsoft.com/ai/shell-iot-ai-safety-intelligent-tools/.

[6] https://www.offshore-technology.com/news/shell-microsoft-offshore-innovation/.

[7] https://news.microsoft.com/2018/09/20/shell-expands-strategic-collaboration-with-microsoft-to-drive-industry-transformation-and-innovation/.

4.3. HR-TECH: IBM, Generali, Company X

4.3.1. Artificial intelligence

Box 4.3. The IBM case study

The International Business Machines Corporation (IBM) is an American multinational information technology company founded in 1911, that operates in more than 170 countries.

IBM provides software, middleware and hardware components to companies as well as hosting and consulting services for IT. IBM is also dedicated to the research field and has invented some of the most notorious and important technologies, like the floppy disk, the hard disk drive, the SQL programming language.

In recent years, IBM developed a computer system with the aim to answer specific questions, using natural language processing and machine learning algorithms. In 2014, the Watson Group was created to make business on Watson.

Currently, it is used for customer services, financial services, cybersecurity and expert services.[8]

Watson applications are not only for business but its current major applications are the HR department of the company. In fact, what makes Watson so important for the future of HRM is that it's capable of predictig, with 95 percent accuracy, if a worker is planning to quit a job.

As a technology giant, for IBM it is very important to search for new applicants but it is also important to retain the most skilled and profitable workers it owns.

Watson, with its predictive ability, is working alongside the human resources department to gain data about the employees thanks to a performance-tracking program that discovers skills and weakness and tracks their projects to provide promotions and increase efficiency.

Watson is providing career feedback which helps employees to increase their skills as well as to identify future career paths based on the data it has collected.

IBM Watson is following every employee on their journey, producing useful data for the HR managers to use.[9] Watson is improving not only the efficiency of the HR department, but it is also saving money for the company as it is boosting the retention rates.[10]

Artificial Intelligence, integrated in HRM, could uncover new features and practises of the HR department as well as add more value for the organisation.

Watson can engage the workforce directly and solve several business problems, boosting efficiency and productivity, introducing a full-scale automation for tedious, time-consuming tasks and augmenting various human capabilities and functions.

---

[8] https://www.ibm.com/watson.

[9] https://www.cnbc.com/2019/04/03/ibm-ai-can-predict-with-95-percent-accuracy-which-employees-will-quit.html.

[10] https://www.cnbcevents.com/news/ibms-ai-backed-employee-retention-software-can-predict-when-youre-going-to-quit-with-up-to-95-accuracy/.

The IBM Watson case shows how the interaction between human and machine could improve the way we work and live, introducing objective criteria and enabling new solutions that will improve the workplace and workforce of tomorrow.

Source: author's elaboration in collaboration with Pietro Pratense.

4.3.2. People analytics

Box 4.4. The Generali case study

Generali is an excellent example of people analytics: the insurance company, in fact, uses a single platform for accessing personnel data (Generali People Analytics) which provides the normalized data of the various national databases. Following the 2019-2021 strategic plan that focuses on digital innovation, the project was born from the idea of releasing HR staff from Reporting activities to convert them to activities with greater added value, through the use of a simple platform and of immediate use that can provide clear summary statements deriving from selected data. In this way, many decisions are made following a data-driven approach, that is, based on the data available. The Dashboard created for Generali by Oracle provides, in fact, a set of reports that update automatically and allow for customization according to one's needs. This dashboard, four months after launch, was already used by 200 managers in 40 countries and, as commented by Diana Sassu, Project Manager of Generali's People Analytics Tool initiative, the "most important benefit [...] is the cultural change that the Tool was able to generate, because it allowed to change the perception of HR, which today are finally seen in the company as a real business partner."

Source: author's elaboration in collaboration with Pietro Pratense.

4.3.3. Impact on Employees' motivation

Box 4.5. A case study on Digital Transformation and Motivation

Company X, whose values converge on the centrality of the person in the Digital Transformation, maintains that motivation is the basis for the development of people's well-being and has therefore activated the platform under study to be able to fully understand the drivers of intrinsic motivation.

The software on which the People Management platform is based to monitor intrinsic motivation is based on research in cognitive science, positive psychology, neuroscience and game design. By combining Artificial Intelligence with behavioral science, the platform helps in creating an organizational culture aimed at understanding the components of motivation to be able to improve it through a personalized feedback and coaching path that the company must base on the results observed through the software.

The software features a PC platform and an App for tablets and smartphones. The PC platform is reserved for managers who analyze the data collected by the App, which, in turn, is used freely by employees. The App sends notifications to the person who decides to download it twice a day, notifications containing multiple choice questions, whose answers feed each employee's profile individually based on the scores (from 0 to 100) that they obtain in the answers they provide to the App. The software uses the answers that the employee submits to evaluate different dimensions of intrinsic motivation: the clarity of the objectives, the continuity of the feedback, the sociability, the balance of the perceived challenges, a sense of growth and improvement, predisposition to error, and a feeling of control.

The different dimensions of intrinsic motivation are, at the same time, like indicators of how management moves towards its people, providing key indications to better understand which positive actions are taken and which ones to undertake. The platform, therefore, provides an accurate insight into what is the company's reality, while being able to understand the motivation of individual workers and take actions to improve.

Motivation then plays influentially on job performance: higher levels of motivation correspond to better performance.

Here too, the software comes in handy because it allows to be able to check the daily progress of employee motivation and intervene, if necessary, in understanding in depth the reasons for poor motivation and being able to work to ensure the person in question returns to the flow optimal motivation, or a complete balance between all its dimensions.

The potential of this tool, however, lies in its continuity: following up an improvement process through greater communication and continuous feedback is the key to transforming a static photograph, such as the one taken by the motivation, into a real dynamic process which increases and optimizes processes, performance and above all the well-being of workers in the company.

This case shows that new technologies can impact motivation, respect and increase the humane aspect of work. They constitute a necessary and no longer replaceable means in the in-depth understanding of the realities company but, and this will be difficult to replace, the human touch must accompany the Digital Transformation and its means in every process, to ensure that the centrality of the person remains the fulcrum of the entire work-system.

Source: author's elaboration in collaboration with Sara Pennacchini.

4.4. Marketing and Sales

Box 4.6. The NBA case study

Founded in 1946, the **National Basketball Association (NBA)** is part of the four major professional sports leagues of the USA and Canada, composed by the **Major League Baseball** (MLB), the **National Football League** (NFL), and the **National Hockey League** (NHL).

It is one of the most notorious and massive sport businesses, with more than 1 billion viewers (registered in 2017/2018) and a broadcast capacity that covers more than 200 countries and 34 spoken languages, with outstanding revenues across television, merchandising, tickets and sponsorships, with a value per team – the NBA league is composed of 30 teams, in which 29 in USA and 1 in Canada – of 2 Billion dollars, on average.[11]

In 2015, the NBA gained an exclusive and important achievement: it became the first of the majors to bring VR's technology into the sport entertainment system: the aim of the project was to broadcast matches live, using the unique experience of the VR, allowing viewers to watch the games directly from courtside, a new way to enjoy their favourite sport as if they were directly in the stadium. **Virtual reality (VR)** is a simulated experience that uses headsets or specific types of environments to produce sounds, images and other sensations, giving users the ability to look inside an artificial world, to move inside of it and interact with it, with given specific equipment like handles for gripping (used mostly in the videogame industry).

In this case, using a small screen that directly faces the eyes, covering all external visuals, the person could enjoy the game in the most immersive way possible with a high-definition camera and high-quality audio, and feel the passion of the match or different features that will be available in the future. Recently the NBA has partnered with NextVr to livestream one game per week, in order to increase their sales using an extremely powerful marketing campaign: as less than one percent of their watchers enjoy the sport in the stadium using the VR, the fans will now be closer to the action with an interactivity that the TV can't really provide because of its linearity.[12]

In order to develop this possibility, Turner Sports, that manages NBA TV, has partnered with Intel to provide virtual reality contents across the TNT VR app available on VR headsets of different companies (Samsung, Google, Sony, Oculus). Intel has powerful computing technology and it's one of the leading companies in the hardware industry, merging these characteristics it is possible to create a realistic virtual reality giving the users the chance to change their perspective as 360-degrees cameras are used to film the matches. Sales and marketing are only a few of the major improvements that this technology could produce in the professional sport business.[13]

What really stands out in the NBA VR experience is that this technology brings a new type of entertainment with a major focus on the engagement of the spectator that couldn't be reached with previous technologies. Not only improvements in camera's quality or in the audio system will give a better immersion but also the features that could be adopted in the future will likely give the idea of living the matches directly. The spectator may be able to direct the play, to move around the stadium freely and not only wait for different camera angles to show the action.

Source: author's elaboration in collaboration with Pietro Pratense.

---

[11] https://www.forbes.com/sites/forbespr/2019/02/06/forbes-releases-21st-annual-nba-team-valuations/#6e53703611a7.

[12] https://www.alistdaily.com/media/inside-the-nbas-virtual-reality-strategy/.

[13] https://www.marketingdive.com/news/nba-gives-fans-court-side-view-with-vr-content-deal/510339/.

> **Box 4.7.** The Biogen case study

Biogen, founded in 1978, is one of the world's first global biotechnology companies. Its focus revolves around neuroscience and the treatment of neurodegenerative diseases like multiple sclerosis and amyotrophic lateral sclerosis, Alzheimer's disease, dementia, Parkinson's disease, movement disorders and neurocognitive disorders. It has developed one of the first treatments for spinal muscular atrophy and many other rare diseases like progressive supranuclear palsy.

Biogen not only does research in neuroscience, it also commercializes biosimilars and high-quality medicines using its technology and engineering advanced sector. [14]

Recently, Biogen has started working with Lexalytics to create a system that will combine Machine Learning (ML) and Natural Language Processing (NLP) in order to understand what conditions or issue the person is calling for, in order to provide the most efficient answer, that will be much faster than the Medical information Department (MID). Lexalytics is a company that works on SaaS and cloud-based technology, providing sentiment, intent analysis, and even multi-lingual text analysis using NLP with AI transforming the text in data. [15]

Currently, the calls are under the responsibility of an operator that should provide an accurate and a short-timed response, given a database of predeterminate and frequently asked questions with their respective answers, as well as brochures or other information resources, in a given time of 1 minute per call. If the operator is not able to answer within the minute, the call is taken by a medical director, resulting not only in a costly and ill-timed operation for the company but also frustration for the caller.

The Lexalytics system will be used to streamline the process of MID's calls from Biogen constituents by merging Artificial Intelligence and keyword search, using NLP, with the aim to reduce the average call time and the calls directed directly to medical directors while maintaining the quality of responses given an automated systems that uses the institutional knowledge from different databases and sources, that was trained on the Biogen Japan LTD proprietary data, like call logs, information brochures, etc.

The revolutionary part of this project is the use of the NLP on the complex Japanese language, resulting in a transcontinental collaboration that took almost a month to develop. The production should go into full operation in 2020, with future and later instalment on chatbots, social media or any given interaction resource. If the project is successful it will be easy to implement different languages. [16]

Source: author's elaboration in collaboration with Pietro Pratense.

---

[14] https://www.biogen.com/en_us/about-us.html.

[15] https://www.lexalytics.com/.

[16] https://www.lexalytics.com/news/press-releases/biogen-chooses-lexalytics. https://www.lexalytics.com/resources/Lexalytics-Biogen-Medical-Information-Case-Study.pdf.

4.5. Supply chain and Logistics

> **Box 4.8.** Impact of DT on supply side and logistics
>
> In the shift towards the digital economy new processes and business models have emerged that reconfigure the supply and logistics chains of companies and evolve to successfully face the challenge of efficient distribution. These methods such as order delivery, new forms of payment and, in general, digital technologies facilitate the transmission of information and closing transactions. The development of technology, along with a change in consumer behavior related to demand, results in the need for a change in the form of purchase and consumption. Technology must allow the connection of processes within companies and with their suppliers and customers in an efficient and economical way based on an environment of maximum reliability, connectivity, and visibility.
>
> Given this situation, it is clear that the supply chain is no stranger to this development of digitalization and changes in production, purchase, and consumption models. It is in full transformation, and companies in the sector will have to adapt to the new rules of the game. Companies must connect their supply chain beyond their current operational limits if they wish to maintain their competitiveness in a new digital era.
>
> For example, the use of autonomous vehicles, without drivers, drones or robots are ways in which the digital technologies are disrupting the supply chains. Current consumer buying habits and market dynamics are forcing companies to change their supply chains, given that the traditional models used so far show shortages. Industry 4.0 is one of the four pillars that supports one of the many new forms of the supply chain: the digitization of administrative processes. Today the consumer is increasingly demanding in terms of distribution channels, whether physical store or online shopping portals, going to one or the other according to their comfort at the time of purchase.
>
> Furthermore, a digital supply chain can be defined as a set of interconnected processes that revolve around the customer, which is always located in the center, is connected to the internet and is not faithful to any particular purchase channel. The pillars of this supply chain are
> 1. Industry 4.0,
> 2. Process digitalization,
> 3. Real-time visibility and
> 4. Digital planning systems.
>
> In the case of the Pharmaceutical Industry, for example, Miebach Consulting was hired by a global pharmaceutical company to develop an audit of the entire supply chain that would allow it to increase the level of service and decrease logistics costs. This evaluation identified a possible improvement in efficiency in the order-to-cash process through the implementation of a robot that automates processes through the execution of repetitive tasks. The result was a 60% reduction in the workload in this process.
>
> In the case of cement and other construction materials, a cement and concrete production company sought to improve the shopping experience of its customers through an online store. However, the purchase / delivery of their products required some real-time dialectic (Is there inventory? Is there a capacity to store it? When can delivery be made?). For this it was necessary to have a digitized chain. Miebach Consulting defined a global objective model of Order Taking & Fulfillment, selected a computer solution, and developed several pilots that confirmed the value of the project for the cement company and its clients.

Amazon's experience is also adapting its projects in the digital era. It is well known that Amazon is one of the most advanced cases in its digital business model and also favors the integration in this channel of other businesses, opening the path to omni-channel distribution for many of them.

One of the biggest current challenges of the logistics sector is to have highly qualified professionals who are prepared to assume and lead all these changes and help set the course, both for traditional and new businesses. Businesses based on the digital economy, aiming towards the development of a connected, efficient, and sustainable supply chain adapted to new market requirements.

Source: author's elaboration in collaboration with Marta Tremps.

Box 4.9. The Unilever case study

Founded in 1929, Unilever is a British-Dutch transnational consumer goods company that owns more than 400 brands around the world and is organised in four main divisions: beauty & personal care, food, beverages and cleaning products. After years of decline because of bad management, Unilever started growing again when Jane Moran and Alan Jope were respectively appointed as CIO and CEO of the company. The revolution of the company started with digital technologies, leading to a digital transformation that was assigned to the IT department. What makes the digital transformation of Unilever so powerful and disruptive is the massive amount of data, collected over time, that provided the opportunity for the company to sell more and spend less. In Marketing, using small teams (Digital hubs) around the world to elaborate the data and study consumers' needs and behaviours, they provide specific and personalised content for different categories of buyers.[17] The major improvements for Unilever are in the supply-chain thanks to Artificial Intelligence (AI) and Robotic Process Automation (RPA).

In order to increase the efficiency of the factory, Unilever shifted from a project-based strategy to a platform strategy supported by Microsoft: Azure and Internet of Things (IoT) have permitted a powerful data share between the machines, creating an interconnected factory.[18]

The data collected will be elaborated by a machine learning algorithm that will provide insight and patterns that are used to improve the supply chain but also to predict certain outcomes based on previously collected data (historic information). An automated factory will allow operators to make better decisions and move their attentions from manual tasks to value-added functions.[19]

The mission of Unilever is to become a data driven company and it's using various tools to do so. One of these tools, Power BI, allows Unilever to uncover data and visualise it easily. Unilever then used these data to eliminate false or unimportant alerts on production lines, resulting in less intervention and a much more productive environment.

---

[17] https://www.computerweekly.com/news/450402108/Unilever-puts-digital-transformation-in-the-hands-of-IT.

[18] https://news.microsoft.com/transform/now-its-personal-unilevers-digital-journey-leads-to-real-results-for-consumers-and-employees/.

[19] https://www.spglobal.com/marketintelligence/en/news-insights/latest-news-headlines/49355732.

Unilever is rewiring not only their structure but also their supply chain, focusing on generating real-time information and using the AI for planning, benefitting robots as well as building digitally connected factories in order to serve customers in the best way possible as well as improving the whole organisation. [20]

Source: author's elaboration in collaboration with Pietro Pratense.

Box 4.10. AccuWeather Case Study

Global weather company AccuWeather is using Microsoft cloud solutions Azure and Dynamics 365 to gain real-time intelligence into weather and business patterns to answer the challenge of handling of 17 billion requests for data each day.

AccuWeather is the world's top provider of weather information. More than 1.5 billion people rely on the company's products and services.

To better answer its users requests the company expanded its use of Microsoft technologies. First, AccuWeather migrated its application programming interfaces (APIs) to Microsoft Azure, and it began using an increasing array of cloud services including the Cortana Intelligence Suite and Microsoft Dynamics 365.

Moving to the cloud helped the company scale out globally and provided a better foundation for more business opportunities. AccuWeather currently handles more than 17 billion requests per day, more than triple the volume when the migration project started in 2012.

Besides scaling better, the APIs expanded possibilities by integrating new data sources and functionality, including radar feeds, imagery, and device sensors. AccuWeather now provides its Minute by Minute™ forecasts with Superior Accuracy™ for any longitude and latitude on earth.

Thousands of organizations, including more than 240 of Fortune 500 companies, rely on the company's customized enterprise solutions, which AccuWeather delivers with help from Microsoft that enable real-time access to information.

Making these business decisions have also helped to save lives and businesses. For example, on May 26, 2016, an AccuWeather enterprise solution warned Union Pacific Railroad that a tornado was going to cross a track in Kansas in about half an hour. The railroad stopped eight trains that were scheduled on that route, saving lives and millions of dollars. AccuWeather was also the first to predict the historic January 2016 blizzard that slammed the Eastern and Midwestern United States.

To improve supply-chain operations with predictive analytics, the company is using the Cortana Intelligence Suite to integrate sales data with weather information. In a recent project with Starbucks, AccuWeather helped the coffee giant solve seasonal problems like running out of ice and cups in hot weather. And in another example, AccuWeather helped a global candy manufacturer identify which products sold best, and if the sales spikes were weather-related.

Source: author's elaboration in collaboration with Andrea Grieco based on https://customers.microsoft.com/en-in/story/726274-accuweather.

---

[20] https://www.marketingdive.com/news/unilever-builds-stable-of-digital-hubs-as-data-driven-marketing-accelerates/559577/.

4.6. Internet of Things (IoT)

Box 4.11. iRobot Case Study

iRobot created the home-cleaning robot category with the introduction of its Roomba Vacuuming Robot in 2002. Today, iRobot is a global enterprise that has sold more than 20 million robots worldwide. iRobot's product line features proprietary technologies and advanced concepts in cleaning, mapping, and navigation. iRobot engineers are building an ecosystem of robots and data to enable the smart home.

In July 2015, spikes in new Roomba use did not directly impact the company's day-to-day operations. But starting that September, large numbers of people trying out the new connected Roomba vacuums would result in large volumes of traffic through the iRobot HOME App, the mobile app customers would be using to set up and control their connected robots.

iRobot operated primarily as a hardware vendor, and to better answer this spike began to run a high-availability, customer-facing cloud application and an Internet of Things (IoT) platform.

Roomba customers can now use their phones to manage their Roomba, wherever and whenever it's convenient. And to be sure to meet all customers' requests iRobot decided to move its mission-critical platform to the Amazon Web Services (AWS) Cloud.

To run the web applications that connect to the new Wi-Fi-connected Roomba vacuums, iRobot is using about 25 AWS services. At the core of the iRobot platform are AWS Lambda and the AWS IoT platform. AWS IoT can process trillions of messages between billions of devices and AWS or other products and services.

By using this architecture-based iRobot is able to keep the cost of the cloud platform low, avoid the need for subscription services, and manage the solution with fewer than 10 people that are focused on developing applications rather than managing the cloud platform.

According to iRobot, there is a crucial category of data: up-to-date mapping information about the houses where the devices reside.

This could be achieved by removing the burden of programming devices from the consumer and by having the home understand itself: specifically, the layout of the home, the location and purposes of each room, and where the home's various smart devices are located,

Connected robots like the Roomba could help in reaching this result, for example, by using visual simultaneous localization and mapping (vSLAM) technology to navigate an entire level of a home. As the Roomba vacuums, it builds a map of the home, and it is this map that could provide the foundational information to help a smart home understand itself. Today's Roomba is creating maps to clean more effectively, in the future they could combine these maps with additional sensors and new cloud services to manage the other smart devices within a home.

Source: author's elaboration in collaboration with Andrea Grieco, based on https://aws.amazon.com/it/solutions/case-studies/irobot/.

4.7. When Innovations are Disruptive: The Evolution of the mobile TLC Sector

Of all the industries that have undergone the Information Revolution, the telecommunication industry is one of the most interesting. In fact, over the last two decades telecommunications, especially mobile products and services have been deeply reshaped. First of all the penetration rates of mobile communication products and services have dramatically increased in almost every country of the globe.

Though being relatively young, the mobile TLC sector has faced several innovative waves: either technological, or regulatory, or else market driven. Above all, technological innovations related to the telecommunication industry have been introduced very often, replacing each other at a generally high speed. Indeed, at the dawn of a new era for mobile communications and in the face of relevant uncertainty on the development and diffusion of fifth generation services, a deeper understanding of the critical success factors in the mobile business is needed for the formulation of strategies to compete in the emerging business scenario.

Once the core mobile services, voice calls gave way to data services in the years 2010s. At the beginning, person-to-person data communications were the most widely used mobile data services: the success of mobile messaging had been phenomenal and, most unsatisfactory, a surprise to both operators and users. When it comes to mobile services and products, it is arguable that they are supported by networked technologies, whose complexity relies on the need of coordination among a number of actors. As innovation is pursued and new value-added services and products are launched, competition between actors (network operators, content providers, vendors) increases. Moreover, cooperation, collaboration and consolidation are key issues, as alliances are built between firms in complementary industries. As a consequence, redefinition of the balance of economic power among actors occurs, and cross-fertilization between services that are complementors boost the sales of those services. For example, successful apps that are developed for a specific mobile operating system can increase the appeal of mobile phones endowed with that operating system (e.g. (McAfee & Brynjolfsson, 2017).

The Italian mobile TLC market is quite peculiar, and its evolution is a quite interesting case study. The Italian market saw the birth of the mobile TLC industry in the late '80s. Though being relatively young, the mobile industry has faced several innovative waves: either technological, or regulatory, or else market driven. Technological innovations related to the TLC industry have been introduced very often, as elsewhere in the world, replacing each other at a generally high speed. A very fast growth of the penetration rate is a peculiar characteristic of the Italian mobile TLC industry. Also, the liberalization of the telecommunication industry drove the competitive pressure, which in turn remodelled its structure, formerly characterized by the monopoly of the one state backed firm. The deployment of innovative technologies, as well as the evolution of the competitive pressure, drove such an upward diffusion. A boon to the penetration rate was provided at the beginning of the '90s, when the digital TACS technology, labelled as first-generation type appeared, replacing the analogue technology. In addition, the operator began to focus its offering on the differentiation of targets and of tariffs, which turned out to be more affordable, and thus settled the activation of a development phase. In 1995 a wave of radical technological change made the TACS technology enter its maturity phase, when a digital mobile technology, labelled GSM or second-generation type, was deployed. Soon enough, the third generation (3G) of mobile technology has been set through the definition of the UMTS standard. More recently, the fourth generation 4G has been introduced, and the 5G is already in the pipeline.

A second shock to the industry was caused by the entry of the second mobile operator: Omnitel Pronto Italia. OPI not only posed the question of competition for the first time ever in the history of the industry, it also pushed a redefinition of the strategies, resources, and capabilities needed for succeeding. At odds with the incumbent, OPI's strategy has always been focused on a consumer-centric orientation, as well as a high commitment to the quality of the services offered. The cellular services market has continually evolved as operators seek new sources of competitive advantage. However, a key issue within the industry is the introduction of the prepaid charging concept for voice telephony. Not only was it a boon for mobile operators, who previously couldn't provide access to those they considered to present credit risks, but it was also another reason mobile penetration has increased so quickly. The mobile industry was then more profitable than ever, attracting new competitors, namely Wind, which entered in 1999 and Blu, the last mobile operators that entered the market in 2001.

Instant messaging is now very common, and actually it has actually replaced the traditional mobile messaging services like SMS, which allows users to send messages up to 160 characters long via their mobile phone. Although it is possible to trace back the causes of the tremendous success of this service. SMS became extremely popular in the 1990's and early 2000's to the surprise of the mobile operators themselves. Operators hardly expected this simple technology to become a popular service and a significant revenue booster. Indeed, later, innovative Value Adding Services (VAS), which have come to be offered as an innovation of SMS, represented an application of a disruptive technology (Christensen, 1997), which have the strength to modify the predefined evolutionary path of the industry. Innovation brought by new technological platforms, in fact, gave new actors the chance to enter the market, constituting a shakeout of the industry.

The evolution of the mobile telecommunication technologies experienced six steps: from analog to digital, to multimedia. In details, it is classified into subsequent generations.

In particular:

1. The first generation comprises an analog cellular system, which allowed for simple voice calls, and basically within the borders of one single Country.
   Designed to support basic voice and data services, the original GSM system consists of a circuit switched Core Network that provides the routing of calls to mobile subscribers, the Base Station Subsystem for radio access and the Mobile Station. One of the most important factors in GSM's success is the standard open interfaces that have enabled any vendor to supply any elements of the network, and have let operators worldwide deploy multi-vendor systems of their choice.
2. The second generation coincides with the development of the GSM standard. With this standard, digital cellular systems have been introduced, allowing for data exchange among users. Though, data could be exchanged only at a poor level of quality, and they basically consisted of text messages.
3. The 2,5 generation is a transition step towards the third generation. In particular, data exchanges are more sophisticated.
   GSM evolution (now referred to as "2.5G") provides a significant enhancement by adding the General Packet Radio Service (GPRS). This provides an "always on", high-speed connection (up to 171 kbit/s) to packet data networks, which is suited to the "bursty" traffic on the Internet and World Wide Web, either directly or via operators' portals. With GPRS, the core network is enhanced to embrace the packet switched domain, adding new IP-connected network elements. Crucially, this extension lays the foundations of a common core network for 2G and 3G.
   EDGE (Enhanced Data rates for GSM Evolution) further enhances this GSM/GPRS radio interface by adopting new modulation technology to achieve higher data rates using operators' existing GSM radio spectrum. EDGE is the other pre-3G radio access technology directly evolved from GSM. WCDMA and TD-SCDMA will not necessarily replace GPRS or EDGE, but will in reality co-exist with them, and can share one common core network.

4. The third generation is born with the definition of the UMTS standard. 3G Systems are intended to provide a global mobility with a wide range of services including telephony, paging, messaging, Internet and broadband data.
    International Telecommunication Union (ITU) started the process of defining the standard for third generation systems, referred to as International Mobile Telecommunications 2000 (IMT-2000). In Europe European Telecommunications Standards Institute (ETSI) was responsible for the UMTS standardization process. In 1998 Third Generation Partnership Project (3GPP) was formed to continue the technical specification work. 3GPP has five main UMTS standardization areas: Radio Access Network, Core Network, Terminals, Services and System Aspects and GERAN.
    UMTS introduced improved wideband radio access technologies as WCDMA for paired bands, as well as TD-SCDMA and TD-CDMA for unpaired bands. The possibility of evolving either through upgrades to EDGE or by introducing UMTS, or both, gives operators an exceptional set of gradual deployment strategies to suit their situation precisely with regard to their legacy networks, capacity needs, spectrum availability and speed of take-up of the new services in the market.
5. The fourth generation is born with the aim of solving the problem of interoperability of the 3G and its subsequent versions. 4G is a concept of interoperability between different sorts of networks, which is all about high speed data transfer such as 0-100MBPS of either the server or the data receiver set is moving at a speed of 60 Kmph.[21]
    Instead of hybrid technology used in 3G with the combination of CDMA and IS-9, 4G introduces a new technology named OFDMA. In OFDMA, the concept is again of division multiple accesses, but this is neither time like TDMA nor code divided CDMA rather frequency domain equalization process symbolizes as OFDMA.
    The purpose of 4G is to enhance speed, quality and capacity, and at the same time, to improve security and lower the cost of voice and data services, multimedia and internet over IP. The applications, supported by the 4G characteristics, included increased mobile web access, IP telephony, gaming services, high-definition mobile TV, video conferencing, 3D television, and cloud computing.
    The key technologies enabling 4G are MIMO (Multiple Input Multiple Output) and OFDM (Orthogonal Frequency Division Multi-

---

[21] *Sources*: https://pdfs.semanticscholar.org/5fbc/bd38c2f4b0a8c24be47ed8cf5522c3bcad2e.pdf; http://net-informations.com/q/diff/generations.html.

plexing). The two important 4G standards are WiMAX (has now fizzled out) and LTE (Long Term Evolution) which represents an upgrade to the UMTS technology.
6. The fifth generation is currently under development. 5G promises to substantially increase the rates at which data travel, creating higher connection density and a much lower latency Some of the plans for 5G include device-to-device communication, better battery consumption, and improved overall wireless coverage. The max speed of 5G is aimed at being as fast as 35.46 Gbps, which is over 35 times faster than 4G.
Key technologies for enabling 5G are: Massive MIMO, Millimeter Wave Mobile Communications, small cells, Li-Fi. All the new technologies from the previous decade could be used to give 10Gb/s to a user, with an unseen low latency, and allow connections for at least 100 billion devices.
But 5G will also have a formidable impact on all industrial sectors and consequently on the world economy: 5G is already spoken of as the "nervous system of digital society". It is estimated that by 2035 the 5G-enabled economy will be worth 12 trillion dollars in the world and operators are expected to grow revenues by 36% by 2026. Europe considers it one of the main instruments to regain the lost position of technological leadership compared to the United States and Asia [22].

Major trends about mobile products and services have been:

- Phones improving, converging with PDAs, and becoming smart phones always in our hands or pockets;
- The majority of active citizens already mobile;
- Service providers have learned how to overcome restrictions and leverage the advantages of mobile communications;
- The mobile phone is gradually becoming a personalized tool for using and managing services;
- Phones with 5G technology will be able to perform multiple tasks at distance, both for work and home duties, thanks to IoT and Artificial Intelligence technologies.

---

[22] *Source*: https://www.corrierecomunicazioni.it/telco/5g/5g-alle-porte-ecco-lo-stato-dellarte/.

Figure 4.1. Evolution of mobile phone Generations.

Generation	Speed	Technology	Time period	Features
1G	14.4 Kbps	AMPS,NMT, TACS	1970-1980	During 1G Wireless phones are used for voice only.
2G	9.6/14.4 Kbps	TDMA,CDMA	1990 to 2000	2G capabilities are achieved by allowing multiple users on a single channel via multiplexing. During 2G Cellular phones are used for data also along with voice.
2.5G	171.2 Kbps 20-40 Kbps	GPRS	2001-2004	2.5G the internet becomes popular and data becomes more relevant. 2.5G Multimedia services and streaming starts to show growth. Phones start supporting web browsing though limited and very few phones have that.
3G	3.1 Mbps 500700 Kbps	CDMA 200 (1xRTT, EV-DO) UMTS, EDGE	2004-2005	3G has Multimedia services support along with streaming are more popular. In 3G, Universal access and portability across different device types are made possible. (Telephones, PDA's, etc.)
3.5G	14.4 Mbps 1-3 Mbps	HSPA	2006-2010	3.5G supports higher throughput and speeds to support higher data needs of the consumers
4G	100-300 Mbps. 3-5 Mbps 100 Mbps (Wi-Fi)	WiMax LTE Wi-Fi	Now (Read more on Transitioning to 4G)	Speeds for 4G are further increased to keep up with data access demand used by various services. High definition streaming is now supported in 4G. New phones with HD capabilities surface. It gets pretty cool. In 4G, Portability is increased further. World-wide roaming is not a distant dream.
5G	Probably gigabits	Not Yet	Soon (probably 2020)	Currently there is no 5G technology deployed. When this becomes available it will provide very high speeds to the consumers. It would also provide efficient use of available bandwidth

Source: author's elaboration based on https://pdfs.semanticscholar.org/5fbc/bd38c2f4b0a8c24be47ed8cf5522c3bcad2e.pdf.

The evolution of products and services is also related to the higher and higher speed of transmission allowed by new technologies. The WCDMA radio access technology will be enhanced to support High Speed Downlink and Uplink Packet Access (HSDPA), enabling transmission at speeds of up to 14.2 Mbit/s.

Another enhancement is the IP Multimedia Subsystem (IMS). It enables real-time, person-to-person services, such as voice or video telephony, to be provided by means of packet switched technology in common with non-real-time information and data services. Yet further advantages will come in the longer term from the ability to interwork interactively with other networks such as Digital Video Broadcasting (DVB) and Digital Audio Broadcasting (DAB), and to take advantage of the content offerings that can be delivered efficiently to small form factor terminals.

Mobile services are based on a complex technological and organizational infrastructure. Qualified partners with a large span of core competences have to cooperate to make them possible. In fact, as shows, a group of new activities are added to the value-offering path of innovative mobile products and services. Whereas, until the 2nd generation, the network operators kept control over the majority of the activities, the innovative mobile systems require that new actors enter the fields, with new competencies and assets.

The technological innovations, along with the visionary approach of the actors in the industry, gave rise to the concept of an overall m-business, which stands alone as an industry as a whole. It comprises the use of mobile telecommunications technologies and services supporting the exchange of goods, services, information and knowledge within and between businesses and at the interface to customers.

M-business includes both customer-facing applications and mobilization of business processes.

M-business leverages e-business infrastructures already in place to:

1. create new services that are time and location sensitive;
2. improve customer relationship;
3. increase productivity and operate more efficiently;
4. maintain operations, organize employees and keep track of the inventory.

The advent of new technologies and their never-ending evolution have clouded the intrinsic limits that once separated telecom players from the world of information technology (hereinafter IT), and the two sectors are on a collision course.

Many telcos are actively engaged in the attempt of exploiting their existing scale and IT assets to move beyond basic voice and data services and begin selling IT services. A number of telcos are shifting from the offering of their basic services such as the ones based on voice and data and have recently acquired IT companies in order to drive growth in ICT services and related network areas.

However, the convergence taking place is not a one-way street. Many modern IT services such as cloud computing require communication products as integral parts of the offering. Also, a number of IT players are recognizing they have the ability to make inroads into the telecoms space. This is often accomplished by designing substitutes for traditionally delivered telecoms services, such as over-the-top application collaboration and IP-based communication applications.

The competition for telcos is therefore becoming more stringent, since the entrance of other important new actors, that have been able to disrupt the traditional telecommunication technologies and business services.

They consist of a wide range of companies that are known as the "Over the Top" (OTT) companies, cloud service providers, and web-scale operators, such as Google, Microsoft and AWS, just to mention a few. They provide a diverse range of services, from infrastructure to platform and application services. Despite their diversity, they all have one thing in common: they are unlike traditional telecoms operators, the scope of their activities and operating models is based on a very different technology architecture. These companies usually provide services built on virtualized, abstract and programmable compute, storage and networking resource pools based on a technology represented by a multi-tenant platform, accessible on demand to everyone connected to the World Wide Web. In this ecosystem, the only barriers to entry for a new global OTT are software development skills and a credit card. Success has increasingly given power to some cloud companies, building hyper-scale infrastructure and environment around search engines, social media, video distribution, infrastructure and devices. It has attracted services that once were siloed to operate over the global Internet, such as VoIP, IPTV and instant messaging. It has also produced several services and capabilities that would have been inconceivable to create any other way. For traditional telco operators, interposed between OTTs and their customers, the innovation and traffic-growth cycle are constantly pressing operators to upgrade access networks to address the increasing traffic from customers using their smartphones, tablets, apps and every mobile device more and more, and their willingness to pay for more traffic is very low if not null.

Notwithstanding the ability of telcos to innovate, which allowed them to achieve many important results, last but not least the shift from 4G to 5G, several frictions still remain. This is mainly caused by the fact that the typical inward-looking of these companies prevent them from adopting new thinking in a relatively short time. Hence, in an era where new technologies jump from one adoption curve to the next, telcos' system might represent a huge impediment.

Within established telecoms industries, other driving forces have led to compartmentalization and specialization over time. Some of these include disinvestment of the industry into manufacturers and operators, separation of regulated and non- regulated services, framing service definitions into tariffs, network splitting regulations, and long-term, negotiated relationships with suppliers of materials and labor. These specifics might fit for maximizing efficiency within a status quo. However, in order to have access to higher levels of innovation, wider ranges of supplier options, and service options, telecoms should disaggregate system standards and take a fresh look at the business.

At the European level, the tide is already turning. Some of the main European telcos, like Telefonica and Deutsche Telekom, are moving towards a more cloud-comprehensive approach as architectural thinking. The ratio behind it lies in the fact that these companies conceive the cloud-native workload running as a more efficient way for accessing the network, therefore it would open the doors for three appealing opportunities:

1. Cloud technologies better manages the increasing traffic demands;
2. The flexibility of cloud technologies allows for more elastic approaches;
3. This technology does not only ease the access, but many improved services can be built upon it.

To do this, telco industries must adopt or modernize data centres with the most updated technologies and align them with cloud ways of working.

OTTs companies also deal with social media. Today, we spend an ever-increasing amount of time using services such as Twitter, Instagram and WhatsApp. However, these multi-billion-dollar businesses would not exist were it not for the likes of Tim, Vodafone or Telefonica. Their infrastructure enables every tweet, picture, message and internet call. Yet, consumers' perception of their relevance seems to have declined as they focus more on apps and devices, rather than the service provider.

Therefore, telcos have a fundamental choice to make: either redefine themselves as digital communications companies and take on digital disruptors or specialize as pure infrastructure providers.

It is thus evident that a broad new array of market opportunities arises. In fact, not only the network providers find room to differentiate their competencies beyond the provision of "simple voice," but there are also opportunities for emergent actors to enter the industry. In particular, the value offering is made up of interconnected services and products if one looks more specifically at the typologies of market opportunities. This suggests that a networked pool of firms collaborate to deliver the services and products.

Another level of analysis can be adopted, looking at the different fields of applications, where the innovative mobile solutions may be required. From this perspective, for example focusing on the business-to-consumer segment, the following applications emerge:

- Financial, where m-banking services as well as real-time information about the stock market can be offered.
- Entertainment, with applications such as games, gambling, and dating
- Shopping, with new opportunities for purchasing goods, m-auctions.
- Information: maps and routing, directions, local infos, alerts.
- M-payment: public transport, parking.
- Advertising: designing specific loyalty schemes, mobile advertisement (location sensitive).

Whatever the new market opportunity chosen, experiences from the introduction of GPRS and WAP services have taught the industry that easy service provisioning and configuration is a key issue. The explosive growth of services and content that new technologies enable must be accessible to the user with essentially zero configuration work.

Furthermore, it is of utmost importance that mobile devices do not suffer from the same vulnerabilities that have befallen PCs and the Internet. Initiatives such as secure execution environments and signed code downloads must be properly handled. This is a scenario that the industry is already taking major steps to address, but the risks nevertheless need to be highlighted.

The Italian market for mobile communication is one of the most compelling examples of the success of mobile TLC solutions. In fact, ever since the birth of the GSM mobile system, Italy has proven to deeply favor mobile TLC products and services.

The main peculiarities of this country are:

a. Fast evolution.
b. Increasing penetration.
c. Intensification of competitive rivalry.

d. Key – strategic Partnerships with OTTs.
e. 5G upcoming diffusion.

In terms of diffusion, the curve of adoption of the mobile TLC solutions shows a classic S-shaped form. Indeed, it has been sloping upwards very rapidly, and a high penetration rate has been reached very soon. In particular, the take-off time may be traced back to 1996.

4.7.1. The Actors of the new Mobile TLC Industry

In the mobile sector actors could initially be divided into two categories: the service providers (or network operators) and phone manufacturers. Until the '90's the market was in fact run by these two unique actors. With the advent of the first phones containing complex software and applications, the market now faces a new category in the market, one of the programmers. Today it also adds the category of suppliers of Operating Systems, which were previously implemented directly by manufacturers of phones.

Broadly speaking players in the mobile market can be grouped as follows:

- Manufacturer: Apple Inc., Nokia, Samsung, Motorola, HTC, Sony Ericsson, BlackBerry, etc. Huawei: those that produce physical goods.
- Suppliers of internal technology devices.
- Managers of the service: In Italy, TIM, Vodafone, WindTre.
- Suppliers of the base operating system: Android, Microsoft (Windows Mobile), Nokia Symbian, Apple Mac OS X, BlackBerry OS.
- Programmers applications: companies that specialize in programming, private programmers.
- Content providers: providers of media content.

Applications can only be purchased through credit card payments using the application market as a platform, which is directly controlled by the developers of the base operating system. Each operating system has its own market (eg. for Apple this is the Appstore, for Android it is the Android market, Symbian Ovi store, etc. ...).

Of course, in addition to these four categories, even end-users should be considered as users of all services, especially because they are consumers themselves, affecting the success of a product and everything that revolves around it.

As discussed above, in the past, there were mainly two market players, manufacturers of mobile and network operators. The network operators have always been the subjects with more power, because their position is of advantage over other players; they are able to manage the network through which the cell carry out their functions. Over the years, technological innovations have allowed us to see a growth in the number of entities in the mobile business. Particularly relevant is the power that software vendors are acquiring through basic (or operating system) devices. In the past, outside of aesthetic difference or some small functions, mobile phones held almost all the same activities.

3G has allowed us to see the birth of new products that had them carry out different operations. And logically, for such devices to operate in an efficient manner, it was necessary to provide them with an operating system. For the first time, the phone was thought of like a small computer. The first was a Symbian operating system. For about five years it was the best operating system on the market. Its golden age ran in the five year period from 2000/01 to 2005/06. Blackberry was the only serious competitor in the field, but only in regards to high-end products, what are commonly referred to as being in the business area. The appearance of the iPhone marks the dividing line between the old and new phone market. The giants of information technology and network flooding into the market has caused a great shock and change, and consequently the increase of the actors in the sector.

In fact, the suppliers of the operating system were not taken into consideration. Closely connected to the operating system, there is a market for applications. The market is developed by software houses that provide the OS. This virtual platform allows the user to interact directly with the application providers and content providers, and also allows the electronic payment. The latest addition to the producers of components had probably not been lost or merged into consideration before because they were associated with the manufacturers of the phones. Now, however, they appear to be essential, because the hardware components are critical to the success of a smartphone. Just as in the personal computer market, consumers are interested in having a satisfactory package of hardware.

So, factors such as the digital camera, the touch screen, processor, memory, ram, turn out to be elements of great importance in the choice of one product over another. This condition not only affects the trend of the market; the manufacturers are the mirror of the situation. The battles for the intellectual property of a particular technology, whether it's a hardware, software and type, common in the market of computing, as a process of osmosis, have moved into the mobile business. The consequences are, as always, very interesting, and are the cause of shock in the market, especially from the point of view of mergers, outputs, and joint ventures.

The consequences are also very interesting from an organizational point of view. Telcos are typically big traditional organizations that need to redefine their organizational design, their set of core competencies and dynamic capabilities, their managerial practices and HR policies. These changes should foster inter-organizational collaboration and knowledge sharing. Accordingly, the next paragraph reports the results of an experiment based on a telco that introduced a KM platform to overcome the problem of organizational silos.

4.8. KM practices as a tool to overcome organizational silos [23]

Many scholars highlight the importance of network in knowledge management, trying to understand the direct effect of networks on knowledge transfer (e.g. (Reagans, 2002). Networks create access to knowledge because interpersonal relations between a knowledge source and a recipient should facilitate knowledge acquisition by increasing the likelihood that two individuals engage in knowledge transfer (Tortoriello et al., 2012).

In Chapter One, the network perspective of Knowledge Management has shown the critical role played by interpersonal informal networks in the knowledge transfer process. These studies shed light on the network mechanisms that are able to influence knowledge transfer focusing on the effect of a network's characteristics (e.g. network cohesion and network range) on the knowledge sharing processes. The idea underneath this body of literature is that strong interpersonal ties between actors of a network enhance a better access to the personal knowledge of the actors because individuals who communicate frequently or who have a reciprocal emotional tie are more likely to share knowledge than those who communicate infrequently or who are not emotionally attached (Reagans, 2002). Other studies have focused on the formal organizational network as a source of knowledge sharing enhancement. Some scholars have underlined the importance of the network position of the unit within the organizational network, analyzing how a central position can enable better access to knowledge and therefore better working cross-functional knowledge sharing (Tsai, 2001). Other studies have highlighted the issue of how the organizational structural dimensions (formal networks) are related to organizational knowledge sharing. For example, Willem and Buelens (2009) have assessed the direct impact of some classic organizational dimensions such as coordination, centralization formalization and specialization on inter-units knowledge sharing.

---

[23] This paragraph is written on the basis of (Marchegiani & Pileggi, 2018).

In summary, the literature has focused mostly on studying the intra-organizational network as an antecedent of knowledge sharing processes. Scholars have tried to explain why and in which cases certain types of network's characteristic can enable knowledge transfer processes within the organization. The network has been considered as an independent variable that can influence knowledge sharing. In contrast, it is important to assume the opposite perspective and investigate how the knowledge sharing moulds the organizational networks.

This paragraph instead shows the impact of knowledge sharing (enhanced by knowledge management approach and knowledge management practices) on the intra-organizational network. The focus of the research that is presented here is on the network shape derived by the implementation of a knowledge management practice. Given that the goal of a knowledge management practice is to facilitate the flow and the spread of knowledge throughout the organization, what can be its impact on the network shape? Is the adoption itself able to be a reason for the creation of a cross-units and cross functional intra-organizational network? This approach also highlights the role of what can be called the *actual networks*, which can overlap the formal networks within the organization. Actual networks are defined by the actual relationships linking the actors in the network and by the actual exchange of resources and information and knowledge happening between them. Detecting the actual knowledge network is of the utmost importance when implementing a sort of virtuous cycle through which a knowledge management approach can shape a cross functional, horizontal network which, in turn, can be a significant condition for well performed knowledge sharing in the organization.

The actual network can emerge from the implementation of KM practices, as a cross-functional actual knowledge network which is horizontal and heterogeneous. A heterogeneous network involves actors from different organizational areas, with different knowledge backgrounds which otherwise wouldn't be able to get in contact and collaborate. Thus, it would be possible to foster cross-functional knowledge spreading and collaboration.

We study an example of ann actual network, which is a weighted network where intra-organizational relationships are weighted through a relationship Intensity index which better defines the underlying relationship itself.

Therefore, the actual network offers a realistic picture of the actual exchange of knowledge and the actual extent of the relationship, as shown in Figure 4.2.

Figure 4.2. From KM to actual network.

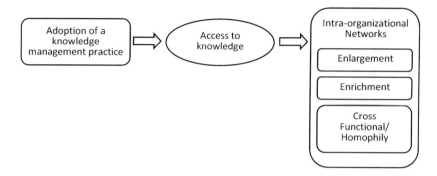

Source: author's elaboration.

It is interesting to test the relation between the evolution of intra-organizational networks and implementation of some knowledge management practices, by measuring how the adoption of KM practices enhances the enlargement and enrichment of the network, making it more cohesive. Moreover, the KM practice is supposed to reduce the tendency to observed homophily over time in the network in order to foster cross-units collaboration and overcome organizational design barriers.

A study conducted within a prominent telco in Italy adopted the social network analysis with a longitudinal perspective to analyse the network at different stages of the knowledge management practice implementation. This enabled them to test the reaction of the social network to the introduction of a knowledge management tool and hence the impact of knowledge management.

Network's enlargement, enrichment and homophily tendency were measured through descriptive statistical analysis and social network analysis. At the empirical level, the experimental setting was provided by the intra-firm network of a big telecommunication company; the knowledge management practice was considered as an independent variable in an online community implemented in the corporate intranet and the network-dependent variable.

The technological variable was also considered as a moderator in the evolution of the network. Information Technologies are in fact critical enablers, as the success of any Information technology system begins with individuals and individuals' acceptance and usage are critical factors (see Chapter Three). Indeed, an information system which is not used does not produce any value. Thus, understanding why users accept or reject an Information system has been and still currently is one of the most challenging issues in

IT research and the outcomes deriving from the related body of literature can also be considered applicable to the analysis of Knowledge Management Systems as well as any other Information System.

This study adopted the technology Acceptance Model (TAM). In its original version by Davis, the Technology Acceptance Model presented five main components: Perceived Usefulness (PU), Perceived Ease Of Use (PEOU), Behavioral Intention to use (BI), Attitude toward using (AT) and Actual usage (U) (Davis, 1989; Legris, Ingham & Collerette, 2003). A prospective user's overall attitude toward using a given system is hypothesized to be a major determinant of whether the user himself actually uses it. The attitude, in turn, is a function of the two beliefs expressed by the Perceived Usefulness and the Perceived Ease Of Use: the former is defined as the degree to which an individual believes that the usage of a particular system is able to improve his work performances; on the other hand, the ease of use is defined as the degree to which an individual believes that using a particular system would be free of physical and mental efforts.

Figure 4.3. From KM to actual networks including TAM.

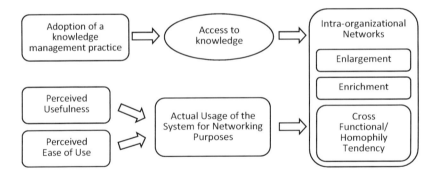

Source: author's elaboration.

The hypothesis stated by Davis claims that the perceived ease of use has a direct and relevant effect on the perceived usefulness, while the opposite is not true, meaning that the perceived usefulness is not hypothesized to have an impact on the ease of use. Furthermore, PEOU and PU are influenced by external variables, including system design features, user's characteristics, and task characteristics. Consequently, those external variables directly influence Perceived Usefulness and Perceived Ease of Use and indirectly influence Attitude toward usage. PU and PEOU are usually measured by a four items measurement scales derived by the six items identified by Davis. Starting from the original model, the Technology Acceptance

Model has evolved over time and many scholars developed it applying some amendments. However, it can overall be defined as a widely accepted model. Nevertheless, the Technology Acceptance Model presents some limits. The most relevant one is related to the concept of technology within the context where it is embedded. The TAM considers information systems as an independent issue from the organizational dynamics in which they are enclosed. Though, research in the innovation and change management field suggests that technological implementation is strictly related with the organizational environment that will have a strong impact on the outcomes. According to Orlikowski and Hofman the effectiveness of any change process relies on the interdependence between the technology, the organizational context, and the change model used to manage the change. This supports the suggestion that it may be difficult to increase the predictive capacity of TAM if it is not integrated into a broader model that includes organizational and social factors (Legris et al., 2003; Money & Turner, 2004).

Beyond its limits, the Technology Acceptance Model is considered to be widely accepted and it is applied in several fields, including Knowledge Management, although there is a surprising paucity of empirical research into the factors affecting individual acceptance and use of information technology implemented in the form of a knowledge management system. One of the causes of the scarcity of research showing the application of TAM to the Knowledge management field, can be considered as related to the model's limit mentioned above. In fact, as it has already been underlined above, organizational dynamics are extremely relevant for Knowledge Management applications and therefore, also for the Knowledge Management technological systems applications. The acceptance of a Knowledge Management System is an extremely complex process as it involves not only the acceptance of a technology system but also the acceptance of all the issues related to the willingness to share knowledge and to collaborate.

Nevertheless, some contributors face the issue and the Technology Acceptance Model appears to be applicable to the Knowledge Management field as well, although the relation needs to be further investigated. Money and Turner propose to use the TAM as a framework to investigate the implementation of a Knowledge Management system within an organizational unit of a large international consulting firm. The analyzed knowledge management system is a web based document repository and management tool intended primarily to support the organizational objectives of improvement of internal software, enhancing and diffusion of R&D products throughout the organization and enhancing business and employee professional development by providing them with convenient electronic access to current and past project information and documentation.

The research model, shown in Figure 4.3 aims to assess the relationship among TAM's main belief constructs, perceived ease of use and perceived usefulness, plus the users' intention to use and their actual usage of the target knowledge management system. Therefore, the model is similar to Davis's original TAM but is lacking the attitude construct and external variables: the former was said by Davis himself, that it is at best a partial mediator of the effect of perceived usefulness on intention to use, and that it added little causal explanatory power; regarding the external variables, they fall outside the aims of the research because there is no immediate intention to investigate antecedents to perceived usefulness and ease of use.

The results of the application developed by Money and Turner are consistent with the results of Davis TAM except for the behavioral intention construct. In fact, Perceived usefulness and perceived ease of use combine to explain a percentage of the variation in behavioral intention that is very consistent with earlier research. However, the individual relative effects of the two belief constructs are not consistent with previous findings. When the effects of perceived usefulness and perceived ease of use are decoupled in multiple regression analysis, perceived ease of use emerges as having a greater influence on behavioral intention than perceived usefulness. Furthermore, the behavioral intention-usage correlation observed in the survey data collected in this research was also lower than observed in most previous TAM research. A possible explanation for inconsistent results related to behavioral intention may lie in the research scenario. Indeed, in previous TAM research, scenarios aimed to predict future acceptance and usage and therefore the behavioral intention construct is critical. In the Money and Turner research, the intent was not to predict usage, but to interpret experience with the target knowledge management system through the lens of the TAM (Money & Turner, 2004).

This framework has been applied to an organizational unit where a Knowledge Management model or practice is in the implementation phase or in the immediately previous stage. We selected a big telecommunication company as an interesting and fitting empirical setting. The target company had recently undergone a change in the HR department, which led to the implementation of a structured KM model. We monitored the early stages through the creation of Pilot Projects aiming to reach knowledge sharing and cross-functional work as objectives, in order to target the firm's overall goal of innovation. A very innovative project was launched, with the basic idea of creating a cross-functional Community. This also requested the convergence of a large amount of knowledge embedded in the company from many different knowledge domains. We collected data during the launching phase when the community was closed, accounting for 39 nodes.

We ran a Social Network Analysis focused on the ego networks of the 39 members of the Community. We collected data through surveys in order to investigate the actual relationships that build up the actual network. In the survey submitted, participants were asked to answer some questions that concern: the existence of relationship of each actor with each other, the content of this relationship, and the tools of interaction. We assessed the intensity of the ties through an intensity index built out of 5 elements: Frequency of relationship, Efficiency of relationships, trust, reputation of other actor's competences related to the project, and willingness to collaborate with the other actors. We collected longitudinal data covering six months. These refer to three phases of the knowledge management practice's implementation: the pre-existence phase (t_0), the first usage stage (t_1), and a further implementation stage (t_2).

Born with the aim of evaluating the impact of a knowledge management practice on the evolution of the network of users, this study has shown extremely relevant effects from the introduction of knowledge management practices. Indeed, the examined KM community has been observed to be able to make the users' network wider and deeper and above all, to be able to connect people from different organizational areas, fostering cross functional collaboration, an essential issue for modern firms.

The results show that, when a knowledge management practice is introduced and implemented, the intra-organizational network evolves over time in terms of enlargement, and depth. Indeed, the Community's network results in the enlargement of the evolution of the community itself over time, and it is observable in terms of the number of active ties increasing from t_0 to t_1 and t_2 as well as in terms of the network's density increasing over the three observation's stages. The increase of actives ties and of the network's density stands for an increase in the network's web of relation and therefore an enlargement of the network for users of the knowledge management practice in exam.

Moreover, the network is observed to evolve in its depth, with underlying relationships becoming deeper over time along the implementation of a knowledge management practice. Indeed, results computed in this analysis show that both descriptive and analytical measures lead to higher network cohesion. Firstly, the average tie strength increased over time from t_0 to t_1 and finally to t_2, but the most interesting results related to network deepening are offered by SNA measures.

Most of the SNA results showed an increase of network cohesion over time, as well as an increase of average degree, connectedness, compactness, and in-degree centrality. Moreover, the results showed a decrease in inverse measure of cohesion such as components and average geodesic distance. However, despite the above mentioned issues, the general tendency of the network is shown to be oriented towards a higher cohesion level, demonstrating that the implementation of the community fosters and enriches the web of connections composing the members network, making it more in-depth.

The increase in cohesion can also be observed just by looking at the visualization of the network at the three stages in time all together in order to visually compared them more easily (Figure 4.4).

The most interesting finding of this piece of research is related to the ability of a knowledge management practice to foster cross unit interaction and collaboration through the creation of a heterogeneous and cross-units/cross-functional network. This issue has been observed through the analysis of the homophily tendency in terms of the organizational units affiliation observed within the network.

Figure 4.4. Evolution of the network over time.

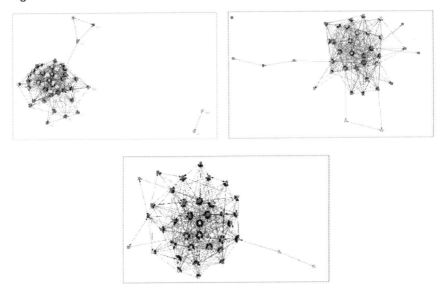

Source: author's elaboration.

Homophily tendency has been measured through descriptive and analytical measures: from a descriptive point of view it has been computed in terms of heterogeneity rate of the relationships while from an analytical point of view, cross units densities and homophily indexes as well as a regression test computing the impact of homogeneity on tie strength, have been considered. We compared three indexes: a) the correlation between homogeneity of the relationships and tie strength; b) the E-I index, inverse similarity measure considering active ties: it ranges from -1 (i.e., perfect homophily) to +1 (i.e., perfect heterophily); c) the Yule's Q Index, measure of similarity contemplating all the potential ties, even the not active ones: it ranges from -1 (i.e., perfect heterophily) to +1 (i.e., perfect homophily). All the obtained results coherently show an increment of homophily in the network from t_0 to t_1, followed by a decrement in homophily measured observed at t_1 to t_2 (Table 4.1).

Table 4.1. Homophily indexes over time.

	T_0	T_1	T_2
Average degree	11,974	13,026	14,34
Density	**0,324**	**0,352**	**0,388**
Components	6	3	2
Connectedness	0,821	0,873	0,949
Compactness	**0,549**	**0,59**	**0,654**
Average Geodesic Distance	1,802	1,768	1,76
Diameter	5	4	5
Closure	0,637	0,618	0,598
Indegree Centrality	1,39	1,393	1,274
Outdegree Centrality	1,028	1,039	1,293

These results show that the implementation of the community actually seems to determine a reduction in homophily tendency of the network, but results have also shown that it does not happen immediately after the introduction. Indeed, in a first phase, when involved in a KM project, actors tend to strengthen homophile relationships interacting mostly with peers coming from the same organizational unit. Regardless, internal networks are enriched through deeper tie strength at this stage. During a second further phase of the implementation, the usage of the community leads to the development of a cross-units interaction, thus fostering cross functional collaboration.

Intra-organizational networks are among the most investigated knowledge sharing elements. However, the literature has focused on networks as antecedents and causes of related events or causes of actors' behaviors.

Therefore, knowledge outcomes have been explained by mainstream literature as functions of different traits characterizing knowledge networks. In contrast, contributions on the impact of knowledge management projects and knowledge sharing processes on the intra-organizational network are scarce: the mainstream literature has only paid little attention in understanding how networks are built up and what shapes networks characteristics, especially considering knowledge networks.

Knowledge management projects are recognized to have the purpose, among others, of connecting people throughout the organization. In general, our research contributes to filling the gap of the intra-organizational networks as a consequence of the knowledge sharing enforced by the implementation of knowledge management practices. The latter are considered antecedents of knowledge networks and furthermore of cross-unit knowledge networks, rather than as a consequence of specific social networks' characteristics.

Our results have important practical implications as we offer practitioners with a very clear understanding on the impact of KM practices in defining the knowledge networks evolution within the organizational boundaries and beyond. This is a powerful outcome as KM practitioners are often challenged by the need to connect knowledge owners to the right co-workers in order to boost knowledge retention and knowledge sharing.

CONCLUSIONS

Knowing and knowledge acquisition is a relational process and higher levels in the pyramid of knowledge, such as intelligence and wisdom, can be reached only through knowledge sharing with others. The digital age has disrupted how we interact with others, when we can interact with them, and who are those whom we can interact with. Faster, real time, and ubiquitous communication tools enable the possibility to interact regardless of time and space. Even more important is the ability to interact with other humans as well as with non-human actors. This book has discussed the organizational implications of these new knowledge sharing processes. Through the overview of the newest digital technologies, and their applications in the redefinition of businesses scope and processes, the chapters have highlighted that the digital transformation is much more than a technological leap. It changes human lives, and it demands radical new ways of organizing economic activities and organizations.

To me, knowledge acquisition starts with the interactions with my family, friends, and closest colleagues. Informal and friendly relations are in fact very powerful as they unlock sharing personal ideas, deepest beliefs, and doubts. Most of all, my kids are to me a powerful source of fresh ideas. When I talked to them asking for their ideas about the relations between robots and humans, they seemed quite interested in the subject. Not surprisingly, they are quite positive about the possibilities of interacting with robots and computers. They think that there are many things that robots can do, and humans cannot-actions like flying, and going to space with no oxygen as they do not need to breathe. Plus, they can compute calculations at a very high speed.

On the other hand, there are many good things that humans can do, and robots cannot. Things like eating cakes or tasty food, thinking on their own, playing with friends. Most importantly, my kids said, robots cannot possibly love. This is indeed a serious shortfall, probably nothing will ever substitute the human capacity of feelings.

I believe this is both a milestone and a steady characteristic of the evolution of human/non-human interaction. Digital technologies can help us overcome some human limits (e.g. limited computational ability, bounded rationality, limited inferential skills) in the pursuit of a sort of *augmented humanity*. Thus, organizations seek to implement those digital additions that can improve productivity, efficiency, innovation, as seen in this book.

Nonetheless, organizations should preserve the human characteristics that make us very distinct and irreplaceable by non-human intelligence. Our capacity of feelings, and especially our capacity of feeling love and empathy for others, should be nurtured in workplaces. Many authors have emphasized that creativity makes us unique, and that no robots could ever invent new ideas like humans do. Also, humans can count on critical thinking, systemic thinking, entrepreneurship, and cultural agility as humans' strength over non-human intelligence (Aoun, 2017). I do believe that this is important, but I would rather stress the importance of keeping our workplaces, both physical and digital, humane. I would refer to the need of keeping, or developing, *Humane phygital workplaces* as they would nurture the ability to share knowledge through networks of relations, and would keep people passionate about their jobs and motivated to collaborate.

Humane phygital workplaces are intended as a synthesis between the concept of the phygital enterprises, that has been introduced by Sica (Sica, 2017, 2018), and the humanistic management approach, that "*regards concern for persons and human aspects in managing organization*" (Melé, 2016). The phygital enterprise, on one side, leverages the huge amount of Big Data to offer better solutions to its customers, while adopting sophisticated machine learning solutions and developing digital/physical experiences based on IoT, while valuing the Employee Experience. On the other side, the humanistic management approach is rooted in a prominent stream of business ethics and management research that views human aspects as central to managing organizations. The combination of the two approaches could lead to the development of humane digital workplaces that leverage the potential value creation of digital technologies while keeping the human experience at its best, fostering passion and love among people.

REFERENCES

Acciarini, C., Bolici, F., Marchegiani, L., & Pirolo, L. (2020). Innovation Diffusion in Tourism: How information about blockchain is exchanged and characterized on Twitter. *Total Quality Management, forthcoming*.

Ackoff, R.L. (1989). From data to wisdom. *Journal of Applied Systems Analysis*, 16(1), 3-9.

Alavi, M., & Leidner, D.E. (2001). Knowledge management and knowledge management systems: Conceptual foundations and research issues. *MIS Quarterly*, 107-136.

Alvesson, M. (2001). Knowledge work: Ambiguity, image and identity. *Human Relations*, 54(7), 863-886.

Alvesson, Mats. (2004). *Knowledge work and knowledge-intensive firms*. OUP Oxford.

Annosi, M.C., Martini, A., Brunetta, F., & Marchegiani, L. (2020). Learning in an agile setting: A multilevel research study on the evolution of organizational routines. *Journal of Business Research*, 110, 554-566.

Aoun, J.E. (2017). *Robot-proof: Higher education in the age of artificial intelligence*. MIT press.

Argote, L. (2011). Organizational learning research: Past, present and future. *Management Learning*, 42(4), 439-446.

Argote, L., & Miron-Spektor, E. (2011). Organizational learning: From experience to knowledge. *Organization Science*, 22(5), 1123-1137.

Argote, L., & Todorova, G. (2007). Organizational learning. *International Review of Industrial and Organizational Psychology*, 22, 193.

Argyris, C., & Schön, D.A. (1997). Organizational learning: A theory of action perspective. *Reis*, 77/78, 345-348.

Armstrong, M. (2006). Competition in two-sided markets. *The RAND Journal of Economics*, 37(3), 668-691.

Attewell, P. (1992). Technology diffusion and organizational learning: The case of business computing. *Organization Science*, 3(1), 1-19.

Atzori, L., Iera, A., & Morabito, G. (2010). The internet of things: A survey. *Computer Networks*, 54(15), 2787-2805.

Baltes, B.B., Briggs, T.E., Huff, W., Wright, J.A., & Neuman, G.A. (1999). Flexible and compressed workweek schedules: A meta-analysis of their effects on work-related criteria. *Journal of Applied Psychology*, 84(4), 496.

Bandura, A. (1988). Organisational applications of social cognitive theory. *Australian Journal of Management*, 13(2), 275-302.

Bandura, A. (2001). Social cognitive theory of mass communication. *Media Psychology*, 3(3), 265-299.

Bandura, A., & Walters, R.H. (1977). *Social learning theory* (Vol. 1). Prentice-hall Englewood Cliffs, NJ.
Barbosa, G., Hernandes, A., Luz, S., Batista, J., Nunes, V., & others (2017). A Conceptual Study Towards Delivery of Consumable Materials to Aircraft Assembly Stations Performed by Mobile Robots Based on Industry 4.0 Principles. *J Aeronaut Aerospace Eng*, 6(187), 2.
Bass, F. (1969). New product growth model for consumer durables. *Management Science*, 15(5), 215-227.
Baum, J.A.C., Li, S.X., & Usher, J.M. (2000). Making the Next Move: How Experiential and Vicarious Learning Shape the Locations of Chains' Acquisitions. *Administrative Science Quarterly*, 45(4), 766-801. https://doi.org/10.2307/2667019.
Beck, K., Beedle, M., Van Bennekum, A., Cockburn, A., Cunningham, W., Fowler, M., Grenning, J., Highsmith, J., Hunt, A., Jeffries, R., & others (2001). *Manifesto for agile software development*.
Bellinger, G., Castro, D., & Mills, A. (2004). *Data, information, knowledge, and wisdom*.
Bettis, R.A., & Hitt, M.A. (1995). The new competitive landscape. *Strategic Management Journal*, 16(S1), 7-19.
Blackman, D.A., & Henderson, S. (2005). Know ways in knowledge management. *The Learning Organization*, 12(2), 152-168. https://doi.org/10.1108/09696470510583539.
Blackman, D.A., & Henderson, S. (2007). Being and Knowing- Ontological Persptectives on Knowledge Management Systems. *The Electronic Journal of Knowlege Management*, 5(3), 283-290.
Bolici, F., Acciarini, C., Marchegiani, L., & Pirolo, L. (2019). Blockchain acceptance and adoption in the tourism industry. *Excellence in Services-22nd International Conference*.
Brown, D.W., & Konrad, A.M. (2001). Granovetter was right: The importance of weak ties to a contemporary job search. *Group & Organization Management*, 26(4), 434-462.

Capdevila, I. (2015). Co-working spaces and the localised dynamics of innovation in Barcelona. *International Journal of Innovation Management*, 19(03), 1540004.
Cashman, K. (2013). *The five dimensions of learning-agile leaders*.
Chan, S., & others (2004). Understanding internet banking adoption and use behavior: A Hong Kong perspective. *Journal of Global Information Management (JGIM)*, 12(3), 21-43.
Chebbi, H., Yahiaoui, D., Thrassou, A., Vrontis, D., & others (2013). The exploration activity's added value into the innovation process. *Global Business and Economics Review*, 15(2-3), 265-278.
Chesbrough, H.W. (2003). *Open innovation: The new imperative for creating and profiting from technology*. Harvard Business Press.
Chesbrough, H.W. (2006). *Open innovation: The new imperative for creating and profiting from technology*. Harvard Business Press.
Chiaroni, D., Chiesa, V., & Frattini, F. (2010). Unravelling the process from Closed

to Open Innovation: Evidence from mature, asset-intensive industries. *R&d Management*, *40*(3), 222-245.

Ciborra, C., Braa, K., Cordella, A., Hepsø, V., Dahlbom, B., Failla, A., Hanseth, O., Ljungberg, J., Monteiro, E., & others (2000). *From control to drift: The dynamics of corporate information infrastructures*. Oxford University Press on Demand.

Cohen, W.M., & Levinthal, D.A. (1990). Absorptive Capacity: A New Perspective on Learning and Innovation. *Administrative Science Quarterly*, *35*(1), 128-152.

Corso, M., & Crespi, F. (2016). Smart Working: Modelli organizzativi e tecnologie, spazi e normative. *Il Sole 24 Ore*.

Damsgaard, J. (2002). Managing an Internet portal. *Communications of the Association for Information Systems*, *9*(1), 26.

Damsgaard, J., & Lyytinen, K. (1998). Contours of diffusion of electronic data interchange in Finland: Overcoming technological barriers and collaborating to make it happen. *The Journal of Strategic Information Systems*, *7*(4), 275-297.

Damsgaard, J., & Marchegiani, L. (2004). Like Rome, a Mobile Operator's Empire Wasn't Built in a Day! A Journey through the Rise and Fall of Mobile Network Operators. *Proceedings of the 6th International Conference on Electronic Commerce*, 639-648. https://doi.org/10.1145/1052220.1052301.

Davenport, T.H., & Prusak, L. (2000a). *Il sapere al lavoro*. Etas, Milano.

Davenport, T.H., & Prusak, L. (2000b). Working knowledge: How organizations manage what they know. *Ubiquity*, *2000*(August), 6.

Davis, F. (1989). Perceived usefulness, perceived ease of use, and user acceptance of information technology. *MIS Quarterly*, *13*(3), 319-340. https://doi.org/10.2307/249008

Delmastro, M., & Nicita, A. (2019). *Big data: come stanno cambiando il nostro mondo*. Società editrice il Mulino.

Del Giudice, M., & Della Peruta, M.R. (2016). The impact of IT-based knowledge management systems on internal venturing and innovation: A structural equation modeling approach to corporate performance. *Journal of Knowledge Management*.

Demerouti, E., Derks, D., Lieke, L., & Bakker, A.B. (2014). New ways of working: Impact on working conditions, work-family balance, and well-being. In *The impact of ICT on quality of working life* (pp. 123-141). Springer.

Duguid, P. (2012). 'The art of knowing': Social and tacit dimensions of knowledge and the limits of the community of practice. In *The Knowledge Economy and Lifelong Learning* (pp. 147-162). Brill Sense.

Dyer, J.H., & Singh, H. (1998). The relational view: Cooperative strategy and sources of interorganizational competitive advantage. *Academy of Management Review*, *23*(4), 660-679.

Earl, M. (2001a). Knowledge management strategies: Toward a taxonomy. *Journal of Management Information Systems*, *18*(1), 215-233.

Earl, M. (2001b). Knowledge management strategies: Toward a taxonomy. *Journal of Management Information Systems*, *18*(I), 215-233.

Enkel, E., Gassmann, O., & Chesbrough, H. (2009). Open R&D and open innovation: Exploring the phenomenon. *R&D Management*, 39(4), 311-316.

Farrell, J., & Klemperer, P. (2007). Coordination and lock-in: Competition with switching costs and network effects. *Handbook of Industrial Organization*, 3, 1967-2072.

Fishbein, M.A., & Ajzen, I. (1975). Belief, attitude, intention and behaviour: An introduction to theory and research. *Reading, Addison-Wesley*.

Fombrun, C.J. (1986). Structural dynamics within and between organizations. *Administrative Science Quarterly*, 403-421.

Fonner, K.L., & Stache, L.C. (2012). All in a day's work, at home: Teleworkers' management of micro role transitions and the work-home boundary. *New Technology, Work and Employment*, 27(3), 242-257.

Friedman, V.J., Lipshitz, R., & Popper, M. (2005). The mystification of organizational learning. *Journal of Management Inquiry*, 14(1), 19-30.

Gandini, A. (2015). The rise of coworking spaces: A literature review. *Ephemera*, 15(1), 193.

Garvin, D.A. (2003). Learning in action: A guide to putting the learning organization to work. *Harvard Business Review Press*.

Gawer, A., & Cusumano, M.A. (2014). Industry platforms and ecosystem innovation. *Journal of Product Innovation Management*, 31(3), 417-433.

Giustiniano, L. (2005). *Strategie, Organizzazione e Sistemi Informativi: dall'IT alignment all'IT governance*. Franco Angeli.

Gold, A.H., Malhotra, A., & Segars, A.H. (2001). Knowledge management: An organizational capabilities perspective. *Journal of Management Information Systems*, 18(1), 185-214.

Gold, M., & Mustafa, M. (2013). 'Work always wins': Client colonisation, time management and the anxieties of connected freelancers. *New Technology, Work and Employment*, 28(3), 197-211.

Grajek, M., & Kretschmer, T. (2012). Identifying critical mass in the global cellular telephony market. *International Journal of Industrial Organization*, 30(6), 496-507.

Granovetter, M. (1983). The strength of weak ties: A network theory revisited. *Sociological Theory*, 201-233.

Gubbi, J., Buyya, R., Marusic, S., & Palaniswami, M. (2013). Internet of Things (IoT): A vision, architectural elements, and future directions. *Future Generation Computer Systems*, 29(7), 1645-1660.

Hagel, J., Brown, J.S., Samoylova, T., & Lui, M. (2013). From exponential technologies to exponential innovation. *Deloitte Center for the Edge, San Jose, California. Http://Www2. Deloitte. Com/Content/Dam/Deloitte/Es/Documents/Sector-Publico/Deloitte_ES_Sector-Publico_From-Exponentialtechnologies-to-Exponential-Innovation. Pdf*.

Hagiu, A. (2009). Multi-sided platforms: From microfoundations to design and expansion strategies. *Harvard Business School Strategy Unit Working Paper*, 09-115.

Hagiu, A., & Wright, J. (2015). Multi-sided platforms. *International Journal of Industrial Organization*, 43, 162-174.

Hall, N.G., Leung, J.Y.-T., & Li, C.-L. (2015). The effects of multitasking on operations scheduling. *Production and Operations Management*, 24(8), 1248-1265.

Handzic, M. (2011). Integrated socio-technical knowledge management model: An empirical evaluation. *Journal of Knowledge Management*, 15(2), 198-211.

Hansen, M.T. (1999). The search-transfer problem: The role of weak ties in sharing knowledge across organization subunits. *Administrative Science Quarterly*, 44(1), 82-111.

Harrison, J.S., & St. John, C.H. (1996). Managing and partnering with external stakeholders. *Academy of Management Perspectives*, 10(2), 46-60.

Henderson, J.C., & Venkatraman, H. (1999). Strategic alignment: Leveraging information technology for transforming organizations. *IBM Systems Journal*, 38(2.3), 472-484.

Henfridsson, O., Mathiassen, L., & Svahn, F. (2014). Managing technological change in the digital age: The role of architectural frames. *Journal of Information Technology*, 29(1), 27-43.

Hess, T., Matt, C., Benlian, A., & Wiesböck, F. (2016). Options for formulating a digital transformation strategy. *MIS Quarterly Executive*, 15(2).

Hicks, R.C., Dattero, R., & Galup, S.D. (2006). The five-tier knowledge management hierarchy. *Journal of Knowledge Management*.

Highsmith, J.A., & Highsmith, J. (2002). *Agile software development ecosystems*. Addison-Wesley Professional.

Hill, E.J., Hawkins, A. J., Ferris, M., & Weitzman, M. (2001). Finding an extra day a week: The positive influence of perceived job flexibility on work and family life balance. *Family Relations*, 50(1), 49-58.

Horlacher, A., & Hess, T. (2016). What does a Chief Digital Officer do? Managerial tasks and roles of a new C-level position in the context of digital transformation. *2016 49th Hawaii International Conference on System Sciences (HICSS)*, 5126-5135.

Inkpen, A.C., & Tsang, E.W. (2005). Social capital, networks, and knowledge transfer. *Academy of Management Review*, 30(1), 146-165.

Kale, P., & Singh, H. (2007). Building firm capabilities through learning: The role of the alliance learning process in alliance capability and firm-level alliance success. *Strategic Management Journal*, 28(10), 981-1000.

Kallinikos, J., Leonardi, P.M., & Nardi, B.A. (2012). The Challenge of Materiality: Origins, Scope, and Prospects. In P.M. Leonardi, B.A. Nardi, & J. Kallinikos (Eds.), *Materiality and organizing* (pp. 3-22). Oxford University Press.

Kane, G.C., Johnson, J., & Majchrzak, A. (2014). Emergent Life Cycle: The Tension Between Knowledge Change and Knowledge Retention in Open Online Co-production Communities. *Management Science*, *60*(12), 3026-3048. https://doi.org/10.1287/mnsc.2013.1855

Kane, G.C., Palmer, D., Phillips, A.N., Kiron, D., Buckley, N., & others (2015). Strategy, not technology, drives digital transformation. *MIT Sloan Management Review and Deloitte University Press*, *14*(1-25).

Katz, M.L., & Shapiro, C. (1985). Network externalities, competition, and compatibility. *The American Economic Review*, *75*(3), 424-440.

Kenney, M., & Zysman, J. (2016). The Rise of the Platform Economy. *Issues in Science and Technology*, *32*, 61-69.

LaRose, R., & Eastin, M.S. (2004). A social cognitive theory of Internet uses and gratifications: Toward a new model of media attendance. *Journal of Broadcasting & Electronic Media*, *48*(3), 358-377.

Laudon, K., & Laudon, J. (2009). Management Information Systems: International Edition, 11/E. *KC Laudon, Management Information Systems: International Edition*, *11*.

Lee, H., & Choi, B. (2003). Knowledge management enablers, processes, and organizational performance: An integrative view and empirical examination. *Journal of Management Information Systems*, *20*(1), 179-228.

Legris, P., Ingham, J., & Collerette, P. (2003). Why do people use information technology? A critical review of the technology acceptance model. *Information & Management*, *40*, 191-204. https://doi.org/10.1016/S0378-7206(01)00143-4.

Leonardi, P.M., & Barley, S.R. (2010). What's Under Construction Here? Social Action, Materiality, and Power in Constructivist Studies of Technology and Organizing. In *The Academy of Management Annals* (Vol. 4). https://doi.org/10.1080/19416521003654160.

Levitt, B., & March, J.G. (1988). Organizational Learning. *Annual Review of Sociology*, *14*(1), 319-338. https://doi.org/10.1146/annurev.so.14.080188.001535.

Lichtenthaler, U., & Lichtenthaler, E. (2009). A capability-based framework for open innovation: Complementing absorptive capacity. *Journal of Management Studies*, *46*(8), 1315-1338.

Lichtenthaler, U., & Lichtenthaler, E. (2010). Technology transfer across organizational boundaries: Absorptive capacity and desorptive capacity. *California Management Review*, *53*(1), 154-170.

Liedtka, J., & Ogilvie, T. (2011). *Designing for growth: A design thinking tool kit for managers*. Columbia University Press.

Lyytinen, K., & Damsgaard, J. (2001). What's wrong with the diffusion of innovation theory? *Working Conference on Diffusing Software Product and Process Innovations*, 173-190.

Mahajan, V., Muller, E., & Wind, Y. (2000). *New-product diffusion models* (Vol. 11). Springer Science & Business Media.

Mahler, A., & Rogers, E.M. (1999). The diffusion of interactive communication innovations and the critical mass: The adoption of telecommunications services by German banks. *Telecommunications Policy*, 23(10-11), 719-740.

Maier, R. (2005). Modeling knowledge work for the design of knowledge infrastructures. *Journal of Universal Computer Science*, 11(4), 429-451.

Malhotra, Y. (2000). Knowledge management for e-business performance: Advancing information strategy to "internet time." *Information Strategy: The Executive's Journal*, 16(4), 5-16.

Marchegiani, L. (2012). *Information, Knowledge, Attention: ICTs and innovative organizations The relation between humans, technology and organizations*. LAP.

Marchegiani, L., Giustiniano, L., & Pirolo, L. (2012). Revitalising the outsourcing discourse within the boundaries of firms debate. *Business Systems Review*, 1(1), 157-177.

Marchegiani, L., & Pileggi, L. (2018, June 19). Birds of a Feather Flock Together: Can Knowledge Management and Communities Prevent Organizational Silos? *Proceedings of Euram 2018 Conference Research in Action, European Academy of Management*. EURAM 2018, University of Iceland - Reykjavík (Iceland).

Maruping, L.M., Venkatesh, V., & Agarwal, R. (2009). A control theory perspective on agile methodology use and changing user requirements. *Information Systems Research*, 20(3), 377-399.

Matt, C., Hess, T., & Benlian, A. (2015). Digital transformation strategies. *Business & Information Systems Engineering*, 57(5), 339-343.

McAfee, A., & Brynjolfsson, E. (2017). *Machine, platform, crowd: Harnessing our digital future*. WW Norton & Company.

Mccormick, M.J., & Martinko, M.J. (2004). Identifying leader social cognitions: Integrating the causal reasoning perspective into social cognitive theory. *Journal of Leadership & Organizational Studies*, 10(4), 2-11.

Meade, N., & Islam, T. (2006). Modelling and forecasting the diffusion of innovation – A 25-year review. *International Journal of Forecasting*, 22(3), 519-545.

Meihami, B., & Meihami, H. (2014). Knowledge Management a way to gain a competitive advantage in firms (evidence of manufacturing companies). *International Letters of Social and Humanistic Sciences*, 3(14), 80-91.

Melé, D. (2016). Understanding humanistic management. *Humanistic Management Journal*, 1(1), 33-55.

Messenger, J. (2018). *Working time and the future of work.*

Midoro, V. (2002). Dalle comunità di pratica alle comunità di apprendimento virtuali. *Italian Journal of Educational Technology*, 10(1), 3-3.

Misra, S., & Stokols, D. (2012). A typology of people-environment relationships in the Digital Age. *Technology in Society*, 34(4), 311-325. https://doi.org/10.1016/j.techsoc.2012.10.003.

Money, W., & Turner, A. (2004). Application of the technology acceptance model to a knowledge management system. *37th Annual Hawaii International Conference on System Sciences, 2004. Proceedings of The*, 00(C), 1-9. https://doi.org/10.1109/HICSS.2004.1265573.

Muegge, S. (2013). Platforms, communities, and business ecosystems: Lessons learned about technology entrepreneurship in an interconnected world. *Technology Innovation Management Review*, 5-15.

Nahapiet, J., & Ghoshal, S. (1998). Social capital, intellectual capital, and the organizational advantage. *Academy of Management Review, 23*(2), 242-266.

Naisbitt, J., & Bisesi, M. (1983). Megatrends: Ten new directions transforming our lives. *Sloan Management Review (Pre-1986), 24*(4), 69.

Nalebuff, B.J., Brandenburger, A., & Maulana, A. (1996). *Co-opetition*. HarperCollinsBusiness London.

Nambisan, S., Wright, M., Feldman, M., & others (2019). The digital transformation of innovation and entrepreneurship: Progress, challenges and key themes. *Research Policy, 48*(8), 103773.

Newell, S., Robertson, M., Scarbrough, H., & Swan, J. (2009). *Managing knowledge work and innovation*. Macmillan International Higher Education.

Njiraine, D., & Le Roux, C. (2011). Applying Earl's KM model in IK management: With reference to Kenya and South Africa. *The Electronic Library*.

Nonaka, I. (1994). A dynamic theory of organizational knowledge creation. *Organization Science, 5*(1), 14-37.

Nonaka, I., Konno, N., Tokuoka, K., & Kawamura, T. (1992). Hypertext organization for accelerating organizational knowledge creation. *Diamond Harvard Business*, 12-22.

Nonaka, I., & Takeuchi, H. (1995a). *The Knowledge-creating company*.

Nonaka, I., & Takeuchi, H. (1995b). *The knowledge-creating company: How Japanese companies create the dynamics of innovation*. Oxford University Press.

Oldenburg, R. (1989). *The great good place: Café, coffee shops, community centers, beauty parlors, general stores, bars, hangouts, and how they get you through the day*. Paragon House Publishers.

Oldenburg, R. (1999). *The great good place: Cafes, coffee shops, bookstores, bars, hair salons, and other hangouts at the heart of a community*. Da Capo Press.

Olson, M. (2009). *The Logic of Collective Action: Public Goods and the Theory of Groups, Second Printing with a New Preface and Appendix* (Vol. 124). Harvard University Press.

Orlikowski, W., & Hoffman, D. (1997). An improvisational model for change management: The case of groupware technologies. *Inventing the Organizations of the 21st Century, 265*, 16-27.

Orlikowski, W.J. (2002). Knowing in practice: Enacting a collective capability in distributed organizing. *Organization Science, 13*(3), 249-273.

Orlikowski, W.J., & Gash, D.C. (1994). Technological frames: Making sense of information technology in organizations. *ACM Transactions on Information Systems (TOIS), 12*(2), 174-207.

Orlikowski, W.J., & Iacono, C.S. (2000). The Truth Is Not Out There: An Enacted View of the "Digital Economy." In *Understanding the Digital Economy: Data,*

Tools, and Research (pp. 352-380). http://s1.downloadmienphi.net/file/downloadfile6/148/1382193.pdf#page=359.

Orlikowski, W.J., & Robey, D. (1991). Information technology and the structuring of organizations. *Information Systems Research*, 2(2), 143-169.

Orlikowski, W.J., & Scott, S.V. (2008). 10 sociomateriality: Challenging the separation of technology, work and organization. *The Academy of Management Annals*, 2(1), 433-474.

Osterwalder, A., & Pigneur, Y. (2010). *Business model generation: A handbook for visionaries, game changers, and challengers*. John Wiley & Sons.

Paganetto, L. (Ed.). (2017). *Knowledge economy, information technologies and growth*. Routledge.

Pagani, M., & Pardo, C. (2017). The impact of digital technology on relationships in a business network. *Industrial Marketing Management*, 67, 185-192.

Parker, G., & Van Alstyne, M. (2018). Innovation, Openness, and Platform Control. *Management Science*, 64(7), 3015-3032. https://doi.org/10.1287/mnsc.2017.2757.

Paschen, J., Wilson, M., & Ferreira, J.J. (2020). Collaborative intelligence: How human and artificial intelligence create value along the B2B sales funnel. *Business Horizons*.

Paunov, C., & Planes-Satorra, S. (2019). *How are digital technologies changing innovation?: Evidence from agriculture, the automotive industry and retail*.

Pedler, M., & Aspinwall, K. (1999). Learning company. In *The Experience of Managing* (pp. 141-154). Springer.

Pedler, M., Boydell, T., & Burgoyne, J. (1989). The learning company. *Studies in Continuing Education*, 11(2), 91-101.

Pendlebury, J., Grouard, B., & Meston, F. (1998). *The ten keys to successful change management*. John Wiley & Sons Incorporated.

Pennacchini, S. (2019). *Trasformazione Digitale e Risorse Umane. La valorizzazione della persona*. Università degli Studi Roma Tre.

Peruffo, E., Marchegiani, L., & Vicentini, F. (2018). Experience as a source of knowledge in divestiture decisions: Emerging issues and knowledge management implications. *Journal of Knowledge Management*.

Phelps, C., Heidl, R., & Wadhwa, A. (2012). Knowledge, networks, and knowledge networks: A review and research agenda. *Journal of Management*, 38(4), 1115-1166.

Plaskoff, J. (2017). Employee experience: The new human resource management approach. *Strategic HR Review.*, 16(3), 136-141.

Plonka, F.E. (1997). Developing a lean and agile work force. *Human Factors and Ergonomics in Manufacturing & Service Industries*, 7(1), 11-20.

Polanyi, M.T. (1966). *1966 The tacit dimension. London: Routledge & Kegan Paul*.

Pólvora, A., Nascimento, S., Lourenço, J.S., & Scapolo, F. (2020). Blockchain for industrial transformations: A forward-looking approach with multi-stakeholder engagement for policy advice. *Technological Forecasting and Social Change, 157,* 120091.

Profili, S. (2004a). *Il knowledge management. Approcci teorici e strumenti gestionali* (Vol. 97). FrancoAngeli.

Profili, S. (2004b). *Il Knowledge Management. Approcci teorici e strumenti gestionali*.

Ratten, V., & Ratten, H. (2007). Social cognitive theory in technological innovations. *European Journal of Innovation Management*.

Reagans, R. (2002). *Network Structure and Knowledge Transfer: The Effects of Cohesion and Range Bill McEvily*. 48(2000), 240-267.

Rochet, J.-C., & Tirole, J. (2006). Two-sided markets: A progress report. *The RAND Journal of Economics*, 37(3), 645-667.

Roda, C. (2010). Attention support in digital environments. Nine questions to be addressed. *New Ideas in Psychology*, 28(3), 354-364.

Roda, C., & Nabeth, T. (2008). Attention management in organizations: Four levels of support in information systems. *Organisational Capital Modelling, Measuring and Contextualising, A. Bonfour, Editor*, 214-233.

Rogers, E.M. (2010). *Diffusion of innovations*. Simon and Schuster.

Roscoe, R.D., Becker, D.V., Branaghan, R.J., Chiou, E.K., Gray, R., Craig, S.D., Gutzwiller, R.S., & Cooke, N.J. (2019). Bridging psychology and engineering to make technology work for people. *American Psychologist*, 74(3), 394.

Rosen, C. (2008). The myth of multitasking. *The New Atlantis*, 20, 105-110.

Rowley, J. (2007). The wisdom hierarchy: Representations of the DIKW hierarchy. *Journal of Information Science*, 33(2), 163-180.

Rullani, E. (2004). *Economia della conoscenza: Creatività e valore nel capitalismo delle reti*. Carocci Roma.

Rüßmann, M., Lorenz, M., Gerbert, P., Waldner, M., Justus, J., Engel, P., & Harnisch, M. (2015). Industry 4.0: The future of productivity and growth in manufacturing industries. *Boston Consulting Group*, 9(1), 54-89.

Rylander, A., & Peppard, J. (2003). From implementing strategy to embodying strategy. *Journal of Intellectual Capital*.

Santoro, G., Vrontis, D., Thrassou, A., & Dezi, L. (2018). The Internet of Things: Building a knowledge management system for open innovation and knowledge management capacity. *Technological Forecasting and Social Change*, 136, 347-354.

Schein, E.H. (1988). *Organizational culture* (American Psychological Association).

Senge, P.M. (2006). *The fifth discipline: The art and practice of the learning organization. Broadway Business*. Broadway Business.

Shapiro, C., & Varian, H.R. (1999). The art of standards wars. *California Management Review*, 41(2), 8-32.

Sherehiy, B., Karwowski, W., & Layer, J.K. (2007). A review of enterprise agility: Concepts, frameworks, and attributes. *International Journal of Industrial Ergonomics*, 37(5), 445-460.

Shy, O. (2002). A quick-and-easy method for estimating switching costs. *International Journal of Industrial Organization*, 20(1), 71-87.

Sica, R. (2017). Dal Digital Workplace alla Phygital Enterprise. *Harvard Business Review Italia*.

Sica, R. (2018). *Employee Experience: Il lato umano delle organizzazioni nella quarta rivoluzione industriale*. FrancoAngeli.

Sica, R. (2019). *Employee experience: The Human Side of Organizations in the Fourth Industrial Revolution*. FrancoAngeli.

Simon, H.A. (1971). Designing organizations for an information-rich world. In *Computers, communications, and the public interest* (Johns Hopkins Press). Martin Greenberger.

Singh, A., & Hess, T. (2017). How Chief Digital Officers promote the digital transformation of their companies. *MIS Quarterly Executive*, 16(1).

Stolwijk, C., & Punter, M. (2018). *Going Digital: Field labs to accelerate the digitization of the Dutch Industry*. Den Haag: TNO.

Sundsted, T., Jones, D., & Bacigalupo, T. (2009). *I'm Outta Here: How Co-Working Is Making the Office Obsolete*. Lulu. com.

Teece, D.J. (2007). Explicating dynamic capabilities: The nature and microfoundations of (sustainable) enterprise performance. *Strategic Management Journal*, 28(13), 1319-1350.

Teece, D.J., Pisano, G., & Shuen, A. (1997). Dynamic capabilities and strategic management. *Strategic Management Journal*, 18(7), 509-533.

Tortoriello, M., Reagans, R., & McEvily, B. (2012). Bridging the Knowledge Gap: The Influence of Strong Ties, Network Cohesion, and Network Range on the Transfer of Knowledge Between Organizational Units. *Organization Science*, 23(January 2015), 1024-1039. https://doi.org/10.1287/orsc.1110.0688.

Turkle, S. (2017). *Alone together: Why we expect more from technology and less from each other*. Hachette UK.

Venkatesh, V., Morris, M.G., Davis, G.B., & Davis, F.D. (2003). User acceptance of information technology: Toward a unified view. *MIS Quarterly*, 425-478.

Venkatraman, N. (1994). IT-enabled business transformation: From automation to business scope redefinition. *Sloan Management Review*, 35, 73-73.

Venkatraman, N.V., El Sawy, O.A., Pavlou, P.A., & Bharadwaj, A. (2014). Theorizing digital business innovation: Platforms and capabilities in ecosystems. *Fox School of Business Research Paper*, 15-080.

Venkatraman, V. (2017). *The digital matrix: New rules for business transformation through technology*. Greystone Books.

Verhoef, P.C., Broekhuizen, T., Bart, Y., Bhattacharya, A., Dong, J.Q., Fabian, N., & Haenlein, M. (2019). Digital transformation: A multidisciplinary reflection and research agenda. *Journal of Business Research*.

Vrontis, D., Thrassou, A., Santoro, G., & Papa, A. (2017). Ambidexterity, external knowledge and performance in knowledge-intensive firms. *The Journal of Technology Transfer*, 42(2), 374-388.

Wang, C.L., & Ahmed, P.K. (2003). Organisational learning: A critical review. *The Learning Organization*.

Waters-Lynch, J., Potts, J., Butcher, T., Dodson, J., & Hurley, J. (2016). *Coworking: A transdisciplinary overview*. Available at SSRN 2712217.

Weill, P., & Woerner, S.L. (2013). The Future of the CIO in a Digital Economy. *MIS Quarterly Executive*, 12(2).

Wright, M., & Esslemont, D. (1994). The logical limitations of target marketing. *Marketing Bulletin*, 5(5), 13-20.

Yeh, Y.-J., Lai, S.-Q., & Ho, C.-T. (2006). Knowledge management enablers: A case study. *Industrial Management & Data Systems*.

Yli-Renko, H., Autio, E., & Sapienza, H.J. (2001). Social capital, knowledge acquisition, and knowledge exploitation in young technology-based firms. *Strategic Management Journal*, 22(6-7), 587-613.

Zeleny, M. (1987). From Knowledge to Wisdom: Strategic Challenges of Global Business Education. *Management*, 7(1), 59-70.

Zheng, W. (2010). A social capital perspective of innovation from individuals to nations: Where is empirical literature directing us? *International Journal of Management Reviews*, 12(2), 151-183.

Zikopoulos, P., Eaton, C., & others (2011). *Understanding big data: Analytics for enterprise class hadoop and streaming data*. McGraw-Hill Osborne Media.

Zollo, M. (2009). Superstitious learning with rare strategic decisions: Theory and evidence from corporate acquisitions. *Organization Science*, 20(5), 894-908.

INDEX

3
3G, 162
3 Vs of Big Data, 65

4
4G, 164

5
5G, 165

A
acceleration, 25
actual networks, 174
Agile Manifesto, 125
Agile Software Development, 125
Agile Working, 147
Agility, 125

B
Bass model, 82
Big Data, 21, 64, 71, 132
blockchain, 54
Business Network Redesign, 96
Business Process Reengineering, 96
Business Scope Redefinition, 97
Business Social Networks, 59
– Online BSN, 36

C
change agent, 86
change catalyst, 86
change management, 57, 99, 103
Chasm model, 87
Chief Digital Officer, 111
Cloud Computing, 24, 131, 136,
Cognitive Computing, 138
complementors, 18; 23; 161
creative chaos, 115
creativity, 41, 45, 114
critical mass, 86
crowdsourcing platforms, 26

D
data
– structured and unstructured, 65
dematerialization, 79
design thinking, 62
Diffusion models
– Bass model, 82
– Chasm model, 87
– Rogers' model, 82, 85
– S-curve, 85
Diffusion of Innovations, 81
Digital
– Age, 5, 8, 12, 21
– Business Ecosystems, 53, 58
– evangelist, 112
– leadership, 17
– platforms, 23, 58
– Transformation, 103, 105, 110
Digital Transformation Framework, 110
digitalization, 11, 53, 108
digitization, 108
dynamic capabilities, 9, 42, 173

E
electronic identity, 72
Employee Experience, 41, 44, 184
Explicit knowledge, 16, 32, 113

F

Flexible working, 144

G

GSM, 90, 162

H

hackathons, 26
Home Working, 147
Humane phygital workplaces, 184
humanistic management, 184

I

increasing returns, 43, 79
incubation, 25, 144
industry platform, 25
influencers, 61
infrastructure, 14, 167
Infrastructure as a Service, 68
internal integration, 96
IT alignment, 110

K

Knowledge Economy, 11, 40
Knowledge Intensive Firms, 121
Knowledge Management System, 103, 109, 177
knowledge network, 36, 59

L

Learning
– Superstitious, 116
– Vicarious, 117
Learning Organizations, 112, 117
Local automation, 96

M

Machine Learning, 45, 71, 132, 137
Megatrends, 6
Multicloud, 70
multiple-helix of innovation, 26
multi-sided platforms, 21

N

network approach, 88
network effects, 21
– positive, 78
network externalities, 18, 61, 80, 89

O

open innovation, 56
organizational
– culture, 97, 113, 123
– flexibility, 15
– silos, 112, 173

P

phygital enterprises, 184
Platform Economy, 22
platform organizations, 15, 21, 54

Q

QR codes, 72

R

redundancy, 115
resistance to change, 97
Revolution
– Industrial, 9
– Internet, 6
RFID, 72

S

Sensemaking, 43, 109
servitization, 55
Smart Working, 148
Social Cognitive Theory, 101
Social Network Analysis, 59, 175
sociostructure, 95
standards, 79
strategic agility, 15
strategic knowledge renewal, 16
superstructure, 95

T

Tacit knowledge, 32, 36, 113
TACS, 162
Technology acceptance, 98
– TAM, 98
– UTAUT, 99
Technology Acceptance Model, 177
Telework, 145
triple-helix model of innovation, 26
Two-sided markets, 18